Evader

The epic story
of
the first British airman to be rescued
by
the Comète Escape Line in World War II

EVADER

THE EPIC STORY OF
THE FIRST BRITISH AIRMAN TO BE
RESCUED BY THE COMÈTE ESCAPE
LINE IN WORLD WAR II

by

Derek Shuff

SPELLMOUNT
Staplehurst

British Library Cataloguing in Publication Data:
A catalogue record for this book is available
from the British Library

Copyright © Derek Shuff 2003
Map copyright © Spellmount Ltd 2003

ISBN 1-86227-226-3

Published in the UK in 2003 by
Spellmount Limited
The Old Rectory
Staplehurst
Kent TN12 0AZ

Tel: 01580 893730
Fax: 01580 893731
E-mail: enquiries@spellmount.com
Website: www.spellmount.com

1 3 5 7 9 8 6 4 2

Typeset in Palatino by MATS, Southend-on-Sea, Essex
Printed in Great Britain by
T.J.International Ltd
Padstow, Cornwall

Contents

Dedications

To Flt Lt Roy Langlois, DFC who saved my life; to Countess A de Jongh, who gave me those extra years of freedom. And to my wife, Mary, who never gave up hope.

Jack Newton

To the Jack Newtons of World War II who willingly took a step into hell that the rest of us would live in peace and freedom. To my mother, Hilda Shuff, who braved Hitler's wrath throughout the duration of the war by carrying on living and working in South Godstone, Surrey, underneath the skyway used by Nazi bombers, flying bombs and rockets. To bravery with honour wherever it is found.

Derek Shuff

Jack Newton was spirited through Belgium and France, then across the Pyrénées into Spain, by a young Resistance girl code named Dédée. Largely through her determination and bravery, Newton was the first British airman in World War II to escape from German-occupied Europe, and get back to Great Britain by the Comète Escape Line.

This biography tells the true story of Jack Newton's bid for freedom, the life-long bond that was formed between himself and Dédée as she put her life on the line to save him, and the many dramas on that journey, including the time Jack was nearly shot by the Resistance which believed him to be a German spy masquerading as a 'downed' British airman.

Acknowledgements

Jack and Mary Newton, for their many memories and their unstinting help (along with many cups of tea and fruit cake!); Countess Andrée de Jongh (Dédée), for making this book possible; to her companion, Thérèse de Wael, for her patience with my questions. To Peter Presence, for his early cooperation; Richard 'Tich' Copley, for his graphic recall of being 'on the run' in Brussels, and to his wife, Betty, who collated his material. I am indebted to Airey Neave's *Little Cyclone* which featured the heroes and heroines of the Comète Escape Line, many of whom, between them, saved Jack's life and, in turn, helped me to convey the horror of the events through which they lived and, in some cases, died. In fact, my thanks to all those who assisted in even the smallest way.

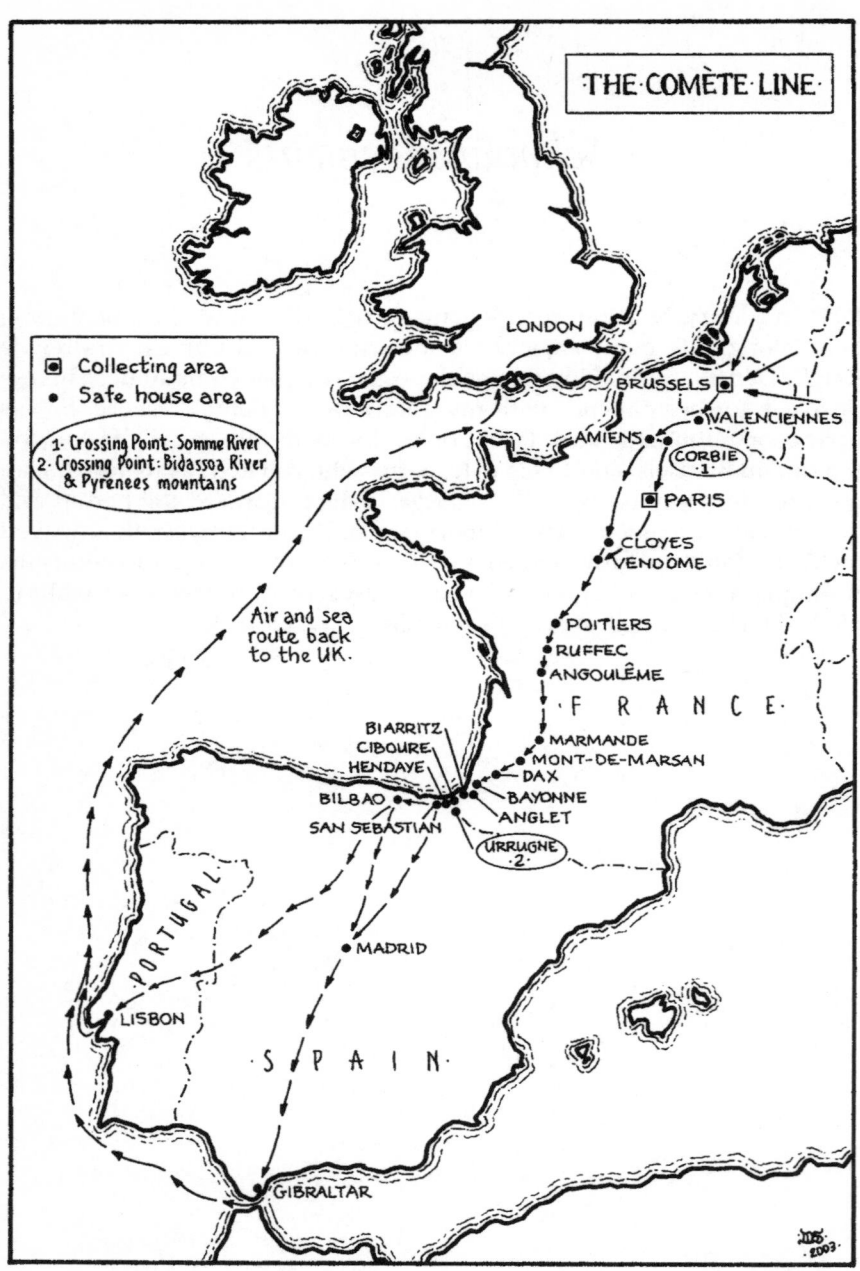

Preface

by

Countess Andrée de Jongh, GM
(Dédée)

I could not accept that a race, because of its blond hair and blue eyes, that this type of people would consider itself to be superior to all others, that it would rule, and that all other races would be considered sub-human. Could one passively allow such a thing to happen? No, it is better to die fighting than to accept such horrors ... even if some of us had to lose family, or friends. Such commitment goes hand-in-hand with great sacrifice, and those of us in the Comète Line had more than our share of personal misery.

For nearly four years we fought our underground campaign to rid our beloved homeland of the German invaders and occupiers. What made our motivation stronger was the privilege of guiding among the escapees so many very young airmen full of courage and so eager to reach Gibraltar in order to return to the battle. And when the Germans finally succumbed, we knew our blood, sweat and many tears had been worth it, even though, in my case, I lost my beloved father who helped me set up the Comète Line. He was executed by a German firing squad in March 1944, sadly just a few months before Belgium was liberated. Many other helpers also gave their lives saving the lives of those like the first English airman I helped, Jack Newton, Royal Air Force, whose story is the subject of this book. Now it is up to present and future generations to ensure that Europe is never again blighted by the cancer of race domination, but this calls for extreme and constant watchfulness.

Enough blood has been spilled. Enough unhappiness unleashed on so many innocent peoples. The future must be paved with tolerance and, above all, with happiness.

As for those of us who helped create this brighter future, I can only add: Don't thank us, we had the joy of fighting, without striking a blow.

Brussels, 2003

Introduction

I first saw Jack Newton on television. He was being interviewed in connection with his visit to Brussels for the last reunion meeting of the Royal Air Forces Escaping Society and the Comète Escape Line. Queen Fabiola was there to pay tribute to her country's Resistance movement and to the Royal Air Force escapers. As one of Belgium's best-known and most decorated members of the Resistance, Andrée de Jongh was at this last reunion, too.

I heard how Jack's Wellington bomber had forced landed in Belgium, that he had been saved by Andrée de Jongh, who had been honoured with the title of Countess for wartime services to her country. That she had been instrumental in getting the young airman, Jack Newton, safely back to Britain. But how? And what had happened between Jack's untimely appearance in Belgium, then under Nazi occupation, and his return to London, via Spain, some five months later? I had to find out!

One phone call and I had an invitation to the Newton home in Broad Oak, ironically barely three miles from my own home in East Sussex. A couple of days later, Jack gave me a shortened account of his amazing story, accompanied by several cups of tea and slices of fruit cake, served up by his equally involved wife, Mary.

Tea at the Newtons' was to be the beginning of our collaboration on Jack and Mary's story. 'Let's hope I am around long enough for you to finish it,' said the sprightly 82-year-old former air gunner, one of the so-called 'tailend Charlies'. There didn't seem to be much doubt that he would be. Jack Newton was still focused, energetic and enthusiastic about the part he played in evading the Nazis whose nationwide dragnet across France failed to catch him. And his recall of those 1941 events remains as crystal clear as the water of the fast flowing Bidassoa river that was nearly his final downfall.

Of Dédée, Jack says he owes her his life. He tells how living on the very edge of life and death for so many weeks created a bond like none other. A bond that survives to this day. Dédée was to suffer inhumanely at the hands of her German captors, but somehow she bravely survived all the horrors of internment and, in 1946, renewed contact with Jack Newton,

'My brave young airman', as she liked to call him. Being the first British airman to evade capture in German-occupied Europe in World War II, he has remained rather special to Dédée, and they have maintained personal and monthly telephone contact with each other for most of the past fifty-eight years, although her failing health is now beginning to make this contact more sporadic.

Jack likes to tell how he has been blessed with two wives – Mary, the woman he married some twelve weeks before he flew to Aachen on that ill-fated raid, and Dédée, to whom he stresses he owes his life. He says he loves them both.

When Jack Newton and those brave souls such as Dédée were existing under Nazi rule, with discovery and death just a bullet away, I was a 6-year-old schoolboy living in South Godstone, Surrey, totally oblivious to the dangers that confronted those given the task of facing and beating the enemy.

So, I hope that Jack Newton's story, and the story of the many brave people who helped to save him, will never be forgotten. And if a book like this helps to keep those memories alive, then the sacrifices of so many dedicated men and women have not been in vain.

Having spent many hours talking to Jack Newton, and researching and writing his story, one questions still remains. That is: Why was Jack Newton's courage never officially recognised? Others involved in his story rightly received the highest honours the British government could bestow on them when the war was over. But for the first airman to make it back to Britain . . . nothing. Not even a letter of commendation. Even the efforts of Naval Lieutenant Commander Griser, who knew what Newton had been through, came to nothing. 'At the time, the Air Ministry simply said I had done nothing out of the ordinary!' says Jack, a little sadly. 'It would have been nice to, at least, have had an official letter, or something. I was the first, and it wasn't exactly a joyride. But I think such personal achievements, especially in the beginning of the war, were largely lost in the increasing momentum of the war effort.'

But, maybe, it is not too late to recognise Jack Newton's bravery, and his incredible achievement. He did more than most for his country. Now is the time his country can do something for him. And make him an even prouder man, if that is possible.

Derek Shuff
2003

CHAPTER 1

The Early Days

Jack Lamport Newton was born in a hayloft on 4 February 1920, although the hayloft had long since been converted into a cosy flat, and the stables below it into a garage where chauffeur John Lamport Newton kept and looked after the guvnor's cars. They lived there for twenty-five years in a very smart part of Hampstead, in north London, through the generosity of John's employer, Mr Johnson, of Johnson and Johnson, the famous baby powder company, who provided his chauffeur with the courtesy flat, and £5 a week wage.

It was in this atmosphere of gracious living, stylish and fast cars, as well as a lifestyle that must have been the envy of his school pals, that young Jack and his elder sister, Babs, spent their formative years enjoying the many benefits and privileges which came their way at 13 Lancaster Mews. Mr Johnson was a kindly man who loved expensive cars, and being well able to afford them, the 'shop' – the family's pet name for the garage – was filled with some of the choicest models around at the time. Cars such as the 90 horse power Fiat, and the superb Issota Frashini, to name just two. A stable once filled with horses was now full of high horse power cars. The irony was not lost on Jack. He became nearly as obsessed with the sleek and beautiful horseless carriages as his father, and Mr Johnson, too. Mr Johnson's cars were his pride and joy, and when he could take a couple of weeks away from his business he liked nothing more than to have chauffeur Newton drive him off to Spain where the roads were long, straight and empty. 'Come on, dear chap, put your foot down. Open up. Let's she what she can do,' he'd say encouragingly, as John put the powerful Fiat through its paces.

On one such trip, the two of them fell foul of some Spanish brigands. Up in the hills around Granada, old Mr Johnson and his chauffeur were suddenly confronted by a gang of ruffians who stood across the road waving guns, hoping to stop the car. Their intentions were pretty clear. 'Go through them, Newton. Drive on . . .' ordered the old man, as though he was leading a cavalry charge. The two men put their heads down, and drove straight at the gang who had to throw themselves either side of the road to avoid being run down. Shots were fired as the car raced away, one

1

missile hitting John Newton in the wrist. Even so, he kept control of the vehicle and continued driving until they reached safety – and a hospital.

John's favourite snack was dripping on toast. He loved it. Gus, as his wife was nicknamed, made him lightly browned toast, and John piled the dripping on so thick it fell off the sides. Then he would cut each slice into four, pop a quarter into his mouth at a time, and savour the flavour for as long as possible before swallowing. After that, he popped in the next piece, and the next until it was all consumed. Jack would watch mesmerised. Jack recalls:

Mum was one of six sisters who all came from Fareham, in Hampshire. Mum's father, Granddad Lamport, was a local butcher, which must have been where dad got his taste for fresh dripping. Each weekend we always had a package from our own family butcher consisting of a couple of pounds of sausages, some pieces of meat, some bacon, and some things unheard of now called chitlings. Also, there would be black pudding and dad's tub of dripping. All delivered promptly on the same day to Lancaster Mews.

We lived in Hampstead until I was about 11, then we moved to what we called the backside of Mr Johnson's house, which was in Avenue Road, St John's Wood. It was quite near to Primrose Hill and Regent's Park. Mr Johnson had a very large garden, with a sizeable plot of undeveloped land one side, and on the other was a little yellow brick house. It was on the plot of vacant land that Mr Johnson had the house built for Dad; our new home, 30-32 Townshend Road, St John's Wood. The big, detached house with two garages and huge glass awnings over both garages, cost about £3,000 in those days. I cannot imagine what it would go for today. But the great thing about living in Townshend Road, I went to Barrow Hill Road School, in St John's Wood High Street, which was barely three minutes' walk away.

By this time Dad chauffeured Mr Johnson around in a Le Mons 3.5 Bentley, as well as an Armstrong Siddeley, both kept and cared for in our double garage. The son had a Lancia, and Dad kept that up to scratch, too. When I bought my favourite little MG, Mr Johnson gave me permission to keep it in one of the garages.

Considering we lived rent free, my Dad's fiver a week take home pay allowed us to live well. We had a wonderful time. On top of that, we had a family holiday in Bournemouth once a year.

My sister and I loved those holidays. London was always interesting, but the sand and the fresh air in Bournemouth was something quite special. My sister's full name is Emalia Hilda Madge Newton, a bit of a mouthful which was why we called her 'Babs'. The Emalia was something to do with my Dad's love of Spain, and anything Spanish. I believe he'd heard the name on one of his Spanish jaunts and when my sister came along, his firstborn, she just had to be named 'Emalia'. Babs wasn't impressed. She liked to be called Babs, or Madge.

There were only the two of us. Like me, Babs is still around, but she hasn't been too well of late, having just lost her husband who was nearly 100. So, at this time of writing, she is in a nursing home in Wales. Babs is seven years older than me, so she is knocking on 90.

Life in Townshend Road was good for the chauffeur's young son, but one day he noticed a family moving into number 42, a few houses along, and suddenly thought being there showed every sign of getting still better! Jack's eye had caught sight of the new family's pretty 13-year-old daughter, Mary. That evening, before bed, he asked his mother if she knew anything about the new people. 'The husband is like your dad, he's a chauffeur,' she told him. 'That's all I know . . .' Apart from the pretty daughter, Jack soon found out she had two younger brothers. Mary's father was a dour Scotsman and a member of the Royal Scots Greys. Apart from being a chauffeur, he was already a friend of Jack's dad. Every Sunday, Mary and the two boys who were turned out in kilts, sporrans, and little buttoned black shoes, were taken to church. After a while, Jack and Mary began talking to each other. Then Jack plucked up courage and started calling at her house. He wasn't always made welcome. Sometimes he would knock, and Mary's father would tell him to 'Go away . . . she's too busy.' 'Yes, I'd get shooed off,' he says. But he persevered. There was an old gas lamp-post outside, and Jack found that if he climbed to the top of it, he could see into Mary's bedroom. When his welcome wore thin at the front door, Mary opened her bedroom window, Jack shinned up the lamp-post and they chatted until Mary was called away.

Jack was getting on well with Mary, but the more it looked that way to her father, the more he showed it irritated him. Some evenings they would take Mary's dog for a walk, but when Jack called at her house to pick her up he was told precisely when Mary had to be back home. If it was nine o'clock, then her dad was on the doorstep waiting, looking at his watch as if he was counting down the seconds. It didn't make courting Mary easy for the lad. But young love conquers, and Mary had conquered Jack's heart. They became sweethearts.

I then passed one or two primary school exams and as Dad always wanted me to do something in the technical line, my parents managed to scrape enough money together to send me to the Regent Street Polytechnic. It was a sort of technical grammar school. The main school was in Regent Street and the technical side in Little

Titchfield Street, alongside Broadcasting House, which was where I went each day. In four years, I did pretty well, passing most of the technical exams I sat in drawing and light engineering.

Then I applied for a job as a draughtsman at the Air Ministry. It had nothing to do with flying because the closest interest I'd shown in anything aeronautical at the time was putting together plastic model planes. Not even a plastic Wellington! Anyway, the Air Ministry didn't want me, or more to the point, they said they hadn't any places left to offer me. The only engineering job I could find was with the Post Office, so I was recruited into the Farm Street Exchange as a 'Cord Boy'; this exchange being the largest in Europe. Well, it was a start.

I went to hotels and big offices to mend switchboard cords. To wire up three-pin plugs, and clean them. I was known as the visiting cord boy. The Dorchester and The Grosvenor hotels were both in my area. I was paid one pound four shillings and sixpence a week, which was pretty good money for a civil servant in those days.

When Germany began throwing its weight around in Europe, war fever began to get a hold of everyone, and I was no exception. I had three pals; one I'd met at work and other two were Fleet Street journalists. We agreed we wanted to become pilots, so in 1938 we trotted along to Store Street, off Tottenham Court Road, and signed on with the RAF Volunteer Reserve. We attended training lectures in Store Street, and took part in weekend camps, which included some flying. Then I was posted to the De Havilland School of Flying, No. 13 Elementary and Reserve Flying Training School, based in Maidenhead. We all trooped off there once or twice a week to familiarise ourselves with flying a couple of the aircraft they kept there – a Tiger Moth and the Hawker Hind. Both planes were painted yellow to show they were trainers.

It was there that I began to get really interested in flying. We'd go off for about half-an-hour, doing circuits and bumps (landing and take-offs), and a bit of cross country flying, too. I loved it, and believed I was becoming a pretty good pilot. Unfortunately, this wasn't a view shared by my instructor, especially after I returned from an afternoon training flight and came in to land just a bit too high. I had the choice of either opening up and going round again, or desperately putting the plane down firmly on the runway and hoping for the best. Unfortunately I made the wrong choice – I went for the landing. It was more of a crash landing. One wingtip hit the ground ahead of the wheels, and bits fell off everywhere before me and my machine came to a crunching halt.

The little man from the control tower insisted I called in with my logbook before I left the airfield. When I reached the tower I could see

4

he hadn't asked me over to sympathise. The little man took my logbook and endorsed it with the comment: 'Sergeant Newton will most likely make a very efficient pilot, but not up to the standards required by His Majesty's Air Force.' In short, there was no way they'd take me as a pilot, though my other three chums passed. It also meant I had lost the sergeant status given to trainee pilots, being instantly demoted back to the humble rank of AC2.

That left me with only one option if I wanted to be a flyer, as I did, and that was to settle for being an air gunner.

Shortly after 3 September 1939, the day war was declared on Germany, Jack had a letter from the Air Ministry addressed to Sergeant JL Newton. It instructed him to go to Store Street to pick up his uniform, his three tapes and little brevet hat. He felt great, and whoopee, he was still a sergeant.

I thought they had forgotten I had smashed up an aircraft, that I had been given another chance. All my friends were thinking, 'Jack must be jolly good. War has only just started and he's already a sergeant!'

But the following week an urgent telegram arrived at the Newton home in St John's Wood informing him there had been a mistake. He was told to hand in his sergeant's tapes because he was back to being an AC2, regarded as the lowest of the low.

His employer, the Post Office, thought he was crazy to want to give up his job to fly. He was a civil servant and in a reserved occupation, so he could have seen the war out as a civilian. That wasn't for Jack Newton, so the only chance he had to get back into the air was to take on a job that nobody else wanted – as a rear gunner, or a 'tail end Charlie', as they were called in those days.

His family, his friends, his girlfriend, Mary, they all suggested there might be a safer job for him to do if he really had his heart set on joining the Royal Air Force. 'I'd been bitten by the flying bug at Maidenhead, so it didn't bother me a damn that being a rear gunner was dangerous. Just as long as I was back in an aircraft.'

After some hanging around at home, waiting to be called up as a trainee air gunner, Jack was posted to the Eversfield Hotel, in Hastings, to do his initial training. It was the home of all the gunners and wireless operators. The next hotel along the road was for observers, and the palatial Marine Court was for pilots. 'So, the RAF didn't think much of us gunners, stuck in the lowly Eversfield, the worst hotel of the three!' said Jack. He did nine months' training without even catching sight of an aeroplane, other than the ones over-flying the town. Nor did he get his hands on a gun, not even those in the seaside town's amusement arcades! There were plenty of lectures, aircraft recognition tests, cross country running – presumably to keep him fit – and once a week pay parades in the underground car park. When it was wet, some of the outdoor activities took place in what was called 'Bottle Alley', a covered walkway beneath the seafront promenade that got its name because its walls were made with broken beer bottles and glasses. And when the NCOs (Non Commissioned Officers) in charge felt really bloody minded, they sent the men to run round Warrior Square ten times before collecting their pay.

Jack Newton stuck it out for nine months. Then came the plethora of inoculations for tetanus, yellow fever, smallpox, 'flu ... everything, it seemed, except swine fever!

They gave us those at the Grand Hotel, on the seafront. I had to sit on a long form, put my right arm on my hip, leaving it there until this medic had given me the three jabs in one arm, and another two in the other arm. That was OK because they gave us our jabs on a Friday so we could have a free weekend to get over them. I made my way up through Warrior Square to the railway station to get myself back to St John's Wood. On the way, I remember seeing quite a few AC2s hanging onto railings trying to catch their breath, groaning with their aches and pains from the effects of the inoculations!

Now for some real action. A posting to an operational training, No. 11 OTU Bassingbourn, in Cambridgeshire. Jack was able to familiarise himself with the Wellington 1c, the version with radial engines, and log a good number of hours in the process. Not too far away, in Gloucestershire, Frank Whittle was assembling his revolutionary jet engine at this time in 1940 and there were fears the Germans might parachute in saboteurs to wreck his work. Jack was one of those selected to undertake special guard duties on the site where the engine was being put together. Night fighters at Staverton, Jack's new posting, patrolled the skies in the area ready to confront any possible German attack. Fortunately, the Jerries stayed away.

Intense training continued on the ground and in the air as Newton went from Fairey Battles to Defiants, to Wellingtons, to understand all the complexities of the weapons that might help to save his own life, and those of his crew mates when he eventually went on operational bombing raids over Germany.

Then it was celebration time once more when the Royal Air Force gave him back his three stripes. He was a sergeant aircrew again, proudly wearing his stripes and his air gunner's winged brevet with AG embossed on it.

Aircrew were given minimum sergeant's rank, rather than LAC (Leading Aircraftsman) because if they were shot down the Germans treated the higher rank of a non-commissioned officer with more respect than an LAC.

What about Mary? Was she concerned that the man who was now her fiancé (they became engaged just before she was 18) was putting his life well and truly on the line as an air gunner?

> I don't think she looked at it that way. Mary was happy that I was doing what I wanted to do. In any case, with war now a part of everyone's life, we each lived one day at a time. When I saw Mary, we'd go to the cinema, take walks together, and we did a lot of cycling. I had a racing bike and Mary often came to see me speeding round the wooden race track in Paddington. Then there was my favourite MG sports car which we enjoyed taking out for a spin. Mary wrote to me every day, as she did when I was miles from her and home at Grimsby, in Lancashire, but there were never any recriminations in her letters at what I was doing, and the risks involved.

From gunnery school Newton was posted back to Bassingbourn around the end of 1940 and remained there training on Wellingtons. He hadn't seen any action, as yet. That happened when he flew as air gunner in Defiants, but this turned out to be primarily defensive patrolling. There was always the chance the Jerries might send over Junkers 52, loaded with paratroopers, in which case he'd have been up there in the front line. But they got cold feet!

> I can't say I was itching to get into action. I was quite happy with what I was doing. Then at the end of 1940 I was posted to RAF Binbrook, just outside Grimsby, to be attached to 12 Squadron which was known as 'The Dirty Dozen'. Or 'Thirteen Bar One'. The squadron emblem was a fox's head, with the motto 'We Lead the Field'. In fact, 12 Squadron did lead the field, too. It was the first squadron to gain VCs (Victoria Cross) on Fairey Battles and its crews bombed the Maastricht bridges on the Meuse. Tich Copley, my Wimpy wireless operator, actually bailed out of his Fairey Battle over the Meuse. The Germans sent out a team to pick him up, as did the British. Luckily for him, the Brits got to him first! So he had been in action before we got together on 'G for George'.

The crew began operational flights littering occupied France and Belgium with thousands of leaflets to reassure the local populations the British were their friends. And fighting for their freedom.

It was the beginning of a bizarre story that was to give air gunner Jack

Newton experiences he would cherish for the rest of his life. And many friends all bonded by their defiance of an enemy that tried – and eventually failed – to dominate Europe and its peoples.

CHAPTER 2
Doing the Business

Jack Newton checks his watch. It is 2320 precisely on a blustery, moonlit night with very little left of Tuesday 5 August 1941. From his front gun turret he can see heavily broken low-layer cloud scudding across the sky, the snowy-white face of the old man in the moon popping in and out of view like the star of some heavenly peep show, and casting its reflected eerie glow on their bomber which will shortly be lined up for take-off. Binbrook's main runway is still glistening from a heavy evening dew. Nine of the ten Wellingtons from 12 Squadron on this bombing mission have already lifted off the concrete strip and are now climbing steadily eastwards, outward bound over the surrounding Lincolnshire countryside. But 'G for George' is forty minutes late, delayed by a faulty rear gun turret. It is to have interesting consequences.

'We're off,' says Jack to himself as skipper Roy Langlois gets the green light from the runway air traffic control caravan.

Langlois turns the 'Wimpy' onto the runway, and lines up ready for take-off. At 2325 it is time to go. A Verey flare, fired from the caravan, arcs high into the summer night sky. 'Power on,' snaps Langlois as he eases the twin throttles forward. The Wellington's two high performance Merlin engines roar into life, but with its brakes applied it remains restrained like a big bull elephant eager to taste freedom, yet held fast because it is still tethered to its post. Suddenly there's a jolt as the skipper releases the brakes, unshackling the beast, allowing the huge, trembling machine to begin its lumbering take-off. From his front gunner's turret – the 'office' as he likes to call his metal and plastic gun bubble – Sergeant Jack Newton has the best view of the flight ahead. But it is also one of the two most dangerous crew positions on board, the other being the rear gun turret.

His eyes scan the concrete strip. His ears tune into the healthy whine of the hardworking Merlins as they pull the heavily laden bomber faster and faster over the ground. The tail rises gracefully as though some unseen force is giving it a helping hand into the sky. There is one small bounce, and she is airborne. 'We're on our way ... at last,' calls the skipper cheerily over the intercom to his five other crew members. His confident and reassuring voice crackling into their headsets is now the only contact they have with their skipper, and with each other.

Langlois eases W5421G, callsign 'G for George', slowly into the night sky on the first leg of the flight which will take it above enemy territory for its operational bombing raid over Aachen, on the Belgian/German border, a border that Hitler's ruthless military machine erased in a single crushing invasion on 10 May 1940. 'Binbrook control. G for George airborne at 2330 . . .'. 'Roger, G for George. Continue your climb. Call when you clear the coast off Grimsby . . .' 'Binbrook – wilco.'

Up to now Jack and the crew have been largely engaged on leaflet raids over Paris, Brussels and Innsbruck. Not really the kind of action Jack had in mind when he signed on as aircrew, but these raids still carry considerable risk and are classed as operational. It always amuses him that he is being a bit of a litterbug, dumping thousands of leaflets over Paris on these flights. In May 1941 it is a popular form of propaganda, although by 1943 other crews are dropping what look like mini French newspapers called 'Le Courier de l'Aire'. The Paris street cleaners must be thoroughly fed up, unless the Germans pay them overtime!

In 1941 the war is still in its relative infancy, but this particular sortie to Aachen is completely different. Crew training completed, it is now time to take their own war into Germany. Instead of leaflet raids, this time the deliveries are an arsenal of bombs they hope will help blast a tyre factory and an important railway marshalling yard into oblivion. One 1,000lb general purpose bomb, three 500lb general purpose bombs, one 250lb general purpose bomb and sixteen 25lb incendiaries will certainly bloody Hitler's nose. But first they, and the four other 12 Squadron Wellingtons on this Aachen raid must get to their target, do the business, and make it back home safely. Another five Wimpys are on a simultaneous bombing mission to Karlsruhe. It is going to be a long night for each one of them.

The heavy, sweaty odour of nervousness hangs in the air inside Jack's aircraft. The crew's training has been thorough and Jack hopes this is the first of many such bombing raids which will give him the personal pleasure of striking back at Jerry. He has already come to terms with the fact that front and tail gunners are the most vulnerable, with a life expectancy that at the height of the war is to become as low as five ops. This night, however, Jack should have been tucked snugly into the tailend gun pod, but for some reason – and he didn't ask why – Doug Porteous, the crew's usual front gunner, asked Jack to change places. The skipper had no objection so Jack happily obliged. 'What the hell. Might as well get blasted with German cannon in the front turret as the rear one!' But behind this skittishness he has a strange belief in his own immortality. It just never occurs to him that something so awful might really happen. Besides, he married his childhood sweetheart, Mary, some twelve weeks before, with only time for just three nights' proper honeymoon together at Bourton-on-the-Water, in the Cotswolds. Then Mary came up from London to Binbrook to the rented cottage Jack had booked for them over that August Bank Holiday weekend; a two-day extension of their honeymoon that was sadly so short, but happily so sweet. That sweetness is still uppermost in his mind. During the quieter moments on the flight to Germany, his heart and head are full of thoughts of Mary, rather than of the Aachen factories and marshalling yards he knows he will have to concentrate on soon enough. In any case, Jack believes that by 0800 the following morning, 'G for George' will be touching down at Binbrook – its job done. Back to a huge breakfast. Back to his beloved Mary.

Right now, though, he must focus on the outward trip. It is so easy to leap ahead, make plans, but Jack knows the reality is to live each moment as it happens. This way disappointments are reduced to a minimum. War is like that. So he focuses on RAF Binbrook which is just visible down below, perched on a hilltop; the hilltop that gave 12 Squadron its nickname 'Squadron on the Hill'. Great for flying in and out, but not so great for the guys on a pub crawl in Binbrook village, at the foot of the hill, when it is time to stagger back to camp! Having said that, RAF Binbrook is home sweet home at this stage of the war so there is considerable loyalty to its presence, and a tolerance of its shortcomings. It is where they train, eat, sleep and play. And it is where Jack and his crewmates will be expecting to return in about eight hours' time. Good ole Binbrook. It's no Monte Carlo, but it's not a bad place to be stationed. Comfortable quarters. Not bad mess facilities. As well as . . . . 'Jack, keep a look out for Jerry. You, too, Doug,' crackles the skipper's voice through their headsets. Both acknowledge.

Their earlier late-afternoon briefing had been interesting. And this being their first active bombing mission over enemy territory, Jack didn't want to miss a thing. His life might depend on something that at this time could seem quite insignificant, although nobody ever thought he would be the one shot down. The one who might die in a burning plane. It always happened to the other guy.

As Sergeant Jack Newton leaves the crew briefing room, the words of Royal Air Force Binbrook's station commanding officer still ring in his ears. 'Your efforts tonight will bloody Hitler's nose where it will hurt him most. At the heart of his capacity to wage war. Hit hell out of him. Good luck to you all, and get back safely.' Stirring stuff, and it strikes a very special chord with the impressionable young Newton. It is as though the CO had stuck a picture of Adolf on the sergeants' mess wall and challenged everyone to pepper it with darts. Only it won't be a picture of Adolf's face Jack and his fellow crew members will be peppering in a few hours' time, it will be his German homeland. The ancient city of Aachen, barely seventeen miles from the Belgian border.

And the crew's arsenal of 'darts' weigh up to 1,000lbs apiece, along with a basket of incendiary bombs. Aachen is definitely not a place to be tonight. It also has to be said, this being Newton's first operational sortie into Germany, it is not one he particularly relishes, although he remains unemotional about the trip ahead. He has already learned to 'switch off' his emotions. There is a job to be done. A flight into the unknown for him, and he has very little idea what to expect, other than that it will be a flight into hell. Certainly, it will be very different to the leaflet drops he has been making over the past few months above France and Holland, and the many hours spent on numerous training flights down to Land's End, over Suffolk and Norfolk, designed to see if his crew can find their way back home. Cheeky! There is no way they will find their way back to Binbrook from Germany tonight if they had got lost on training flights out to Norwich! 'Anyway, we didn't, so there is no reason to believe it will be a problem now,' muses Jack as many thoughts flicker through his adrenaline-pumped mind. Besides, the skipper of their Wellington, with its distinctive registration, is the equally distinctive Flight Lieutenant Roy Brouard Langlois, holder of the Distinguished Flying Cross, awarded to him before the war, though he never told any of his crew for what! He has a DFC, so he'd have earned it for something pretty sensational. Now it is his destiny to lead this new crew of young airmen, to be blooded in the Royal Air Force's increasingly heavy and effective bombardment! Langlois, his second pilot, Sgt Pat McLarnon; navigator Harold Burrell (nicknamed 'Burry'); wireless operator Richard 'Tich' Copley; Doug Porteous, usually the front gunner, and Jack Newton, usually the rear gunner, are a great bunch of guys and Langlois is pleased to be with them, as they are happy to have him running the show at the business end of their Wimpy.

Apart from the skipper, the only other member of the crew with previous aerial warfare experience is wireless operator Richard Copley. Born in Farnborough, Hampshire, on 13 October 1919 and educated at the local Farnborough Grammar School, Richard was called up on 3 September 1939 and sent straight to Hamble, in Southampton, on a radio operator's course. He saw action soon after his posting to 12 Squadron in France on 12 May 1940. Over the next month he had logged eleven operational flights, including three during daylight. It was on his twelfth, on 13 June, that he got unlucky in his Fairey Battle. He was shot up by four marauding ME109 German fighters over the Forêt de Gault, near Paris, as he was bombing Panzer tanks reportedly refuelling under the wooded cover there. The plane caught fire and crashed near St Barthelemy (Seine-et-Marne), some twenty miles north of Provine. Of the three crew, Pilot Officer Shorthouse and LAC Copley managed to bail out, but Sergeant Cotterell, the observer, was badly hurt and died in the burning plane. Shorthouse suffered burns, but Copley got off reasonably lightly with a wounded right foot.

In his graphic official report of the incident, Copley said:

Four ME 109 aircraft attacked from the rear in line astern and slightly below. I returned fire, but German tactics were such as to deprive me of any chance of effective gunnery. Our Battle aircraft caught fire, the observer was badly hit. I stayed with him until the altimeter indicated 900 feet, then I realised the pilot had already bailed out. Unable to help the observer in any way, I baled out. I landed in a field, approximately a quarter of a mile from a German ground gun crew engaging our aircraft, and then realised that my right flying boot was missing and my foot was bleeding badly from bullet wounds. I bound up my foot with emergency dressing and crawled away from the German ground gunners, who had not noticed me. I was picked up by French patrols and taken south to Sens, where I was put aboard a hospital train bound for Bordeaux.

Richard Copley made it safely to the south-west French port of Bordeaux, where he was transferred to a British Indies liner and taken on to Falmouth, in England. In January 1941 he was back at 12 Squadron, but this time flying on Rolls Royce Merlin-engined Wellingtons. After a number of operational flights across the continent between February and June of that year, on 24 July under the captaincy of Wing Commander Roger Maw, he went on a daylight raid to Brest against the notorious German battleship *Scharnhorst*, as well as battleships *Gneisenau* and *Prinz Eugen*. The crew's gunners shot down an ME 109. The pilot Wing Commander Maw called it 'a dicey do'. Anti-aircraft fire was very intense, there was no fighter escort and a considerable number of aircraft and crews were lost in this operation . . . 'but we made it back to Binbrook in one piece,' said the skipper, who was awarded a DFC (Distinguished Flying Cross) for the crew's successful part in the operation.

Now, on 5 August it is this fateful bombing raid over Aachen, in the company of skipper Roy Langlois, and three others, McLarnon, Burrell and Porteous, which is occupying front gunner Jack Newton's thoughts.

Jack recalls his 21st birthday celebration, only last February, in his parents' home in Townshend Road, St John's Wood, a posh part of north London. How he blew out a single candle on the cake made for him so lovingly by his mum, a candle she had rustled up from one of her neighbours. It had been a small and happy family party for Jack, with his fiancée, Mary, by his side to help him through the evening's low-key celebrations, prior to their marriage in April.

Now it is August, with the war against Germany gaining momentum as each day passes, and it is not the time to make too many plans. Who knows if any of them even has a future? The depressing thought is there, but few care to acknowledge it with gloomy sentiments or predictions. Each day is lived as it happens; each happiness savoured as it is experienced. And yet there is a national feeling of optimism because Britain is taking its fight with Hitler to his troops now occupying an increasing number of European countries, France among them.

Mary is so proud of the airman who is now her husband. He has promised to love her, 'till death us do part'. 'Why marry Jack with war and so much uncertainty in the air?' asked her family, and so many of her friends. That was easy for Mary to answer. Jack was barely 21, bullish with so much energy, enthusiasm and patriotism. He was good looking; tall and lean, with black hair greased and combed back. His dark features gave him a swarthy look; he was the personification of Britain's young blood eager to serve their country at this time of great need. Jack had no intention of standing on the sidelines. He had wanted to be in the thick of the action as a pilot, but as that was not possible, he was happy to settle for being an air gunner. That training flight landing, when he unhappily 'dumped' his light aircraft too heavily on the runway, and bent it a little, was the cause of him being turned down as a pilot and, of course, it saddened the young Newton, but he didn't let the disappointment dampen his spirits. Half his wings (as an air gunner) was better than no wings which he would have earned as a pilot. Mary just knew she'd got a good 'un. Her heart as well as her head told her so.

Mary's heart overflows with her love for her Jack, and each night she makes it quite clear to God that she is relying on Him to keep Jack safe. There are to be no slip-ups. No excuses. God certainly knows the score!

In any case, at work Jack is much nearer to God than most people, so they can keep an eye on each other. If things look like getting a bit tough, then Jack doesn't have to shout too loud to call for a bit of heavenly help.

Jack smiles. Funny how the mind can race along so many of life's nostalgic highways without actually reaching anywhere. Yet, they bring great comfort to him, as the mesmeric hum of the Wimpy's engines takes him deeper and deeper into his thoughts, as well as nearer and nearer to the target.

Suddenly the spell is broken. As the hypnotist clicks his fingers to bring his subject instantly out of a trance, so the commanding tone of the skipper's voice snaps Jack instantly back to the here and now. What had been the soothing, sense-numbing hum of the twin engines again becomes an ear-shattering roar less than ten feet either side of his turret. The vibration that rings through every rivet, every panel of the aircraft's flimsy thin shell, even rises through his feet, his legs, his chest to his teeth. They tingle with the unseen, unchecked shaking.

'Keep your eyes peeled, you guys. We don't want Jerry joining our little party unannounced. Much better that we give him a warm welcome if he looks like dropping in uninvited!' says Langlois, a touch impishly.

'It's so quiet back here you'd think the Luftwaffe had given up, and gone home,' chips in Porteous from the back office.

'Don't count on it, Doug,' says Langlois.

'Maybe they all booked their summer holidays in the Black Forest for the last two weeks in August,' intervenes Newton, unable to resist a chortle at the prospect.

'Ok guys, keep alert. We don't want Jerry sneaking up on us . . .' says Langlois, gently reminding his crew that this is not a tourist flight to northern Germany. That they are not there by invitation. Everyone needs to be absolutely tuned in and focused on what they are doing, and should be doing. The point doesn't have to be made twice.

Newton scans his twin Browning 303s, the shiny clipped ammo neatly snaking back into its boxes at his feet. Strapped into his swivelled seat, he looks around and reminds himself that in the event of something going badly wrong, it is not as easy to escape from the front gun turret, as it is from the rear one, his usual Wimpy workplace. In the 'back office', he is used to four Brownings set two on top of each other. Controls move the Fraser Nash 23s up and down. Hydraulics rotate the turrets quickly and smoothly. And most air gunners keep their parachutes inside the aircraft to give them more room in their turrets. When things get a bit busy, they snap their chutes into position across their chest for a bit of added protection, but the chute's bulkiness can restrict movement. The back or front office are just about the worst places to be on board!

Getting out of the rear turret in a hurry is almost as tricky as getting into it. Jack has practised until it has become second nature. He turns the turret sideways, and by raising his elbows quickly and firmly, the two so-called dead man's levers open the turret doors, the strength of the wind forcing the doors free. Then he throws himself through the opening – and, as he floats down under his inflated parachute, he prays for a soft and safe landing. So far, it is all theory. Jack wants it to remain that way!

Back or front turret? For Jack it is the rear turret, his usual position on the Wellington, even though that puts him in the firing line with the Luftwaffe fighter pilots mostly attacking from behind. It's easier to bail out of the rear turret! This time, Jack knows that if the Wimpy gets into difficulties, he will be a goner because it is unlikely he will have time to get himself out of the front gun turret, and back into the fuselage. A lever which controls the opening and closing of the bulkhead door is usually operated by the wireless operator, or the observer if he is in his bomb aiming position. So the front turret is a lonely place, a bit like a cage. Once the front gunner is in position, he cannot bail out so there is little point in wearing a parachute. With two powerful Merlins, their triple-bladed props cutting through the air a few feet either side of the turret, no front gunner in his right mind would want to try leaving it, even it was possible! So why did Jack Newton agree to change places with Doug Porteous on this operational flight? 'He asked to change, and I'd never been upfront before, so I thought it might be an interesting experience,' says Jack. Little did he know, at the time, just how interesting it is going to prove to be.

'Jack and Doug, it's time for you to zap a few seagulls before we reach the Dutch coast,' orders the skipper over the intercom.

'OK, skip . . .' acknowledges Newton.

'Right skipper,' checks Porteous from the rear gun turret.

The aircraft shudders as both gunners let go several short burst to test their armaments. Their guns must be in good working order and reliable; if they jam with Messerschmitt 109s homing in on them, it will be a recipe for disaster. But all is well.

'Guns checked, skip,' reports Newton.

'Guns checked, skip,' says Porteous.

'No sign of a welcoming party, skip,' repeats Newton. 'Maybe the Luftwaffe boys are all tucked up in bed, having an early night!'

'Don't count on it, Jack,' responds Langlois.

Nobody likes a ducking and the last thing any of the crew wants is to come across a patrolling German fighter plane that might get lucky and send them into the drink before they have even delivered their surprise 'pressies'. Jack looks down and thinks how beautiful the sea is, the waves shimmering in the moonlight thousands of feet below. If only he knew how to swim! A shooting star dives into the earth's atmosphere and splinters into a myriad of flaming fragments. In his front gun turret, Jack braces himself, his hands tightening on one of his two Browning machine guns. For a split second he mistakes the high altitude lights for diving Messerschmitts, then he relaxes again as he realises his mistake. He sits back. It's onward and upwards, still climbing gently as the Wimpy's droning twin engines take it ever nearer to its 12,000 feet ceiling which it will reach over the bombing zone.

It is still quiet, but Jack knows that things will get considerably livelier when they reach the enemy coastline. Searchlights will be one of the biggest problems. If one of these enemy searchlight batteries gets lucky and picks them up, others will pick them up too. Then the anti-aircraft fire will lock on and it will be hard to escape the lethal concentration of fire power that follows. In any case, the anti-aircraft batteries down below pick up an aircraft's altitude and lay a carpet of deadly flak in its path, shells that explode like puffballs, deadly balls of fire and smoke spitting out equally deadly flak that peppers anything within a couple of hundred yards. It is hit and miss gunfire, but it is eerie, deadly and effective because it is so frightening.

Jack knows that keeping busy and keeping calm is the secret. With his left hand on one of his guns, he uses his right hand to fish around in his flying jacket for his sandwiches. 'Nice of them to provide us with a packed meal, as well as a bar of chocolate and bottle of fresh orange juice,' he mumbles happily. He gets stuck in before he will need to turn on his oxygen. He stuffs the last bit of chocolate into his mouth as the skipper tells his crew to do just that. Not too long after, the skipper is on the intercom again – 'Target coming up. We'll be over Aachen in ten minutes. Keep you heads down, there's a bit of flak ahead.'

Jack tells Mary he loves her, and puts a hand to his battledress top pocket where he keeps her picture.

'Bomb doors open,' orders Langlois. Kerbooomph . . . an anti-aircraft shell explodes dangerously near, and small shreds of white hot metal pepper parts of the fuselage to the rear of the Wimpy. It only takes one small piece of this shrapnel to penetrate a fuel tank or sever an aileron control to put a plane out of action. Porteous is quick to report that he is in the firing line! Flak activity increases. Bomb aimer Burrell gets into position above the bomb doors. As the bomb doors lock into place, there's a clunk, and a brief shudder. The Wimpy is buffeted by the increasingly active and effective flak explosions, still too close for comfort. The acrid, sulphurous smell of spent TNT filters through the fuselage causing some of the crew to cough uncontrollably.

'Approaching first target. All yours Burry . . .'

'Got it skip . . . left, left, hold it, hold it, right a little. Hold it . . . Bombs away.'

The Big One, the 1,000 pounder drops out of the bomb bay like a mother rhino giving birth to her first baby. Its heaviest occupant unloaded, the Wimpy does a little jump for joy. The three 500 pounders go next. 'Some party they will be having in Aachen tonight,' snorts Jack, who still hasn't seen even one ME 109.

'They turned the lights on, or switched them off, which way you care to look at it,' quips rear gunner Porteous excitedly. He has a clear view of their exploding bombs and incendiaries lighting up the tyre factory. The skipper nurses the Wimpy round on its port wing, straightens up, and turns for his final run over the marshalling yards. The bomb doors still open, Langlois hands over again to Burrell. In moments the rest of their deadly load is delivered onto German soil. Langlois turns for the Belgian coast and the home run back across the North Sea.

The Wimpy is now some 3,250lbs lighter. That's the way to slim! And she seems to be in good heart, the engines still purring contentedly, as the aircraft and its six crew, their job done, congratulate themselves on their night's work.

But their joy is premature.

'Christ, what was that?' shouts Copley as the Wimpy suddenly flips starboard as if cuffed by some giant hand. Has it been hit by flak, or by an incoming ME 109? The starboard engine starts 'racing', its pitch now out of sync with the port engine.

'My God,' yells Jack as he sees heavy flames licking from the cowling of the starboard engine. It could blow any moment, and he is the nearest to it. But before he can draw attention to the flaming engine, another crew member has seen it, too, and shouts over the intercom, 'Fire, starboard engine'. Langlois presses the Merlin's fire extinguisher button. For a moment, the flames are quenched. But they quickly return. The extinguisher again momentarily damps the flames, before they envelop the engine once more. None of the crew is under any illusion that they are now in serious trouble as the skipper feathers the blazing engine to give the foam a chance to do its job. He can no longer risk what will be a terminal explosion if the flames spread and reach the fuel tanks.

With the starboard engine now shut down, the Wimpy is already starting to lose height. 'Throw out anything we don't need,' orders Langlois. Whatever the crew can lay their hands on, and they can do without, goes overboard through the flare chute; including some rather unpleasant little mementos from 'G for George' which are quickly despatched to rain down on the residents of Aachen. Jack explains:

> Before flying off on ops, the crew would go to the officers mess after a party to 'borrow' big champagne bottles the officers had emptied. It was almost the done thing, especially for gunners, who, stuck in their small turrets, found the big champagne bottles ideal as portable piss pots. I found my willy fitted into the neck of a champagne bottle a treat, especially at 12,000 feet where any man's willy is just about as shrivelled by the cold as it can be! So I could sit there, clamp the neck of the champers bottle in place, have a relaxing pee and still keep a look out for enemy fighters. Anyway, in the kind of serious situation we were in, these filled bottles had to go too. The wireless operator Doug's bottle went, but not mine from the front turret because I was inaccessible at that stage. So it was Doug's unstoppered bottle that got delivered through the flare chute to rain down on the long-suffering folk of Aachen. This was seemingly the last indignity for them. Also the corkless champagne bottles made a frighteningly shrill whistling noise as they plummeted through the air onto enemy territory. And it was not unknown for bomber crews to take a crate of empties on a trip to send them menacingly whistling down over German cities just to scare hell out of the locals!

Now it is the turn of the six crew of 'G for George' to be scared. They are flying on just one engine, and they are losing height. They all know they are slowly crashing. Burrell is heard to mutter: 'So much for Aachen. We should call it "Amen"!' And Porteous good humouredly blames Jack for their bad luck because, for the first time, he isn't wearing his lucky heart-shaped badge on his Sidcott flying suit. He has left that behind at Binbrook, choosing to wear leathers instead. But what to do now? Tich is all for bailing out, having done it before from his Fairey Battle, but the others prefer to take their chance ditching in the sea.

'The decision made, we flew on,' said Tich, reliving this dramatic moment from his home in Canada, where he now lives with his wife Betty.

In order to help the skipper, I went forward into the area below the pilot's position, where Burrell had been during the drop, and I cut the rope which is normally intended for use in bailing out injured crew members, but now I used it to help the pilot. By kneeling in the observer's bombing position with my back to the front turret where Jack was watching out for any ME 109s that might get the idea they can finish us off, I looped the rope round the rudder bar and was able to take some of the strain off the skipper's legs. Temporarily I tied the rope in this position and returned to my wireless set to send a number of SOS calls so back at 12 Squadron they could get a fix on us. I switched on another of our radio aids, but because this seemed to be attracting too much attention from searchlights, I had to quickly switch it off again.

The skipper believes their only hope is to make the coast of Belgium and flop down in the North Sea. Even that is a slim hope because the single dinghy housed behind the burning engine has now been barbecued to a crisp. Everything begins to look utterly hopeless. Reflecting on the terrible odds against him that night, Jack says:

I just could not believe that here I was on my very first operational flight over Germany and I was now facing death in the freezing North Sea. In my front gun turret there was little chance I would even survive the crash landing on water because my position would take the full impact of the crash landing. I would be killed instantly. Even if a miracle happened and I survived the initial crash, then I knew I might be trapped, and drown. As I have said, I couldn't even swim!

As he continues to weigh up his chances of survival, another member of the crew panics and shouts . . . 'Bail out!' But it certainly is not an order from skipper Langlois. And it isn't a call from Jack Newton. Both of them up front can see they are much too close to the ground. They would not stand a chance if they jumped. 'Jump? Not bloody likely,' shouts Jack to the bail out call. 'We can't be more than a few hundred feet.'

Not only are they perilously low, Jack suddenly sees the beautifully architectured spire of Antwerp Cathedral less than two hundred yards to starboard, its spiked pinnacle – above them! Clocks front four sides of the spire two-thirds of the way up, and Jack is quick to point out that their Wimpy is at the same height as the clocks. The Scheldt Estuary is coming up fast, and Langlois tells his crew to brace themselves for the only place in the heavily populated city where they might be able to put down in one piece. In the estuary. It is now clear they have no chance of making the North Sea some fifty miles farther on.

'We need a miracle,' shouts Newton. God must have been listening, just as Mary had told Him He must do, because a miracle is what he gets. From his front gun turret, Jack spots a possible way out of their dilemma. 'Down there, skip. An airfield. Port side. Can we make it?'

'I've got it. Let's give it a go,' says Langlois, calmly putting the limping Wimpy into a sharp left turn. There is no room for manoeuvre. There will be only one chance to land safely on the blacked out runway the skipper can now just make out below. He has only one functioning engine and he hasn't even got the benefit of runway lighting to help guide him in; nor can he use his own landing lights for fear the Germans defending the airfield will shoot the Wimpy out of the sky before its wheels touch down. It is all or nothing.

From his position inside the fuselage, Tich feels the aircraft make a sharp left turn and fears the worst. 'I really thought we had stalled,' he says, 'and that we were about to go into a dive, and crash. In those milliseconds the mind takes to appraise the situation, I prayed, "I hope it doesn't hurt" .'

Langlois wrestles with the controls as the underpowered bomber responds lazily to his demands. The rest of the crew hold their breath knowing they can have only a few more minutes to live if they get shot up by enemy ground fire. Or if their crippled plane doesn't make the runway. Jack hears the undercarriage clunk into the locked position. 'At least the wheels are down and locked,' he says to himself. The concrete runway, dark and deserted, lit only by moonlight, is coming up fast as Langlois makes his final adjustments, battling to keep the one-engined 'crabbing' Wimpy on line. 'Whatever airfield it is, here we come,' shouts Jack, crouching, bracing himself in the best seat in the house as 'G for George' sweeps in low over houses bordering the airfield. He spots parked Dorniers and Messerschmitts. 'Oh, if only I could send a few rounds from the Brownings into them,' he mutters, but right now that is not his priority. A happy landing is all Jack asks God to grant them as the Wimpy straightens up halfway down the runway. Langlois cuts the remaining engine, and flares the controls to let the old girl flop wearily down onto the runway. Its wheels give a quick squeal, like the cries from a stuck pig, as they bite into terra firma. And she rolls to a stop with fifty feet to spare. Jack checks his watch. Touch down time 0134 which, incredibly, was to be confirmed after the war when the German airfield air traffic control records were checked. 'That was an amazing landing. We all owe our lives to you, skip,' says Newton, as he wriggles out of his 'front office' through the cockpit end of the fuselage. But there is no time for niceties. The six crew know they must get out as quickly as possible, fire the plane, and make a run for it.

'Suddenly there was peace and quiet surrounding us,' adds Tich Copley.

I realised that Roy, no doubt aided by the full moon, had made a perfect landing. We hadn't stalled and hadn't crashed after all! Ex-Cranwell pilots were always very competent. We opened the hatch, lowered the ladder and I left the aircraft expecting to be surrounded by armed Germans.

Jack is surprised too. Amazingly, there isn't a single German in sight. With a bombing raid in progress, most of them have taken to the shelters. Those defending the airfield are well outside the perimeter, and haven't even spotted the distinctive, dark shape of the Wimpy make its low run in. Or have they? Just as Jack thinks they have got away with their cheeky landing on the German occupied airfield, there is a volley of shots from some way off, that seem to be aimed in their direction. Langlois quickly rallies his crew, and identifies them. 'Is everyone all right?' he asks.

'Yep, fine,' they say in unison.

'Then let's fire this baby,' says Langlois. They heave their unwanted parachutes into the open fuselage, and Tich fires a flare that ricochets off the now blackened starboard engine, and it fizzles out harmlessly on the ground. 'Jack and I then entered the aircraft and fired another six cartridges inside until we saw a healthy heat haze where the plane was now well alight. Time to go,' reveals Tich.

Now the Germans will know they have visitors. Their calling card is well alight! 'Let's go lads,' shouts the skipper, as they hear the distant noise of revving vehicles heading their way.

Hampered by their heavy leather flying gear and heavy boots, they dash as best they can to the edge of the airfield. They want to get into wooded countryside as quickly as possible, well away from the now blazing remains of their Wimpy. As he starts to run with the others, Jack feels a searing hot pain over his right eye. He rubs his forehead and realises he has caught a piece of phosphorous flashback from one of the ignited flares, possible the first that ricocheted off the engine. But there is nothing he can do except grin and bear it. Running in flying gear proves difficult, especially across grassy, rough ground. But they all make it some two hundred yards to the high barbed-wire perimeter fence, into woodland and beyond that into open countryside. Still no sign of German patrols. Sheer adrenaline keeps them stumbling on for a good fifteen minutes, until they feel it is safe to stop and consider their situation. Breathless and confused, they stop under cover of a small copse to discuss what to do next. Behind them, above the tree line, they can still see the glow of their burning plane.

'We are not going to stand a chance of avoiding capture if we stay as we are. We must split into two threes,' says Langlois. 'Me, Jack and Tich in one group. McLarnon, Burry and Porteous in the other. Good luck guys,' snaps the skipper, beckoning his two to follow him without further delay.

'Good luck, skip,' second pilot McLarnon calls back, as the two groups set off in different directions. It is the last time, until the end of the war, that Jack will see his other three crew mates. In four weeks, they will all be rounded up by the Germans and interned in Germany for the remaining four years of the war.

But for Jack Newton, Langlois and Tich Copley, the radio operator, an extraordinary adventure is just beginning.

CHAPTER 3

Dropping in on Antwerp

Their luck is holding. Langlois, Copley and Newton are only three hours into their bid for freedom from German-occupied Belgium, hedge-hopping from field to field, across country roads, warily alert for signs of patrols out looking for them. But in all honesty, they haven't much idea where they are or, for that matter, where they are going. They just want to put as much distance between what they hope is the now burned out Wimpy, and themselves. They estimate this is about seven miles.

They are having to rely on their instinct and the tips they were given in training should they find themselves in enemy-held territory. Jack explains:

> That advice, should we be unlucky enough to come down, is to seek out a monk, or somebody religious. Go to a church, they told us. We were given some currency, too, the equivalent of about ten pounds worth of Belgian, Dutch and French notes to help us along, and we had James Bond style compasses. If you were a smoker, a compass was concealed in your pipe; three of us were smokers so we weren't short of compasses. We also had special buttons to which we attached our braces. By taking two of the magnetised buttons and placing them one on top of the other, being magnetised, the top one always turned to the north. Clever stuff.
>
> First of all we broke open one of our pipes to get to the compass concealed inside the stem. Then we took a bearing to show the right way to go for England. But, of course, it wasn't quite as simple as that.

It wasn't going to be a hitchhike to the Channel coast, and thumb a lift over on a passing ferry!

So far luck has been with the trio. These three of the six-man crew have survived the desperate landing on a German-occupied airfield, they have escaped into the countryside, and they haven't – as yet – set eyes on the enemy.

Now the sky on the eastern horizon is starting to lighten. A new day is dawning and they are feeling nervous.

'I think it is time to find ourselves a bolt hole. The workers will be out soon. It will be foolish to try and continue in daylight. We must hide, decide how we are going to make contact with the Resistance, and only move on under the cover of darkness,' says Langlois. Newton and Copley agree. They have reached a cornfield, bordered by a thick hedge alongside what looks like a country lane. 'This is probably as good a place as any. We'll put down here,' decides Langlois.

Jack looks around. They are in a cornfield all right, and one that has only recently been cut. The stooks have been stacked together in threes, looking like small tepees. Langlois has been quick to appreciate their potential and is soon nestling inside one, encouraging the other two to do the same. Jack picks his, and soon follows. But even though Tich, being short, would probably find it easier than the other two to squeeze inside the stacked stooks, he decides they're not for him. Instead, he prepares his nest at the foot of the hedge, spreading a couple of sheaves across the ground to lie on, buffing up the corn at one end to give himself a pillow. He seems quite pleased with his handiwork as he settles down for what looks like becoming a very long day!

Langlois and Newton are asleep within minutes. Tich knows this because he can hear their heavy breathing, and an occasional low, rumbling snore. Tich muses that anyone innocently passing by on their way to work could be forgiven for thinking the field on the other side of the hedge was filled with grunting pigs! They'd never believe it was giving some comfort and considerable camouflage to three dishevelled British airmen. Tich cannot help thinking that he should be looking forward to his well-earned sergeant's mess breakfast; not sleeping rough under a hedge like some forlorn vagrant. He cannot even get comfortable. He tries resting, first on his left side, then his right side. Then on his back, giving him a view of the sky filled with trillions of twinkling stars, their light now slowly being snuffed out as the sun comes up over the horizon. Why can't he drop off like the other two? Tich thrashes around for a good hour and is still wide awake. He has tried counting sheep, tried imagining himself back at Binbrook in his own bed; he has pulled straw over his face but that proved too itchy. It's no good. The ground is simply too bumpy, and however much he tries to imagine otherwise, he is in a field – a Belgian field – and that is why he is so dog-tired, yet cannot sleep. It doesn't help that insects are finding their way up his sleeves, into his hair and down his collar. Now every limb is aching. Instinctively, he stands up for a stretch . . . maybe that will do the trick. Then he can start again.

Tich is so nicknamed by the crew because he is not a lot over five feet two inches tall, though with a reputation as a first-rate radio operator as tall as the Eiffel Tower. He can stand up in a Wimpy, raise his hands above his head and still not touch the roof. Something he does quite often on a long flight in quite cramped conditions. So it comes quite naturally to Tich, who is now cramped and quite stressed through lack of sleep, to have a long, lingering therapeutic stretch. But, as he stands up and raises his hands above his head he is not at all prepared for the outcome . . .

A young cyclist, on his way to work along the lane, can hardly believe his eyes when he suddenly spots two hands appear over the hedge top. As he brakes hard to stop and investigate, Tich realises he has given his position away. The rattling bicycle being brought to a skidding stop awakens both Langlois and Newton.

A face peers cautiously over the hedge. 'Ello, are you Engleesh airmen?' it asks.

Copley is dumbstruck. He just gawps not knowing quite how to respond. But Langlois, ever alert, crawls over to the hedge. 'Yes, we are. We need help,' he says.

'Wait here. I come back after dark,' instructs the cyclist. 'I am with the Resistance,' he says proudly as he gets back on his bike and pedals off in a cloud of dust.

'What do we do now?' asks Jack, rubbing his eyes as he lets loose a yawn so enormous that it threatens to swallow his face!

'We have no choice. We wait until the lad comes back,' says Langlois.

'If he does come back. Or he comes back with a German patrol,' says Tich, now clearly alarmed by the situation.

All three agree it could be a trap. Maybe the cyclist will find the nearest German patrol and tell them about his encounter. Maybe they should move on quickly and put still more distance between them and the airfield. Or they can sit tight, and hope the young man keeps his word. Tich ponders the issue for a moment, and decides he is in favour of taking a chance, hoping the cyclist is really with the Resistance; that way, he says, he stands a much better chance of getting into a proper bed where he can have a proper sleep. 'Yes, I am for hanging on until he returns,' says Tich.

'Me, too,' adds Newton.

'That's good because it's my gut feeling as well,' says Langlois. They each know that their only hope of evading capture is to link up with the Resistance and by now the village grapevine will be buzzing with the news that a British bomber has landed on the airfield, and that the crew has escaped. The Germans will be out in force trying to find them before the Resistance does.

'All right chaps, let's get back to bed. We've a day to kill,' says Langlois. They know they must not talk, must not move around. Must not be seen. They just pray for a sunny day and a happier ending to it.

The next thirteen or more hours of 6 August 1941 go by without event. They hear a number of bicycles pass along the lane, as well as people on foot, though none of them German if their conversations are anything to go by. They spot over-flying Dorniers and Messerschmitts, possibly from the same airfield where their burned out Wimpy still litters one end of the main runway.

The watery sun has passed from east to west, giving little joy on the way, and is now setting below the distant tree line as a new night gets underway. Dusk is falling fast and the three men are twitchy with anticipation, wondering if their young cyclist friend will put in an appearance, as promised. They are not disappointed.

'Ello, plees. Are you there Engleesh airmen?' The unmistakable, squeaky voice of the young Belgian patriot brings grins to the faces of the three airmen.

'Yes, here,' says Langlois, as he rouses the other two.

'I am back,' says the young man, peering over the hedge. He must be in his early 20s. He is wearing glasses, and his dark hair flops across one side of his happy, flushed face. He looks as nervous as the three apprehensive airmen huddled by the hedge.

'Yes, that's good. Can you help us?' says Langlois.

'You come with me,' says the young Belgian, who leads them out onto the lane and indicates that they should walk together behind him.

They have gone barely one hundred yards when the young man turns into a farm entrance – the same farm so close to where they had been hiding all day. A few minutes more and their saviour, Richard Dumoulin, delivers them into the safe care of the farmer, Alphonse de Voegt, and his wife. There are handshakes all round, as they are told they are in the village of Kapellenveld in Bouchout, on the outskirts of Antwerp. The de Voegts also tell their new guests how word is already getting round that a British bomber landed on Duerne airfield during the night, and that the crew had escaped. The Germans are scouring the countryside looking for them, but the de Voegts are quick to reassure the airmen that the Germans won't find them there.

The three men are led to a hayloft in one of the barns, and that is where they are told to rest overnight. In minutes, they are pressing steaming mugs of weak coffee to their lips, and for the first time since the crash landing, they are feeling just a little more relaxed about their situation. Within an hour they have eaten a small snack, and have fallen asleep under blankets, curled up on mattresses spread out on the floor. Over the next thirteen hours all their worries melt away in the oblivion of a good night's sleep, and they are left to enjoy every moment of it. The de Voegts, though, know it will not last.

When Langlois, Newton and Copley are woken the next morning there is the ritual of washing, and shaving with a so-called cut-throat, though with a near spent piece of elderly shaving soap. Trying to work up a foam in tepid water is impossible. The pursuit of personal hygiene quickly becomes a nightmare. Jack decides it is time to grow a moustache so that he only has to scrape half his face. The three share a well-worn toothbrush, but there is no toothpaste to put on it. They all agree that life at Binbrook wasn't so bad after all, and vow never to complain again if they ever get back to the base.

The hospitality shown by their hosts continues as generously as circumstances permit, but all three sense it is not without some kind of strange reservation. In stilted English, M. de Voegt is reassuring, but in his eyes there is a perceptible coldness. Perhaps it is the fear of being caught, perhaps it is the suddenness with which this ordinary Belgian farmer has been caught up in a situation over which he has very little control. Perhaps it is something rather more sinister for the three airmen?

With the Germans now intensifying their search for the missing bomber crew, there is a new urgency for the Resistance group to spirit the men away (the Resistance group, which they will later learn is known as the Comète Line).

'We will have what you call a fashion parade. You see,' laughs M. de Voegt, as he leaves the room. A fashion show? Jack thinks the old farmer must have a translation problem! When he returns his arms are full of secondhand clothes. A huge pile which he dumps on the floor.

'You have what you like,' says de Voegt. Within minutes they are all in fits of laughter as the men slip into trousers three times too big for them; and try to squeeze into jackets two sizes too small; shirts that were probably fashionable a good twenty years before. Tich has to settle for a pair of shoes two sizes too big for him, but it's the best he can do.

'We had the time of our lives for a good couple of hours sorting through the coats, suits, shoes, berets, scarves, socks, jumpers,' says Jack. 'Eventually, we all found outfits that fitted us, or nearly fitted us, and I ended up with a fine grey suit that I'd have been proud to wear in St John's Wood,' he adds. It is just a shade on the large size, but this allows him to continue to wear his Royal Air Force battledress jacket underneath so that if he is caught, he will not be accused of being a spy and possibly shot. A long grey overcoat, black beret and black shoes completes Jack's outfit. Alphonse de Voegt, with his little knowledge of English, many gestures and sign language, manages to tell Jack that with his naturally dark complexion and jet black hair nobody would give him a second look in Bouchout. He would blend in like one of the locals. His growing moustache is a bonus!

When the three airmen are kitted out as civilians, with clothes collected from villagers and brought in by three cyclists, their own flying gear and personal possessions are collected, wrapped and buried in a deep hole near the farmhouse, including Jack's Boy Scout penknife which he'd kept tucked in his flying boot, ready to cut the lanyard on the Wimpy's dinghy had they landed in the sea. A shed is moved over the hole so that it is not disturbed by foxes – or by German soldiers! And that is where everything remains until 1945. Undiscovered and undisturbed.

Jack can only think of his beloved Mary. She will have had the dreaded telegram that he is missing. And she will be worried sick about his fate. Is he dead? Is he alive? Is he hurt? Where is he? So many questions will be on her lips, and she won't have any of the answers. Even the Air Ministry won't have answers, not at this stage. There is nothing she can do but pray, hope and wait. Jack knows that Mary will be doing all three, as he also knows she will not lose faith that he is alive.

Back in Bouchout, things happen quickly. The three British airmen are told it is time to move nearer to Antwerp. It is too dangerous for them to stay any longer in the farmhouse.

Jack's thoughts leapfrog through all the problems now facing him. He thinks, 'What a difference a day makes'. In less than twenty-four hours, his life has been turned upside down. On 5 August home was RAF Binbrook. Twenty-four hours later, he is in a stranger's home in German-occupied Belgium wondering how the hell he is going to get back to Britain. A few days on, and doubts start to creep into his mind. Will he ever get home?

Only the one Wellington failed to return home from the Aachen bombing raid, and none of the other crews saw what happened to it.

Jack knows his fate is now out of his hands. He has to do as he is told, and put his trust in the Resistance, those who are, after all, risking their own lives to save his. He recalls:

> The de Voegts had been good hosts. Sometimes I would hear them around the house, at other times we seemed to be on our own. We had newspapers and some magazines to read, but because I didn't speak Flemish, and only a little French, I just looked at the pictures. The isolation was almost unbearable. We'd lie on our beds, doing silly things like studying a fly as it flew around the room! We'd lay bets with each other, where it would land next. And whoever was right would chuckle out loud. Even mealtimes brought very little relief from the monotony. The soup, which was plentiful, was always a frothy potato concoction, served with a small piece of bread. There would be an apple to follow or, occasionally, an orange. There were small pieces of meat in the soup, but was the meat rabbit, as Mme de Voegt assured us it was, or was it the remnants of some unfortunate farm cat, of which there were many? I was never quite sure, although I knew enough about cats to know they have round skulls, whereas a rabbit has an elongated skull. Unfortunately, I was not allowed into the kitchen to find out, so I suspected the worst. Because such thoughts whirled round and round in my head, when soup was served up I'd imagine Mme de Voegt chasing and slaughtering one of the farmyard cats so that we could have some meat. Sometimes I'd heave at these thoughts. It became a bit of a vicious circle and I quickly began picking out anything that looked like meat, just in case.
>
> I know I shouldn't have been so fussy. These were hard times, and those who took us into their homes at great personal risk often

sacrificed their own food so that British airmen like me could be fed. I certainly never went hungry. None of us did.

But at this time my bigger worry was my fear of being caught by the Nazis, and tortured. Would I be strong enough to keep my mouth shut, or would I reveal the names of the Resistance people helping me? I had had no instruction about coping with enemy interrogation. How to cope with possible torture, and some horrifying stories were in circulation telling how evil the Nazis could be when interrogating.

Another less life-threatening worry was the burn over my right eyelid where the Verey flare stuff hit me as we torched the Wellington. My eye was now sore, swollen and closing fast. I was going to have to get some treatment for it soon, or I would need to find a white stick!

Thankfully, the time came for us to be moved to the next safe house some distance away in Antwerp. A local Antwerp Resistance girl named Mlle van Eeckhove had the job of taking us to the home of a M. Paul Duquenne, at 146 avenue de Belgique, in Antwerp. So, we were off to the big city all decked out in our new Belgian clothes. Would we look the part? We would soon find out!

To be honest, I cannot remember the sequence of safe houses I was taken to in and around Antwerp at this time, although I do know there were as many as seven or eight, so I am largely relying on one of the leading Comète Line patriots who, in 1945, completed his own detailed report of our movements. In some houses, I stayed only for a very short time. In fact, it was from one of these Antwerp safe houses that I was soon separated from Langlois and Copley. They were moved off together to yet another safe house because it was considered safer to split us up – or, that is what we were told.

The young girl entrusted with taking us into Antwerp was a happy soul. She couldn't have been much more than twenty, with all the innocence of youth, a disposition worth a king's ransom to the patriots; it was the way things were done in those scary days. Who'd have thought she'd be leading escaped British airmen through the city of Antwerp? Certainly not many Germans, so smug with their new occupation of this neighbouring country. Before we left the de Voegts we were briefed and each given our tram tickets. We were told not to bunch, but to walk separately and casually behind Mlle van Eeckhove, keeping her well in sight. And when she stopped for a tram, we must do the same. There were handshakes all round, and the four of us left with almost indecent haste. Though the way we dutifully spaced out, as we were told to do, you wouldn't have known we were one party!

This was going to be my biggest test so far because I believed I now looked more like one of the locals than many of the locals! Would the

Germans think so? Would my disguise get me through? The journey to the new safe house, the superb home of banker Paul Duquenne, in the avenue de Belgique, was a good thirty minutes tram ride from Bouchout, and we had to get there as though we were on our own. We weren't, of course, because we had to 'shadow' Mlle Eeckhove. Do whatever she did . . .

The girl leaves the farmhouse first, turning to give her friends, the de Voegts, a friendly wave as she walks away. Jack and his two pals follow twelve to twenty paces behind each other, having said their goodbyes and thanks to the de Voegts earlier. Jack thrusts his hands into his pockets and wills himself to look as natural as possible. The biggest giveaway to the German soldiers, he had been told, is to see someone with shifty eyes, continually looking to see if anyone is watching them. So Jack keeps telling himself to think Belgian or French, as he is supposed to be, and to keep his eyes on his guide ahead without it being obvious. If he senses anyone looking at him he must not look back. He has to avoid eye contact.

So far so good. In a short while they are walking into the more residential area of Bouchout. Shops are open but they seem to have very little to sell. A pretty little girl holding her mother's hand looks up at Jack as they pass, and she gives him a smile. He smiles back. And walks on, taking an occasional look in a shop window, and making sure he doesn't lose sight of Mlle Eeckhove, fascinated by her long, black hair swinging from side to side as she walks.

Some one hundred yards ahead, Jack sees four German soldiers chatting, their rifles slung across their shoulders. As he walks towards them he sees that they seem more interested in each other than in the shoppers. That's good. But well before they reach the soldiers, Jack sees the girl stop for a tram. He does the same; Langlois and Copley, behind him, do likewise. The wait seems like an eternity, an uncomfortable eternity, with the Germans little more than thirty yards away. Jack adjusts his beret. And doesn't once catch the eyes of the girl, or his pals, until the tram arrives. When it does, with a sweep of her eyes, Mlle Eeckhove indicates that this is the one they must catch. They step aboard and Jack sits behind the girl; Langlois and Copley in other seats. The airmen already have their tickets so all they have to do is show them when the ticket collector approaches. As the tram sets off, shuddering and shaking, its wheels screeching along the shiny rails, Jack tries to relax for the thirty-minute journey into Antwerp, looking out of the window at the passing shops and the people. Who'd have thought there was a war on? Only the sight of several army trucks filled with uniformed men, grey coloured cars in a great hurry, and Belgian police standing around, are reminders that this is not a free country. Jack begins to feel easier. Perhaps he does look Belgian or French, after all.

How does he handle this new and quite dangerous experience?

The tram ride is the easy bit. Jack says:

I noticed a couple in front of our girl chatting away, but I hadn't a clue what they were saying. The woman kept pointing out things in the city streets that caught her eye. The man with her would laugh, and she carried on talking. But I kept my head buried in my newspaper; like the conversation going on in front of me, it might just as well have been double Dutch for all the sense I could make of it.

Finally, our girl stood up. She gave me, and the other two, a fleeting glance as she passed my seat on her way to the exit. The shuddering monster on rails was by no means full, and as I got up and joined the queue for the next offloading stop I could see that nobody was interested in anyone else. There was little conversation, though this could have been because it was difficult to be heard above the noise and vibration of the tram. Such awful conveyances! No wonder trolley buses, so smooth and on rubber tyres, mostly put the clumsy trams out of business in Britain. Anyway, that was Antwerp's business. I wasn't there to praise or criticise their trams. I just couldn't stand them; but they had their uses. If only their bored passengers had realised I was an evader, a shadowy figure passing through their city!

I didn't know it at the time, but I was on my way to a house that was more than a cut above any others in which I would be hidden.

After a good twenty minutes brisk walk, Mlle Eeckhove turns into the tree-lined avenue de Belgique, and then into the drive of what is a luxurious looking three-storey tall house of great character, with huge wooden garage doors, and a palatial oak front door. Someone from inside has seen her approaching, because as soon as Mlle Eeckhove reaches the front door ahead of Jack, it is quickly opened, then half closed again until Jack and the other two reach it. They are let in without ceremony, and ushered into a large entrance hall, with glistening white marble steps that lead upstairs to the drawing room, where it is indicated the airmen should go. Although, at this moment, none of them know whose home it is, most certainly it is not the home of one of the city road sweepers. This owner has money; lots of it. The pictures that hang on the walls, the rugs that cover the polished wooden floors on the first-floor landing, and the drapes across the windows, all show the owner is not only rich, but has good taste, too. Yes, this is the home of the remarkable Paul Duquenne, an Antwerp city banker; and a man of impeccably good taste. Once she has safely delivered the three men to M. Duquenne, Mlle Eeckhove leaves almost immediately. It is the last Jack sees of her, and he regrets he is not even able to thank the young woman for what she has done.

This safe house is to be a brief respite from dodging the enemy. Just one day. But long enough for M. Duquenne to call in medical help for Jack's painfully swollen eye. A 'tame' doctor, a friend of the banker, squirts a few drops into Jack's affected eye, and that is that. Happily, the outcome being instant relief for the wounded front gunner, the whole procedure taking less than five minutes. Then the doc is off back to his surgery. Or, Jack presumes that is where he goes, assuming he even has a surgery! Ironically, the next safe house is that of a practising doctor by the name of de Bie, in rue de la Station, in Liège.

The Germans had been taken by surprise. When the Wellington apparently crashed on Deurne airfield, and went up in flames, the Germans thought the crew had perished inside it. Shot down, they believed, by their own guns. It was not until dawn the next day that they discovered the truth, that the crew had escaped, and were now at large. German patrols flooded the area, roadblocks were set up, spotter planes put into the air in the desperate search for the missing British airmen. The pressure was on, making it necessary for the Resistance to keep the airmen on the move, and to put as much distance as possible between themselves and the Germans.

With this in mind, the airmen are told to prepare for yet another move, from M. Duquenne's home to the Liège home of the aforementioned elderly Resistance sympathiser, Doctor de Bie.

This time their guide is Mlle Raymonde Trockay, girlfriend of Richard Dumoulin, who took the airmen from the cornfield to the de Voegts' farm. Mlle Trockay lives in Liège so she knows the area well, which is largely why she is called in to undertake this particularly dangerous mission. With the German authorities on full alert, and searching for the escaped airmen throughout the region, any movement is very risky, but it has to be undertaken.

Langlois, Copley and Newton are successfully transferred to Doctor de Bie's house. At the same time, the Resistance leaders are becoming increasingly concerned about the safety of the airmen, so the decision is taken to separate Newton, the convalescing air gunner, from his two fellow crewmen, Langlois and Copley. The three are told it will be safer if they are split up. Less chance of the Germans being tipped off that something unusual is going on. Collaborators are in the most unlikely places, hoping to gain favours from their wretched occupiers, and they will not hesitate to tell what they know for a few francs.

Is this the true reason? Or, is there another reason they don't want to keep the airmen together? At least Langlois, Newton and Copley are unaware of any other background drama being played out – assuming there is one!

But first Raymonde Trockay, whose home is at 32 Quai Orban in Liège, and M. Duquenne, set off for the new Liège safe house via Brussels where Duquenne has left the group to continue without him. He has other business to attend to in the city. From Brussels, it is a short train ride to Liège, risky in its own right because many German soldiers use the same line. But the journey is made without incident. None of their fellow travellers suspects they are rubbing shoulders with evading British airmen! It is reassuring for the three aircrew.

On arrival it quickly becomes clear that Dr de Bie's house is not exactly a quiet little hideaway for escaping Allied airmen. On the contrary, it is like Piccadilly Circus, and nearly as busy because of the doctor's association with the Belgian equivalent of the Red Cross. There is even an office on the premises with workers handling the collection and distribution of parcels for prisoners of war. The arrival of the three men is not a secret for very long. Word spreads quickly that 'special guests' are in residence, and by the third day it is the talk in every bar in the city that in the suburb of Chenée, the Resistance are harbouring the crew of the British bomber that had landed on Deurne airfield! It is decided they have to be moved before word reaches the ears of the Gestapo that they have Allied 'guests' in their midst. Chevalier AG Pasteger, Belgian patriot and a well known citizen of Liège, visits the three airmen and introduces himself. He had been a liaison officer attached to the Royal Flying Corps in World War I, so his English is near perfect. Langlois tells him how they'd had to force land their Wellington on Deurne airfield after a bombing raid on Aachen. Pasteger tells Langlois that he and the other crews had done a good job; that the Englebert tyre and rubber factory had been flattened. He also tells them that the Aachen factory was the German branch of the Englebert works of Liège, and he (Pasteger) was a former manager of the wrecked plant. They are soon celebrating the news and the highly successful raid!

Pasteger reassures his new Allied friends how important it is to keep one step ahead of the Gestapo, now even more desperate to get their hands on the British crew. Together with fellow Comète Line member M. Pierre Hacha, it is decided to transfer the airmen to Hacha's sister's house. It will be safer at Henry de Rijcker's home even though it is still in Liège. Henry is a professor at the University of Liège, and a respected citizen, even with the Germans. It is in the professor's – and Belgium's – best interests to be seen to be above suspicion!

But the pressure continues. After three days in the Rijcker home, with the Rijckers' two young children taking so much interest in their new friends, it is considered best for the men to be moved yet again. Jack recalls:

> The youngsters were so curious about us that they asked so many questions. Of course, we talked to them. It was the one small bit of sanity at the time, being in a family with these children around. But Pierre Hacha wasn't comfortable that the children got to know so

much about us. It was a difficult secret for them to keep from their school friends, and it would not be long before word was passed on, endangering the Rijcker family, and us. But before we were hurriedly moved on to another part of Liège, there was one very special moment. One afternoon, Madame Rijcker managed to pick up a radio broadcast from Britain, the King speaking over the BBC. The three of us airmen sat on the carpeted floor listening to every word. It was the pick-me-up we all needed. Suddenly, my home sickness left me for a short while. It restored my determination to get back to Britain – at any cost.

But where now? There is almost a state of panic permeating through the brave members of the Liège Resistance network. The Gestapo is closing in fast as the three airmen are moved from one safe house to another, the risk of the authorities being tipped off is growing each day, but most alarming of all – and the flyers are unaware of this – some patriots are having grave doubts that the men they are sheltering really are Allied airmen. Word is circulating that they could well be Germans posing as British aircrew. Opinion is split. And the fears they might be German plants is kept from the men themselves. Nobody wants to put them on their guard, or risk exposing them before it is proved they are infiltrators.

One thing is certain, the Liège Resistance group, known as 'Beaver-Baton', is determined to find out the truth. It has radio links with Great Britain. Checks can be made.

But, as has been said, at this point, Langlois, Newton and Copley are unaware of the suspicions they have aroused.

Pierre Hacha is given the task of taking the men on to their next safe house, this time to the cottage belonging to a M. François, at 'Bois le Comte', Gomzé-Andoumont. Though the Francois' have chosen to live at their other home at Remicourt.

Jack takes up the story. His first impressions are favourable as they arrive in the Bois le Comte, Gomzé-Andoumont, some fifteen miles from Liège.

Our guide led us into a road heavy with trees and spacious parkland, with fine houses set back from the road by tidy, open front gardens.

'Welcome,' said Pierre Hacha once we were inside our new safe house. 'You are in Spa, on the outskirts of Liège. You will be very comfortable here.' But for how long? I was beginning to feel very unsettled, very insecure.

'I expect you will want to get to your room and settle in. Please follow me,' invited Hacha. He led the way along a darkened panelled corridor that reminded me of an upmarket private hotel. 'This is where you will all stay. In this one room,' said Pierre, opening the door and beckoning the three of us inside.

It was quite a large room, with a huge double bed taking up a good half of the available space. It was covered with a plain blanket, puffed up pillows, and I noted that the bed looked quite bouncy! The floor was shiny brown and wooden, with two or three individual carpets over the boards. A dark wooden clothes cupboard occupied half of one wall, and there were three easy chairs. A window, its shutters in place, was now our only link to the outside world. But for how long? And who would get to share the double bed – with whom?

That first night it was me, and Langlois. We tossed for it. I found it so easy to fall into that big bed early that evening. Hacha told us we must stay in the room, unless asked to move out of it to another part of the house. He reassured us we would be perfectly safe if we did as we were told. However, we were definitely not to go to the window and look out. Germans were everywhere, and vigilant. One of us just might be tempted and get caught the first time. We reassured him we wouldn't chance it.

'That's good,' said Hacha, giving me a friendly pat on my right shoulder. 'Then I will wish you all good night, and I will see you again first thing tomorrow,' he added, as he turned and left, closing the door gently behind him. I waited to hear if the key would be turned in the lock but it was not. Even so, I knew they would know if one of us tried to snoop round during the night. What they didn't know was that once my head hit my pillow, there wouldn't be a peep out of me till first light next day!

And that is how it was for all of us, even for poor old Tich who got the short straw and had to sleep on the floor the first time round. I felt much better when I woke after some ten hours of uninterrupted sleep. Breakfast came and went. Then Pierre returned.

Big issues are now being raised.

The Resistance are getting jittery. Is the Gestapo suspicious of the François family? Hearing that they might be, M. François invites his friend, the Italian Consul, to his home for the evening, hoping this grand gesture will deflect any possible suspicions that he might be involved in something devious. In any case, François knows full well that if the Gestapo called on him that particular evening they would not have been foolishly heavy-handed and insisted on searching his home, knowing that he was entertaining the Italian Consul. It works. He is left alone. But François cannot help feeling just a little pleased with himself, that whilst he is entertaining the enemy, he is also sheltering three British airmen. And even the Italian Consul hasn't a clue!

Then there is the fact that the airmen are beginning to become a considerable liability. What if they are Germans? Everyone's cover will be

35

blown. There will be wholesale arrests, and deaths, and the Resistance organisation will be blown apart.

A secret meeting is arranged between Hacha and a man named Emile Witmeur, who lives at 195 rue de Campine, in Liège. Although only about 21, he is an ex-pilot in the Belgian Air Force, has penetrating steely blue eyes, and is a leading man in the Liège Beaver-Baton Resistance organisation.

Suspicions about the airmen have to be resolved before any damage is done. On the afternoon of 14 August 1941 the two men arrive unannounced at the François home in Gomzé-Andoumont. Tich Copley is taking a bath, whilst Roy Langlois and Jack Newton are relaxing in their room listening to the radio.

Hearing heavy footsteps tramping up the stairs, Tich fears the worst. A towel wrapped round his lower body, he comes out of the bathroom half expecting to see Gestapo brandishing their pistols. Instead he sees Witmeur, followed soon after by François. There is relief all round.

Witmeur is introduced to Langlois, Copley and Newton, and explains to all three that he needs to ask them some questions. In fact, he asks lots of questions. But Witmeur and Hacha decide further interrogation is still necessary – elsewhere.

At one point, traffic noise on the road immediately outside interrupts this preliminary meeting. Hacha and Witmeur are seriously anxious because on their way to the house they spotted a car of the Feldgendarmerie nearby. Are the police keeping watch on the François house? Suddenly, there is a knock on the front door. By now Tich Copley has finished his bath and has dressed. Langlois and Newton freeze as the loud knocking reverberates through the house. But it is not possible to see who is at the front door. The knocking stops and from inside the house, the men can hear footsteps cross the gravel path round the side of the building. After several more minutes they see a man go into the back garden and steal vegetables. So, it is not the Gestapo; it is a thief after food. The relief shows on all their faces.

There can be no further delays. Witmeur knows they have to either clear or convict the airmen. If they are British aircrew then they need to get them on their way, out of Belgium, through France and to the Pyrénées. If they are Germans . . . Witmeur puts two fingers to his head. He doesn't have to say anymore. François knows the men's fate is now in Witmeur's hands.

Jack is more than relieved to hear Witmeur speak excellent English. He is of medium build, tall, dark-haired, and good looking. Clearly very muscular, very fit. Having said that, Jack decides Emile is friendly and likeable enough.

So, the atmosphere is relaxed. There is an older woman in the house, there to look after their cooking and domestic needs. She serves up mugs of coffee, and slices of plain bread. No butter. No jam.

And there are more questions.

It's Jack's turn.

'Was I a fighter pilot, shot down on my own? Or, were there any other members of my crew on the loose? I think he knew the answer, but it was no time to be clever.'

Emile asks Jack how things are going for him. Did he like the de Voegts? How lucky Jack was to find them, he tells him.

Is Witmeur fishing? Does he know about the bomber landing on Deurne? Is this an informal kind of interrogation? These thoughts flash through Jack's mind as they talk. He decides not to volunteer too much information, at least not at this stage, so he sidesteps direct questions, preferring to make general conversation about the weather, oncoming winter and his first impressions of Antwerp. Emile doesn't press him for more, nor does he seem to want to volunteer much information himself. It is a stand-off which both of them – at least for the moment – respect.

Langlois had his own views which were later found out to be spot on. He had said the Resistance might think they were German spies, rather than British bomber crew.

But at that point, none of us really knew if there was some kind of drama, or what was worrying the Resistance, and Emile Witmeur in particular. No doubt we would find out soon enough. As it happened, 'soon enough' was a couple of days later.

We were given bicycles and had to ride in the rain into Liège, then to the Hôtel de Provence where we were put in three separate rooms. I was interrogated again by Witmeur.

We knew now that our worst fears were confirmed. Witmeur and the others were obviously not yet convinced we were Allied aircrew, although Witmeur didn't let on as such.

Langlois and Tich are each taken to separate rooms, leaving Jack with Witmeur. The other two are interrogated by different Resistance agents.

Jack is concerned. 'Alone with the one man who had power of life and death over me, and seeing this concern on my face, Witmeur said, "This is just a routine interrogation. Don't let it worry you." '

Witmeur: 'We need to know that you are who you say you are. So, let's start. Your name rank and number . . .'

Newton: 'Jack Lamport Newton. Sergeant. Number 742570'

Witmeur: 'What is your father's name? What is his job?'

Newton: 'John. He is a chauffeur . . .'

The questions come from Witmeur like bullets exiting the barrel of a machine gun. Newton does his best to keep up, but feels under pressure. Why does he think Witmeur is trying to trip him up?

Witmeur: 'What is the name of the road at the end of the road in which you live?'

Newton: 'Avenue Road, St John's Wood, north-west London.'

Witmeur: 'Which way does it go in one direction, and which way in the other direction?'

Newton (to himself): What kind of question is that? Here we are having survived a crash landing on enemy territory, and this man wants me to tell him what's at one end of Avenue Road, London, and at the other. What is that going to tell him?

Jack can see that Witmeur is in no mood for argument. This is the business end of the man, and he means business. So, he tells him . . . the Zoological Gardens along the 74 bus route and the other Baker Street, also on the 74 bus route. Witmeur busily scribbles down Jack's answers on scraps of paper.

There is a slight pause, and Jack thinks it's all over. But Witmeur straightens his back, turns toward Jack again and snaps:

'How long have you been married?'

That's an easy one. 'Less than five months . . . on 19 April 1941,' says Jack. 'Your wife's name?' Jack gives him the lot . . .' Mary Emily Newton. Or Mary Emily Sutherland, if you want her maiden name.'

The questioning gets still more bizarre.

'When you leave your RAF station guard room, what part of the form do you leave behind?' asks Witmeur.

'Jesus . . .' stutters Jack, shaken by the apparent pointlessness of the question. But he knows he must answer just the same.

'This is form 295. The part you leave behind in the guardroom is doubled-checked with the stamped half you take with you . . .' says Jack, wishing to seem to be as helpful as possible, even though he cannot understand why this interrogation is now so strangely intimate.

'Why do you carry a picture of a sports car?' blasts Witmeur. '. . . and why a prayer book?'

Jack is quick to answer both. The MG sports car is his pride and joy. The prayer book was given to him by his wife, Mary, who is also his pride and joy.

With some visible relief, Jack realises his half-hour grilling has come to an end. Witmeur thanks him for being so cooperative, and leaves the room. No doubt to check out the other two agents.

The interrogations over, his crewmates join Jack back in his hotel room, where they have to remain until the following morning. They draw straws for the two who are going to sleep on the bed that night. The odd one out will have to bed down on blankets on the floor. But they cannot sleep. The interrogations are still on their minds, and they discuss what is behind such strange questioning.

'I know I'm right,' says Langlois again. 'They do think we might be Jerries. God help us if they decide we are . . .'

With the outcome in the balance, how can Witmeur and his friends possible find out for certain? It turns out to be a long, long night for the three airmen. They discover they've even been locked in their room. Morning light doesn't come round any too soon. And surprise, surprise . . . Witmeur with it!

They hear the key turn in the lock, and Witmeur enters with a big grin across his face. 'I hope you have all slept well,' he says cheerily. 'Well, I have some good news for all of you. You are who you say you are. London confirms it, and they checked your files. That's good.'

'That's good,' repeats Newton.

'That's bloody good,' adds Langlois.

'Yes, very bloody good,' pipes up Tich.

All four men break into laughter and shake hands, as Emile Witmeur again turns serious for a moment.

Is there more? Emile says:

> We had some reason to think you might be Germans in RAF uniforms trying to infiltrate our Liège organisation, so we had to be sure you were not. Now there is no doubt that you are from the bomber that landed on the airfield.
>
> If your answers had been wrong, it would have been very bad for all of you. If there had been any serious doubt then I would have taken you into the yard and shot each of you in the head. There would have been no second chance.

Tich's legs give way under him, and he flops down onto the bed. Newton and Langlois turn white, and in unison exhale a huge . . . phew!

'Now please, gentlemen, relax. Let us take good care of you and get you all safely back to England,' adds Emile, as he turns to leave the room, and his stunned house guests – flaked out in a state of euphoric shock!

The three are then split up yet again. Langlois and Copley ending up in the house of Jean Vandenhove, at 66 rue Washington. It is to be a bad move.

Events from this point on move swiftly and dangerously. And what happens next is well-documented, most graphically by the man largely responsible for them – Emile Witmeur.

In 1945 Emile Witmeur wrote his own detailed report about the landing of Wellington 'G for George' on Deurne airfield during the early hours of 6 August 1941. He graphically described the build up of the war over Belgium and Germany at this time, and the fate of W-5421G and its six crew; how they came into the safe care of the Resistance escape line 'Beaver-Baton', and how they were so nearly mistaken for German agents.

Some of the events described by Emile Witmeur have been recounted earlier in this chapter, and in some instances, may vary slightly, according to the viewpoint of those involved and the accuracy of Jack Newton's own recall of events. However, Witmeur's own recall is from a different perspective and is stunning in its detail.

At the end of the war, he wrote his own graphic account.

This is Witmeur's translation of his original report:

The night raids of the RAF intensified with the good weather conditions. A nonstop offensive over Aachen and Cologne began. The course of the bombers passed over the city of Liège and the Germans had soon installed a row of two hundred and forty searchlights cooperating with a dozen ME110 night fighters between Liège and the Dutch border. It was the last barrage the Allied planes had to cross before reaching Germany and the many beams of light were often converging on the same bomber. The people of Liège, my home city, could see the tracer shells of the defence of Aachen and were anxiously following the combats.

Since a few months already, patriots had entered secret organisations connected with London. Their main job was to collect general information about the German installations. Incidentally, they helped Allied airmen who had been obliged to bail out with parachutes or were forced to land. Other groups had specialised in sabotage of the high tension posts and cables bringing the electricity to the batteries of searchlights.

As more planes had been brought down since the beginning of August, the agents spread all over Belgium were advised to be on the look out for lost airmen. They had to take care of them personally and to hand them over to their chief of sector. The latter knew where to contact the special 'Escape Service' (as Resistance groups were called) leading to UK, via France, Spain, Portugal or Gibraltar at that time.

August 6 1941. Liège. At zero o'clock Central European time, the German interceptors took off and passed over Liège whilst the searchlights all switched on. The moon was full and the beams were not very efficient. The first British pathfinder crossed the barrage. Then minutes later we watched the first combats. A bomber escaped by releasing its bombs which fell a half-mile distance from my house. The alarm was given at 0045. A plane was brought down in flames, north of Liège. A few minutes later, I saw another one diving in the direction of the harbour. She was blazing and exploded in the air. During an hour we heard about a dozen combats seeing only the flares and the cones of light working like scissors and trying to get the planes. At half past two, one of them passed south of Liège on her way home. An engine did not work well. Every time she was putting on full throttle, the flames of exhaust were clearly visible so that the searchlights could easily catch her again when she tried to escape. A German fighter intercepted her. They machine gunned on both sides but no result was seen. At 0300 everything was over.

The next morning I got the following information: nine allied planes had been brought down in our area. A Wellington had fallen in flames into the harbour of Liège. Her wreckage lay partly on the embankment, partly in the river. The Germans allowed the people to watch. They were always proud to show that they were able to bring down RAF planes. Three bodies were still in the water and were removed. I heard that one of the airmen, probably belonging to that plane, had bailed out and had been rescued in a tree near Cheratte. Doctor Gilles, who belong to our organisation, had already sent him to safety in a shelter near Huy. Two other members of the plane were missing. The people had run to rescue an airman coming down on a parachute. 'English!', they said. But he was a German pilot. He uttered some unpleasant words, as the people ran off and kept out of the way for the rest of the night!

In town, the fires caused by explosive bombs and incendiaries had been stopped. Thirty people had been killed. An agent coming from Verviers told us that the tyre and rubber plant 'Englebert', in Aachen, had been completely destroyed.

On August 10, bills were stuck on walls around town and a note was issued in all Belgian newspapers, which read: 'The German headquarters warn all Belgians that anyone convinced to bring aid to enemy aviators will be sentenced to death. Anybody who knows where an airmen is hidden and does not report to the Feldgendarmerie, will be sentenced even if he did not contact him. A reward of 5000 marks will be given to the person whose information will lead to the capture of an enemy. Name of informer will not be disclosed.'

Two days later, a lady friend, Mme Masson, called on the telephone and told me that she had found tobacco for me. She asked me to come and visit her in the evening, which I did.

'You told me once,' she said, 'that if I ever heard of Allied airmen lost in this country, you could perhaps do something for them.'

'Yes, where are they?'

'In a cottage ten miles from here. If you agree, I will introduce you to a man who can lead you there.'

'Who is he?

'Maybe you know him. M. Hacha?'

'I know him from school. I will go to him, but I do not want to see other people, only the airman. I will give you my answer tomorrow. I must first contact some friends.'

August 13 and I saw several agents of my group. Doctor Gilles said that he would look for accommodation and I had to hand the airmen to M. Doneux after having crossed the bridge of the Meuse. The best time was at six o'clock in the evening the next day. 'Be careful,' he added. 'I do not know what the Germans have eaten, but they are patrolling everywhere. You saw the warning in the newspapers and on the walls?'

'Yes, I have cut it out of the paper.'

'Ask them a lot of questions and make sure that they are British!'

On the afternoon of August 14 I entered the cottage where the airmen were hidden, accompanied by Hacha. That is how I made the acquaintance of Roy B Langlois, Jack L Newton and Richard A Copley.

Emile Witmeur continues his report, describing the results of this interrogation . . .

From information I collected, or from what I saw myself, the Wellington bomber W-5421G on her return from a mission over Aachen was hit by anti aircraft gun fire and began to lose altitude. The pilot, realising that his plane would not be able to get home, landed on a large field. It was around 2.10 am on 6 August 1941 (though the actual landing time on Deurne airfield was verified by the crew and also in a German report as 0120). The plane had landed on a German airfield in Deurne, outskirts of Antwerp, Belgium.

The crew, numbering six was composed as follows:

Roy B Langlois, pilot and captain of the plane, service number 37938.

Jack L Newton, nr 742570. Front gunner.

Richard A Copley, nr 748217. Radio

MacLaren [should have read: 'McLarnon']. Second pilot.

H Burrel [should have read 'Burrell']. Navigator.

R Porteous. Rear gunner.

Realising that they had landed on an enemy airfield, the crew set fire to the plane and climbed the fence surrounding the airstrip. The crew ran away and was split into two parties. One of them was composed of Langlois, Newton and Copley. I shall not speak of the three others. Langlois and his two friends walked in circles all night in the neighbourhood of Antwerp and were contacted the next morning by a Belgian patriot M. R Demoulin, living presently 14 rue Montebello, Antwerp. He hid the three airmen in a wheat field and supplied them with food and cigarettes. In the evening, he came back and took the British to the farm of . . .

M. Alphonse de Voegt, farmer at Bouchout, Antwerp, where they slept one night. In the morning they were given civilian clothes and taken by . . .

Mlle van Eeckhove, 14 rue Montebello, Antwerp, to the house of M. P Duquenne, 146 avenue de Belgique (now Belgiëlaan), Antwerp, where they slept the night.

The Germans had been so surprised to see the plane take fire on their airfield that they did not think at first that the crew was safe. Moreover, they tried to fight the fire with their extinguishers. At dawn they knew that the airmen were not in the wreckage and they sent patrols everywhere. It was most urgent to put space between the British and the Germans.

Mlle Raymonde Trockay, 32 quai Orban, Liège, together with M. Duquenne, took our friends to Brussels where M. Duquenne left and Mlle Trockay, knowing people in Liège, took again the train and arrived in Liège with Langlois, Newton and Copley at the house of the old Doctor de Bie, in rue de la Station, Chenée, Liège. This house was visited by a lot of people as Doctor de Bie belonged to the Red Cross and had an office sending parcels to prisoners of war. Therefore, the three airmen did not like to stay too long in that house fearing that people would speak . . . which they did, of course. Two days after their arrival there, a big part of the city already knew about British airmen being hidden in Chenée and Chevalier A G Pasteger, living in 'Le Bercail', Embourg, Liège, thought that it was high time to move them before the Germans also heard the story. He visited them and introduced himself. He had been belonging to the Royal Flying Corps as a liaison officer of the Belgian Army during the previous world war and could speak English. He learned that the airmen had just bombed Aachen. The tyre and rubber factory Englebert, was flat. When he told Langlois that this factory was the German branch of the Englebert works of Liège and that he had been the manager of the destroyed plant there, there was some excitement.

Together with M. Pierre Hacha, 5 rue J B Meunier, Brussels, they took the decision to transfer the airmen to the house of Hacha's sister.

Mme Henry de Rijcker, of Embourg-par-Chenée, Liège. Henry de Rijcker is professor at the University of Liège. In this house they stayed three days. The two young children were asking so many questions that it seemed better to move again. Maybe our friends will remember that they heard a speech of HM the King at the BBC, while staying there.

Up to now, nobody had succeeded to contact a line of evacuation. Hacha transferred the airmen to the cottage of M. François, 'Bois le Comte', Gomzé-Andoumont. M. François lives presently at Usines, Melotte, Remicourt, Belgium. As the Germans had heard something, the François' were anxious not to be discovered and they had invited the Consul of Italy for the evening. Of course, the latter did not know that his hosts were sheltering airmen. If the Germans had come for a search, they would not have insisted when seeing the Italian Consul. Hacha had contacted a lot of friends and among them was Mme Henry Masson, 34 quai Mativa, Liège, who knew an agent connected with an information service. She arranged a meeting between Hacha and Emile V Witmeur, 195 rue de Campine, Liège, who was a pilot of the Belgian Air Force and belonged to the organisation Beaver-Baton, connected with the UK. Hacha and Witmeur arrived in Gomzé-Andoumont, in the afternoon of 14 August 1941. The François had left their house and they found the three airmen in the first storey of the house. Langlois and Newton were listening to the radio and Copley was just having a bath. Hearing noises, he came out of the bathroom and saw Witmeur climbing the stairs, alone and was rather excited. Witmeur asked a lot of questions, names, serial numbers, kind of mission, location of landing. Hacha and Witmeur were anxious because they had seen a motor car of the Feldgendarmerie on the road, as they were reaching the cottage. There was a knock at the door. It was not possible to see who it was. Then they heard the visitor walking in the gravel, round the cottage. After several minutes, they saw what it was – a man realising there was nobody in the house, had gone to the kitchen garden and stolen vegetables.

The transfer to Liège was settled for the same afternoon. Witmeur started first to see if the way was clear in Liège. Hacha and a friend named Georges Marchand, Ingénieur à Ougrée-Maribaye, accompanied the airmen in the bus. It was raining heavily. As the people were staring at the airmen who kept silent, Hacha feared that they would be recognised and came out of the bus before the spot of the rendezvous. He asked Langlois to follow the avenue and take the first street to the left. He could not miss it . . . but there was a misunderstanding and he missed it. When Witmeur arrived he saw Hacha with Newton and Copley. The rain was pouring down. They had stopped before the German firm 'Acier Marathon', exactly where they could meet Germans. Hacha said that Langlois was lost. Fortunately, after having taken the second street to the left, Langlois came back. The bridge was clear. Witmeur passed, followed by the three friends. There was nobody in sight. As they reached the other side of the bridge, Witmeur saw the German Consul, who knew him. They stared at each other and he did not even notice the three English airmen following. The airmen had to follow Witmeur until he spoke to a man waiting on the avenue, along the river. This one was Paul Doneux, 30, rue Louis Jammes, Liège. Instead of being alone, as had been agreed, he was speaking to another man named Eugène Vandeweerdt, rue Albert de Cuyck, Liège. Witmeur did not know the latter. He stopped, the airmen stopped. Doneux and the man seemed to be discussing him. As Witmeur approached they said 'What have you done? These three men are not English, they are German. They have taken the papers on the corpses of the three airmen who have been taken out of the water.'

Witmeur: 'I am sure they are British. They were forced to land in Antwerp, on the airfield of Deurne.'

Doneux said, 'Where? On the German airfield? You fool, why not on the moon? They have told you that because they know that you will not be able to enter the field and confirm their story. I do not take them.'

Witmeur: 'I can't go backwards. I shall take them in my house then.' To which Doneux responded: 'You'll be taken.'

44

Witmeur: 'I am sure that they are true British, though their story is amazing.' Vandeweerdt left. Doneux and Witmeur entered the long street where the latter lived. Doneux said again: 'What makes you think that they are British?'

Witmeur: 'Because they showed me photos of a motor car with a British registration plate. I recognised well the man. Moreover, I can speak sufficient English to notice a foreign accent. Look at the smallest of the three. He is typical Anglo-Saxon.'

Doneux: 'Have they got money with them?'

Witmeur: 'Yes, Belgian, French and Dutch. There has been doubt at the beginning because some of their bank notes had been issued here during the occupation. I saw it from the signature of the manager of the National Bank, but they told me that the people in Antwerp had given them some money and they were able to tell the ones they received in England and the notes they were given here. So that it seems all right.'

Doneux: 'Look out. Two German officers are standing at the corner of the street near your house . . .'

Witmeur: 'Maybe they are waiting for the street car?'

Doneux: 'Not on that side . . . turn back.'

Witmeur and Doneux turned back, followed by the airmen. Vandeweerdt had alerted other agents of Beaver-Baton.

From his report of the turn of events at the time, it is clear that, with the exception of Emile Witmeur, his fellow Resistance agents are now seriously concerned that they are harbouring three German infiltrators. And that they are not convinced by the stories they gave when first questioned. Doneux, though, believes all is not lost even if they are Germans. He and Witmeur will interrogate the airmen further and check them out by radio with London. If they are still unconvinced, the airmen will be shot.

Doctor Georges Gilles, 32 rue des Guillemins, Liège, and Fernand Farlier, 48 rue Albert de Cuyek, Liège, had a meeting in the café where they were waiting. Witmeur and Doneux turned round, Doneux said: 'Even if they are Germans, everything is not lost if I can reach the hotel with them, but we must make sure that nobody follows us. I shall put them there till we are sure. Leave me now and wait for news. We shall send a message by radio, after we have confirmed supplementary details. If they are not OK, we shall kill them.

It was seven o'clock in the evening when they entered the Hôtel de Provence, whose owner was Eugène Demeure, living now in 12 rue Roul, Liège.

The airmen had to tell again their story. They did not agree on the hour of the take off in England. One said they had left at midnight, another said forty minutes later. Finally they remembered that the time of departure had been fixed at midnight, but that there was something wrong with the rear turret and they had been obliged to wait forty minutes before it was repaired.

They refused to give the name of the airfield, but gave three names of dromes and also the number of their squadron. It was necessary because of the circumstances. A message was sent by radio during the night, and it was answered favourably. They were not German.

Carlier and Edgard Defau, 47 avenue de l'Observatoire, Liège, had found shelters for them. On 15 August, Defau came to the Hôtel de Provence with a friend his, M. René Debaets, 82 rue du Coq, Liège, and took Newton to his house. M. Jean Hufkens, of place Saint Paul, Liège, took Langlois, and M. Armand Lovenfosse, 252 rue du Laveu, Liège, sheltered Copley. They remained in these houses till 8 September.

Witmeur, in his report, records an incident concerning Roy Langlois and his stay at M. Hufkens' house . . .

While he was staying at M. Hufkens', the latter was obliged to receive a member of the German Luftwaffe, who spent part of the evening in his company. Langlois, in the next room could see the German pilot through the keyhole. During that time, the chief of the organisation 'Beaver-Baton', M. Nicolas Monami, 4 quai des Pêcheurs, Liège, visited our friends and contacted the 'Escape Service'. It was necessary to wait as a lot of airmen had been rescued during the month and it was not possible to pass them all at the same time.

However, M. Monami took further steps and it was arranged to transfer the airmen to Brussels where they would wait their false papers. On the 8 September, Defau arrived with Copley at the house of Hufkens, Newton came also and M. Monami took the three airmen to the square before the post office where M. Louis Rademecker, commissary of police, rue Auguste Donnay 49, Liège, took care of them.

Emile Witmeur is not clear what happened from this point on, but he surmises . . .

M. Rademecker must have accompanied the airmen to the station of Ans where a man or a woman (I could not find who) took them in the train to Brussels. They passed the night at the house of a Lieutenant of the Belgian Army and his sister. Who they are and where they lived, I do not know. They stayed there the 8, 9, 10 and 11 September. Newton must already have been separated from Langlois and Copley, who remained together. Newton must have met afterwards a young girl about twenty years old, rather small whose name was perhaps Jacqueline de Jonghe. He arrived in France safely, passed into Spain, and arrived in the UK in 1942.

Langlois and Copley were visited in their shelter, between the 8th and 11th by Baron Jacques Dony, 18 rue Jacques de Lalaing, Brussels. He could not offer accommodation in his own house as he lived at his mother's, but he had a lot of friends and transferred Langlois and Copley to the house of M. and Mme X (I do not know the name). They slept the night of 12 September. Baron Dony came again and took our two airmen in the house of M. Jean Vandenhove, 56, rue Washington, Brussels. They remained there till the 2 October 1941. The German Geheime Feld Polizei raided the house on 2 October and took Langlois, Copley and their host Jean Vandenhove, after a pursuit in the sewers running from the house. It took them seven hours to get hold of them. Transferred to the prison of Saint Gilles, Langlois and Copley remained about a fortnight before being sent to Germany. Langlois had been taken with secret papers containing information which had been given to him by Hufkens and hidden in a cake. The Germans must have found them, but at that time, and during several months, nobody in the organisation Beaver-Baton knew what had happened to the airmen. Vandenhove, who was probably only an indicator of Baron Dony, never spoke. He must have been specially courageous, because though terribly beaten, the Germans never succeeded to get something from him. Last time he was seen by two fellow prisoners, he had been transferred to Germany and tortured in such a way that his fellows had been obliged to carry him. He died two days later.

This is what happened to members of Beaver-Baton.

All except one, were searched by the Germans. The owner of the Hôtel de Provence, Eugène Demeure escaped. Witmeur was arrested the first time in April 1942. Monami succeeded to go to the UK in Spring 1942, but was taken again when landing with parachute in June 1942. Doctor Gilles, Commissaire Rademecker and Baron Dony were sentenced to death and shot. Vanderweerdt was killed. Doneux obliged to hide himself was found dying alone in an abandoned house at the liberation of Brussels and died. Carlier and Debaets died from starvation in the concentration camps of Germany. Defau, Hufkens, Monami and Lovenfosse remained about two years in Dachau or Oranienburg and came back in a bad shape. There is still a doubt about Debaets whose death is not official. As to the three other members of the crew of the Wellington, MacLaren, H Burrel and Porteous, they had taken the direction of Antwerp and were sheltered during a period of several weeks by Mme de Beuckelaer, 21, rue Gaullincks, Antwerp. They were visited there several times by Lt Commander W Grisar, Royal Navy, HMS 'Royal Athelstan', rue du Prince, Antwerp.

At the end of August 1941 I was informed that three airmen belonging to the crew of Wellington W5421 G wanted to go back home. The information came via Pasteger-Hacha. I gave the names of Langlois, Newton and Copley, telling that in order to get the OK, the others had to give the same names. They never succeeded to reach England, but I know nothing more about the story.

When Lt Commander Grisar arrived in England in 1942, he went to the Air Ministry and gave a report of what he knew about the landing of the Wellington on the German airfield and helped thus to confirm the report of Newton who had been alone lucky to get back safely.

I realise that my style is smokey and excuse me to have been so long.

Signed: Emile V Witmeur
195 rue de Campine, Liège.
Report dated: 7 December 1945

CHAPTER 4
Tangle with the Enemy

It took a while for Langlois, Copley and Newton to come to terms with their close brush with death at the hands of Witmeur and the Liège Resistance group. If there had been a slip-up in London a terrible mistake might have been made with the swift execution of all three Allied airmen. An irony that up to that point the airmen hadn't even considered. At the same time, they admired the dedication of local Resistance leader Emile Witmeur to get to the truth because it strengthened their faith in his leadership. They knew they were in good hands.

The following day, in September 1941, an autumnal chill in the air and a clear blue sky heralded the first throes of approaching winter. There was still warmth in the sun's smile but Belgian citizens – as well as their German 'masters' – visibly preferred their warmer winter coats as they went about their business, or simply through the motions of living under the stress and the humiliation of military occupation. For them, summer was now becoming a memory, as were the smiles of a happy and contented nation.

Jack Newton, again on his own, was escorted back to the villa on bicycles. Emile Witmeur returned to the villa later that same day. He slipped out of his heavy black overcoat, which he threw casually over the banister at the foot of the stairs, before he joined Jack in his room. 'Why did you have doubts about us?' asked Jack curiously. Emile replied:

> We had doubts about you when you first arrived at the de Voegts'. As far as I was concerned, not necessarily big doubts, but they were big enough for us to be concerned. I have to tell you that some people in our organisation felt there was sufficient doubt that you were a threat to many of our people. They wanted the three of you shot, better that and risk killing three innocent people, rather than find out later that you were German agents and risk one hundred or more people losing their lives.
>
> We had known for some time that the Germans were trying to infiltrate Belgian escape lines, but they hadn't been successful. Then, only a few weeks ago a Wellington bomber crashed in the Meuse

river, drowning the whole crew. The Germans pulled the bodies out of the aircraft, removed their uniforms, dry cleaned them, and gave them to six English-speaking German airmen. Word was leaked out that the crew had escaped; that there were no bodies on board.

The German imposters then went 'on the run' to make contact with the Resistance. The aim was to infiltrate our organisation. They succeeded, but not for long because we soon had serious doubts about these people. We questioned them as I questioned you, but whereas you had the right answers, they didn't. London was quick to let us know that these other men were imposters, not British aircrew. Their stories were seriously flawed and when it became clear they had been found out, they confessed. But for the Germans it was too late. They were quickly dealt with. There can be no sentiment in our shadowy war, no mercy. Too many lives are at stake.

Newton nodded his agreement. Perhaps for the first time in his service career, he said a silent word of appreciation for Air Ministry personnel files, and all the seemingly irrelevant information kept in them. On this occasion, it looked as though it may well have helped save his life.

There was no doubt that Emile Witmeur was prepared to die for his country. His allegiance to Belgium was rock solid and he hated with a passion the Germans who marched in and conquered it. He was no more than 21 and yet he had a much older and wiser head on his shoulders. Until the Germans moved into Belgium, Emile was a pilot in the Belgian Air Force. Now he was leading the region's Resistance movement, and he carried a concealed knife that Jack had no doubts he would use if any German was to get in his way. And yet, he was a man who looked more like a banker than a fighter. A man of the shadows. He also did a little writing and publishing, largely producing propaganda material; he also wrote for a Liège newspaper, though this had no connection with the war. Even so, it made a good cover for his more nefarious, cloak and dagger activities. Jack recalls:

In one conversation I had with Emile he told me at some length that our story that we had landed our crippled bomber on a German occupied airfield just didn't ring true. The Resistance thought we were lying. If we had done what we claimed, why weren't we shot out of the sky as we came in to land? Why weren't we captured on the airfield? They believed we must have had some help from the Germans. To them, our story was so improbable the ruse must have been planned; it was simply another attempt to try and infiltrate the Comète Line. It was hoped the Resistance would think the Wellington was crewed by British airmen, when really it was crewed by Germans. Only a week or so earlier Witmeur had rumbled the other

German plan to infiltrate Comète. Was this another attempt? He told me they knew the Wellington which crashed into the Meuse was brought out virtually intact; maybe this was the one 'dumped' by the Germans on Deurne airfield?

Well, I could see their point. When we suddenly turned up at the de Voegts' and told them we'd just walked away from our bomber which we had landed on a German-occupied airfield, I can see now that it must have sounded highly unlikely. Because it was true, we didn't even consider it might sound unlikely.

Well, it was true, and fortunately we were eventually believed. It was a near thing though. That Spa villa garden was so nearly our graveyard.

So, I was on my own again. There was no further wartime reunion. At least I now had a room and the bed to myself, but I guessed it wouldn't be too long before they'd send me farther downline – though in which direction? I had no idea how they intended to get me back to England. I thought it was bound to be the quickest way, across the Channel. I was so wrong!

I was now allowed the free run of the house, which made life a little more bearable. For most of the time Emile stayed in the villa, although he would sometimes be out for a few hours. Every time we spoke he made a point of telling me that I must not go near the windows, nor answer the door. Often the hours dragged by. I looked at more pictures in more magazines; I slept, and I talked to myself quite a lot. I listened to Junker 52s flying over, an occasional Dornier 217, and Messerschmitt 109s. I kept telling myself that at least I was still free. The irony of my situation at this time was that I had been moved back nearer to Aachen . . . the scene of the crime, so to speak! It was probably less than twenty miles away across the border, where all my troubles first started. Where we got shot up.

I was moved to about seven safe houses in the Antwerp area . . . as well as in Liège, Spa and Waterloo, near Brussels (as I say, in some instances with stays of less than a day). I was told that from Brussels I would have to make the hairy river crossing over the Belgian border into France. Ah, maybe a visit to the Moulin Rouge would soon be on the cards? But before thoughts of the Moulin Rouge over-excited me, there was still a great deal of excitement to be experienced in Belgium. Though of a different calibre!

It was in one Liège safe house, over a bicycle manufacturer's huge workshop, that Jack met the joker of the pack, René Debaets, and his wife, Lisette. René, the owner, seemed to fear nothing, especially the Germans. With a chuckle Jack recalls:

He was a great one for wandering around Liège, and on a couple of occasions I went with him. First we jumped on a tram that took us into the city centre, we walked for a bit, and then we boarded another tram. At first I couldn't understand why he liked riding on trams, until he told me that his favourite pastime was slapping offensive stickers on German soldiers as they brushed past him – on trams! René's stickers became quite famous in Liège; I even kept one for my book of memories. They were pieces of paper, with sticky stuff on one side, and on the other the French Croix de Lorraine (the Freedom Cross), with 'RAF' printed underneath it. To René RAF meant Royal Air Force. But the Germans, showing a surprising sense of humour, printed thousands of their own stickers and wrote underneath the Croix de Lorraine – 'Rien à Faire', meaning 'Nothing to Worry About'.

This didn't impress René one little bit. He continued peeling off his own stickers from a pad he carried around with him, slapping them on Jerries whenever he could. I actually saw him doing it. Before I left his home, he told me that if I had the chance to go back to Liège after the war he would supply me and my family with a bike each to our specifications. Alas, it was not to be. René died before the war ended.

The Germans had recklessly sent their imposter aircrew to their deaths, and they had failed to apprehend the aircrew of 'G for George' which so audaciously landed on their airfield under their noses. The Antwerp Resistance was proving to be a big embarrassment to the Nazis desperate to break the Comète Line, so they turned on the heat in their attempt to infiltrate the organisation. No sooner was Jack Newton moved to one safe house, than he had to be moved to another as the 'men in black', the Gestapo, came too close for comfort.

This was how Jack found himself at 97 rue de la Station, in Waterloo, a strange place for a so-called safe house because it had been requisitioned by the Germans, and two young soldiers even shared a room and double bed on the top floor! This was the home of Max and Céline Evrard, two very cool customers when it came to deceiving their country's occupiers. They reasoned that the Gestapo would never suspect Allied evaders, such as Jack Newton, would be hidden under the same roof as their own troops. And they were proved right.

The Evrards lived in two back rooms on the ground floor where they spent much of their leisure time doing what comes naturally to a happily married couple with a king-size bed at their disposal. No way was the war going to interrupt their healthy sex life! They also had a small dog, a Westland terrier, that hated Germans. It took an instant dislike to all uniformed soldiers, and made no exception for the young patrol bike duo, who had a rather nasty habit of removing their mounted MP-40

Schmeisser sub-machine gun from their bike, and dragging it upstairs to their room for overnight safe keeping. A trail of oil led from the front door all the way up the stairs to their room, where they left the gun on the oil-soaked carpet alongside their bed. It was disgusting and infuriated Mme Evrard enormously, but the lodgers were unmoved by her protests. They said the Schmeisser had to be protected, and had to take priority.

The fact that the little Westland barked angrily at the Germans was good news for Jack because it let him know when they were about. More than once he was tempted to sneak a look when he could hear the terrier snapping at their ankles as they tried to manhandle their messy gun up the stairs, but, of course, he didn't. Jack's hideaway was in the basement and whenever it got the chance, the little terrier called on its English friend and snuggled up with him on his bed. 'That little Westland hated the Germans, but it loved me to bits,' said Jack.

Within a couple of days of his arrival, the German bikers moved on to other digs. They were not replaced, which was good news for Jack because Mme Evrard – as he always respectfully called her – considered it safe enough for him to change to a much more comfortable first floor bedroom. This room also had a huge double bed, with flowery quilt and big drapes that extended to the floor.

Life with the Evrards quickly settled into a routine that was almost normal, a cut above most safe houses, and Jack remained there to enjoy it for nearly three weeks, one of his longest stays in a safe house. He had a hand basin in his room, even a little hot water, so shaving was possible if he was sparing with the soap. Then he would be called down – or up – to the breakfast room where a steaming cup of coffee would already be on the table waiting for him. Coffee? Well, not real coffee. This was largely ground acorns, mixed with a very small amount of real black market coffee. Household supplies of proper coffee had been used up months before, so the only source of new supplies was through the black market at an extortionate price. There was never any tea; bad news for the tea-loving English such as Jack! However, for some reason he never quite worked out, there seemed to be endless supplies of Stella Artois beer. He only had to ask for one of the large, porcelain bottles of beer and it was provided. He drank a large number because he felt it helped numb his senses. Bread was also quite plentiful. At breakfast it was cut into slices by Mme Evrard and left on a wooden platter. Most days a boiled egg was served up, sometimes even fresh eggs from local farms, but they were always undercooked and Jack couldn't stand runny eggs. Nor could he make Mme Evrard understand that he needed them to be boiled for a good five minutes, rather than two! But somehow he made sure he always emptied the shell! 'My attempts to speak French often had the Evrards in fits of laughter. As I often laughed at their English. I could just about manage . . . "morceau de pain". But we all got by with a great deal of laughing and affection. They were both so kind to me,' says Jack.

In fact, it was with this kindness in mind that on one occasion Mme Evrard suggested that Jack might like her to give him a head massage and shampoo.

> Would I! What a treat. So, the next morning I went to her bathroom where she had opened a big bottle of Eau de Cologne shampoo, or whatever it was. In one corner was a huge porcelain sink, with hair brushes, towels and all the paraphernalia set out, ready for me. Even the little Westland wanted to be present, eagerly awaiting the fun. It wasn't disappointed. With me stripped to the waist, Madame E quickly worked my hair into a fantastic lather. There were bubbles everywhere . . . over the sink, over the floor; even over the little dog that, by this time, was in a bit of a lather itself. Barking, yapping, jumping up trying to catch the suds we both blew at it, and at each other. It was pandemonium. But terrific fun. We all had a great time, and we laughed till tears ran down our faces. Then Mme Evrard gave me a wonderful head massage. I just sat back and enjoyed every moment of it before she rinsed and dried my hair.
>
> That became a twice weekly ritual, and I looked forward to it enormously. I have very fond memories of the Evrard family; they were wonderful, loving people. They even had a radio and we'd listen to English programmes together when it was safe to do so, as I did with a good friend of theirs who lived in his own house across the road from the villa.

Before Jack left, as it happened in a great hurry, Céline Evrard asked her favourite Englishman if he would leave a souvenir.

> I told her I had nothing, apart from my wife's prayer book and I said I couldn't leave that. Mme E asked me if I would sign my name under one of the many pictures in her sitting room, which, of course, I was pleased to do. I wrote 'Jack N'. Max was a gem, too. During my stay, I noticed that he spent many hours in his garden tending his much-loved roses, though I wasn't allowed to go into the garden to see them close-up. But he did me the great honour of naming a new rose he had created after my wife, calling it a Mary Elaine rose. It was a climber on an outhouse wall, and in bud at the time. Just as I left, it produced a wonderful creamy white flower.
>
> Mary was always on my mind, and it helped me to talk about her to those many wonderful people who risked so much to get me through those traumatic days. It concerned me that Mary didn't know if I was dead or alive. By this time, the Air Ministry knew my

fate (Emile Witmeur had established this when he checked me out through his Resistance radio link with SOE – Special Operations Executive – but I doubted they would pass this information on to Mary for fear it might jeopardise my situation, in fact, as was the case), but Mary remained uninformed. Anyway, it must have touched the Evrards' hearts rather more than I had realised, because after I left their home, they did an extraordinary thing which I knew nothing about at the time.

They concocted a coded telegram message which Céline Evrard sent through the Belgian equivalent of the British Red Cross to my sister's home in Pope's Grove Mansions, Twickenham. Their idea was to let Mary know that I was alive. The message was sent as a Christmas greeting, and gave the sender's address as 97 rue de la Station in the province of Brabonne, Belgium. And Céline wrote in French: 'Am in good health, with my friends and I hope that you are well yourself. Also that Mary has a good anniversary with Papa and Maman (my mother and father). Happy Christmas. I embrace you. And have a good New Year. From: Jacques Céline, 27 October 1941.'

Well, the clues were there all right but even though she duly received the telegram, unfortunately Mary didn't pick up any of them! The telegram was a total mystery to her, and she could only come to the conclusion that it must have been from some distant relative. It never occurred to her that it was about me! So, she still didn't know I was alive . . .

Then high drama. The young Newton was about to commit the cardinal sin of evading capture – taking a chance. A foolhardy error of judgment, brought on by sheer frustration with his increasingly intolerable confinement.

His friend across the road and the Evrards could see that being cooped up for so long within the villa's four walls was beginning to take its toll on Jack. Nearly three weeks of confinement and being forbidden to even go near a window to see some signs of life in the outside world was unsettling Jack. He was getting restless, even twitchy.

It was to culminate in near disaster.

One particular afternoon, and left alone in the villa, Jack was stretched out on his bed, with just the little Westland terrier snuggled up alongside him for company. He was feeling at a very low ebb. Alone with his thoughts, he began to have serious doubts that he would ever see Britain, or Mary, again. At the same time, it wracked his conscience that he was putting an increasing number of wonderful people like the Evrards at serious risk; ordinary, courageous people putting their own lives on the line trying to help him. His worries started to overwhelm him, and tears welled up in his eyes. It was more than he could take for much longer. He even wondered if he was going crazy.

Maybe a beer would help. Jack swung his legs over the side of his bed, and got to his feet. The light coming through his bedroom window was like a magnet, drawing him to it, but he told himself he must resist. He tried hard, very hard, to fight the urge to take just one long, lingering look . . . after all, it was only into the back garden. And why shouldn't he take a look at the Mary Elaine rose, which Max had named in honour of Mary? 'Why shouldn't I?' Jack called out aloud. Now he had good reason to look through the window, and the need to do so became overwhelming. Impossible to resist any longer. There . . . no harm done, Jack told himself as he sat at the window, his eyes scanning Max's well tended roses, the plants, the little brick footpath, beneath rose arches, that ran down to the hedge at the bottom, and the small gate that led out into the large, empty field beyond.

In his present state of mind Jack was able to find every reason in the world to go just one step farther. Take a short walk round the garden, perhaps. Breathe in the clean, fresh air. Hear the birds. Let his eyes feast on the myriad of colours so generously provided by a bountiful nature. Anyway, he had to go to the kitchen to get a beer. He grabbed his heavy, grey coat, slipped it on over his battledress and was quickly on his way down the stairs, through the hallway, into the kitchen. He unlocked the back door, and within a few steps, he was into the garden. 'No, you stay inside,' Jack told the little terrier, eager to accompany him, its stubby tail wagging excitedly like a wayward windscreen wiper.

Jack took a deep breath, and exhaled . . . Aaaaah. Then he stretched his shoulders, his arms. He was feeling better already.

There was nobody about, and the garden wasn't overlooked by neighbours, so what was the harm? Jack told himself that the Evrards wouldn't be any the wiser, so this one-off bit of mischief wouldn't hurt anyone – and it would do him the world of good. In fact, it had already. Jack ambled along the garden path, looking at Max's horticultural handiwork on the way. There were lots of healthy looking plants, shrubs and small trees. 'Mmmm, he certainly seems to know what he is doing,' mumbled Jack, now feeling much more relaxed. He noticed a small shed alongside the garden path. 'I wonder where the footpath leads to? Seems to be a field beyond. I'll take a look. There's nobody about,' he told himself.

Jack opened the little gate and passed through it into the field. There was a thick hedge to his left, so he decided to follow that. He had gone no more than a hundred feet when he suddenly spotted a German soldier ahead. 'Oh, my God. What now?' he said under his breath. 'Has he spotted me? Yes, I think he has,' As casually as he could, Jack calmly turned round and started to walk slowly back, and away from the German. But there was no escaping the soldier's attention. Before Jack could get back to the garden gate, the soldier caught up with him, shouting to him to stop. He knew he must stop, or risk being shot. The German asked for Jack's identity papers but he hadn't, as yet, been fixed up with false papers.

Jack knew he was in big trouble, but there was no way he could talk his way out of his dilemma. He reached into his pocket as though to retrieve his papers, and as he did so, he lashed out at the German's face, forcing the Jerry's helmet sharply back over his head, the strap almost strangling him in the process. The German fell to the ground, gasping for air, seemingly in a great state of distress. Sprawled out on the grass, close to unconsciousness. His gun was by his side. Should he kill him? No, Jack told himself he hadn't the heart to do it, but he did have the presence of mind to kick the rifle out of reach. Slightly bemused, as though he was looking in on a dream, Jack turned and ran back to the garden gate. He was seeing it all in slow motion. Would he wake up soon? Jack looked back . . . the German now appeared to be out cold. Or even dead.

Jack slipped through the garden gate and back into the house, just as the Evrards were letting themselves in through the front door. 'What is happening?' they asked in their stilted English, and clearly alarmed. Jack's face was white and frightened. He told them that he stupidly went into the garden, and into the field; that he was stopped by a German soldier. That he had knocked him unconscious. 'But I didn't finish him off,' added Jack. Max and Céline appreciated there was no time for recrimination. Knowing that the soldier was either unconscious, or close to it, there was every chance the Germans wouldn't realise Jack was being hidden in a local house. They would think he was passing through the area, using the field believing it would be safer than the road.

The Resistance had to be informed immediately. They would know what to do – and they would do it swiftly. Jack Newton had to be moved out of the district without delay for his own safety and for the safety of the Evrards. Within a few hours, a Resistance worker known to Jack, and who spoke very good English, was taking him by tram to his next safe house, this time in Schaerbeek, a district of Brussels. It was the home of the delightful Madame Antoinette Becquet. A nun!

There were no hard feelings on the part of the Evrards, just remorse that Jack Newton had to leave them so suddenly. Max had told him he was foolish to chance going outside, against all the warnings that he must not even be seen at a window. And what if the dog had followed Jack? That would have been the biggest giveaway, said Max, and could have been very serious for him and for Céline. As it happened, the Germans failed to pinpoint the Evrards, concluding that the soldier's attacker had simply been passing through the district.

For something like three weeks, Jack had been hiding in the Evrards' house in Waterloo. His solitary confinement had made him feel like a caged bird. He yearned for the freedom to walk a street, see people, see some life – even ride on a tram. And suddenly he had it all. A punch-up with a German soldier, an emergency change of location, and a tram ride to busy Brussels. A city also bustling with German military. Was this excitement enough?

No, because it was the wrong kind of excitement. The wrong kind of freedom. In fact, Jack Newton was soon to realise that his next safe house had much more to offer! Apart from the attentions of the owner, a nun who lived there alone, there were the visits of her gun-toting brother, a heavyweight friar. Two great characters who gave their airman such a good time he was almost reluctant to move on!

By now Jack was used to being on the open streets, moving around as though he was a resident. He looked so much a part of the local scene nobody in any kind of authority thought to question him. Especially, the military. Besides, it quickly became obvious to Jack that those in uniform weren't really the biggest threat; it was the Gestapo, the plain clothes security men who stood on street corners and in shop doorways, who were more likely to prove a problem. They were skilled at reading body language, and would quickly pounce if someone's unusual behaviour caught their attention. As yet, he didn't even have identity papers, and he couldn't speak fluent French, so it would be the end of the road if he was stopped. Jack had already decided not to risk trying again to escape from arrest. It had worked once, he was unlikely to get a second chance. He would just raise his hands, and say 'Fair cop'!

Sadly, it was about this time that a Resistance man showed Jack a French newspaper write-up reporting that two British airmen had been picked up and arrested in the south of France, and were being held in a French prison before being moved on to Germany. It was definitely two of the 'G for George' bomber crew (McLarnon, Burrell, Porteous), who went off on their own when the crew split up at Deurne, but it didn't name the two who had been caught. As it happened, all three were eventually picked up and spent the rest of the war in a German prison camp, but not for quite a few weeks. They gave the Jerries a good run for their money.

As Jack approached 24 rue François Polletier, in Schaerbeek, the usual safe distance behind his friendly Resistance guide, he had no idea what kind of safe house he was about to enter, except that he could see it was in a pleasant, tree-lined road with quite tasteful two and three storey individually architectured private houses. Jack knew he was going to the home of a single lady owner who lived there alone, but he had no idea she was a nun. That she spent a couple of days each week helping in a nearby nunnery. The Resistance man thought it was best he found out for himself.

Jack was not disappointed.

As soon as he stepped inside the front door, he was enveloped by what seemed to be a floating black cape. Two big kisses – continental style –

reassured him that the black cape was probably quite harmless, but he had not yet worked out who was inside it. He didn't have to wait long. The introductions followed immediately.

'Mademoiselle Becquet, this is Jack Newton, one of our friends from Britain. Jack, Mademoiselle Antoinette Becquet, who you can see is a nun.'

'Very nice to meet you, Mademoiselle,' stuttered Jack, proffering his right hand with all the English charm he could muster. His hand was taken, shaken enthusiastically, and returned intact, along with two more continental-style kisses.

Mademoiselle Becquet, in a black habit, removed her cape, and slipped it inside a cupboard in the hall of her three-storey home, alongside her 'funny' black hat. Jack estimated she was about 40, with strong features and a proud, upright figure. Then he had the mischievous thought that maybe his new safe house was really a witch's coven. It had all the makings of one! All he had to do now was find the broomsticks! How unkind. He shrugged his shoulders and rejected the idea immediately. It was in very poor taste, he told himself reprovingly.

In fact, the two got off to a very good start. Antoinette took an instant shine to her young airman house guest. She showed him to his basement bedroom and told him that just as soon as her brother called round, they would all sit down to eat. Jack stayed in his room and used the time to settle in. He was on his bed, close to nodding off when he heard the front door slam shut, and the loud, jolly voice of a man in the entrance hall. It must be Antoinette's brother. Then he heard footsteps descending the small stairway to his basement room. There was a knock, and the door swung open. Framed in the half light was a monster of a man who looked as though he had just stepped out of Sherwood Forest. It was surely Friar Tuck! The big man, with a huge, round, red face started laughing heartily . . . 'Ello Jacques,' he said, proud of his excellent English.

A friar, indeed, but this one was Antoinette's brother; a monk and resident in a nearby monastery. A gun-toting monk, no less, who packed two Colt 45 revolvers attached to a Sam Brown belt concealed under his tent of a cloak. Why the guns? asked Jack. He explained that one gun was to use on any German who got in his way, the other was for himself, in an emergency. Then he showed Jack huge poacher's pockets stitched to the inside of his gown, which he used for smuggling bottles of wine and whisky, cigarettes and any other scarce wartime luxuries that came his way. Luxuries such as tins of corned beef buried by the escaping British army on the beaches of Dunkirk, later recovered and ferreted downline by the French Resistance. Apart from being a walking armoury, Jack's new friar friend also spoke quite good English and updated Jack with all the latest news from Britain. 'He was just one hell of a character and I quickly looked forward to his twice weekly visits to his sister's house,' said Jack.

Antoinette was no ordinary nun, and loved every moment playing 'mum' to the fresh-faced young British airman. He even started calling her his 'Nun Mum'. When he went to bed she insisted on making him comfortable, listening to his worries, tucking him in and giving him a parting goodnight kiss on his forehead before she turned out his light as she left his room. She always locked the door behind her so that nobody could get in overnight. Jack was the son she never had. And all she cared about was his safety and his happiness. It was an extraordinary tale of devotion in the lives of two totally different people brought together in the atmosphere of wartime hatred. Number 24 rue François Polletier was a house overflowing with care, love and compassion.

Jack was in need of some of that compassion two days later, when he was suddenly in agony with raging toothache. Two of his teeth had been cracked in the desperate landing on Deurne airfield. Now he was paying the price. Over breakfast with Antoinette, he told her that he needed to see a dentist. He didn't think he could cope with the throbbing pain for very much longer. But how could a British airman on the run in German-occupied Belgium possibly pop into a local dentist and ask to have his teeth fixed?

Antoinette said she had the answer. Jack could visit her dentist friend, and she would introduce him as her Spanish nephew who had been caught short on a holiday visit. 'Me, your Spanish nephew?' asked Jack. 'I cannot speak a word of Spanish.'

'You will not need to. My dentist friend doesn't speak Spanish either, and I will tell him you do not speak French. So you won't have to speak French or Spanish,' said Antoinette.

'She told me that all I needed to know were the words *Diente . . . aquì* – which, she said was 'This tooth . . . here'. And I was to point to the bad teeth.

'Antoinette was confident this plan of hers would work. In any case, I suspected the dentist was sympathetic to the Resistance, and to nuns, so even if he was a bit suspicious he was hardly going to tip off the German authorities. At least, I hoped not.'

Antoinette arranged for her nephew to visit her dentist friend the following morning. Apart from the agonising toothache, Jack was very nervous. What if he had to have his teeth taken out? Antoinette told him to stop worrying, to put on his coat and his beret so they could set off on the five-minute walk to the surgery a couple of streets away.

'I stopped in the hallway to give myself a once over in the full-length mirror. Yes, I looked the part, especially now that I had grown a fine, bristling moustache and long sideburns. "Come, my brave boy," urged Antoinette, opening the door for us to leave.

Antoinette, of course, did all the talking when we got to the dentist's surgery. She looked very impressive in her black habit, black cape and broad brimmed hat, sweeping in through the waiting room where just one young girl was sitting. The girl looked up momentarily, then looked down again at the magazine she was reading. Antoinette, with me hot on her heels, went straight into the surgery. The friendly dentist barely caught my eye as he pointed to the dental chair, indicating me to lie back on it. 'Diente . . . aquì,' I said. 'Diente aquì . . . diente aquì' I kept repeating, my finger in my mouth, pointing to the affected teeth. He seemed to get the message as he moved my hand to one side and plunged his own right hand into my mouth, pulling my upper lip almost over my nose. Then he poked around with a pointed tool, grunted a couple of times and spoke to Antoinette. After a brief conversation, it became clear that I needed two fillings, but the dentist didn't have enough silver filling. Heads were put together and I told Antoinette I might be able to help, fishing out of my battledress pocket two silver British coins given to me by my aunt for good luck. I kept the coins to help prove I was an Allied airman if I was ever arrested. But the coins would give the game away that I was British if the dentist took them to melt down for my filling. Antoinette didn't see this as a problem, and handed them over. With my contributed silver, and the small amount she and the dentist were able to provide, there was enough to get the job done.

In less than one hour Jack walked out of the surgery with two teeth largely filled with metal from two King George VI silver coins. And no more tooth trouble.

[Jack still has one of those fillings in place to this day, sixty years later. The other was lost when the tooth had to be extracted five years ago!]

There was never a dull moment at the Becquet home. Jack was introduced to Hubert Casin, a close neighbour and an excellent pianist. The ever thoughtful Antoinette believed a little light music would be just the thing to relax her airman when she was not around, so Hubert, who was about 26 and just a few years older than Jack, got the job of being Jack's friend as well as his pianist! It so happened that Hubert was another member of the Comète Line, and in peacetime a very fine pilot as well as a pianist. He became a regular caller, tickling the ivories of Antoinette's upright piano with classics, some swing and a little jazz that helped put the war very much into the background for a couple of hours each visit. It was a real treat. But the sad end to this story was that Hubert was to die in such tragic circumstances toward the end of the war. As an active member of the Resistance, he helped a good few downed airmen to freedom through Belgium, France, into Spain, and actually used the escape line himself when his involvement became known to the Germans. He made it safely back to Britain, and was transferred on to Canada as an instructor where he tragically died in a freak air crash. The Spitfire he was piloting developed mechanical problem and went out of control at 20,000 feet, into a spin, and into the ground, taking the trapped Hubert Casin with it. Said Jack: 'What a terrible thing to happen; what rotten luck after all he had been through in Belgium and France.' Jack was to befriend one of Hubert's relatives, a Mrs Chaplin who lived in Streatham. 'She was devastated when he died in that Spitfire, having gone through all the dangers of war in Belgium and France,' added Jack.

Antoinette's big passion was reading. She was a real bookworm, and had an extensive library on shelves, in cupboards, piled up in corridors, in most rooms, even on the upright piano with its wobbly ornate brass candlestick holders, one at each end. Reading was her way of escaping from all the worries of war. She could read herself into another dimension. Into the world of her imagination, beyond the rotten day-to-day one in which she found herself. One afternoon, she and Jack were sitting and chatting; she asked him if he would mind reading to her, in English. Jack said he was more than happy to do so. She reached up to the nearest shelf of books and took down the first paperback to hand.

'This one, Jack. Please read this one to me . . .'

'It was a Penguin novel. It had a gold coloured title, though I have long forgotten what it was. I flicked through its pages and told Antoinette: "This will take me several days to get through." She agreed, so I began reading.'

Antoinette sat back in her chair, closed her eyes and absorbed every word, every image, this little book projected as Jack read slowly down its pages. She was so relaxed, and very much enjoyed this little treat. The first day's reading passed happily, and Antoinette said, 'Will you continue tomorrow at the same time?' Jack said of course he would. He wasn't going anywhere!

The next day they once again made themselves comfortable in the same seats in the same room overlooking the garden. Jack picked up the paperback, found the marker, and said he was ready. Antoinette leant back in her chair, closed her eyes, and Jack began to read what he now knew was a romantic novel. But he had only turned a few pages when he came across a passage that stopped him in his tracks. It left him speechless. 'My brave boy, what is the matter?' asked Antoinette, a little alarmed. He told her that it was the prayer he was reading to her. 'As I read it, I couldn't help thinking it must have been written especially for me. It was Psalm 107, so it was not written for me – but it could have been,' said Jack, emotionally shaken by the meaningful words he was reading out loud.

His voice started to weaken, and suddenly he felt very moved. Even moved near to tears.

Antoinette asked again, 'Tell me, what is upsetting you my brave boy?' she repeated tenderly, using her favourite way of addressing him.

'It is this psalm. It is so meaningful to me. It is as though I am meant to read it. I mean, of all the hundreds of books you have in your home, why did you pick this one? It is just so meaningful, so uncanny,' spluttered Jack, almost lost for words at the significance of what was happening.

Jack couldn't continue. And they stopped the reading. Jack promised to continue the following afternoon. But he took the little paperback to his room and read the psalm over and over again, till he almost knew it off by heart.

He read it out loud: *Let them give thanks whom the Lord hath redeemed and delivered from the hand of the enemy, and gathered them out of the Lands, from the East, and from the West, from the North, and from the South. They went astray in the Wilderness out of the way, and found no city to dwell in. Hungry and thirsty their soul painted in them. So they cried unto the Lord in their trouble, and He delivered them from their distress. He led them forth by the right way, that they might go to the city where they dwelt. Oh, that men would therefore praise the Lord for His goodness, and declare the wonders that He doth for the children of men.*

Jack knew he must keep the verse with him, that it would protect him and get him safely back home to Britain. He carefully removed the page from the book, folded it and slipped it into his pocket. He felt a little guilty that he had defaced Antoinette's book so he decided not to tell her what he had done. Anyway, it was very unlikely she would want to read the book herself, after Jack had read it to her.

[Note: Later, Psalm 107 was adopted as the Royal Air Force Escaping Society's 'Escaper's Prayer', thanks to Jack Newton, who impressed the Society with this particular story, telling them how it had given him the strength – and protection – to get him safely back home.]

Reflecting on the circumstances in which he came to read Psalm 107, Jack recalled: 'Why this particular passage in a very early Penguin book should come to me to read, God only knows. It was just so uncanny. I still have the page from the book. I just wish I could discover the paperback's title.'

After ten days in Antoinette Becquet's home, the Resistance told Newton it was time to move on to 51 rue du Pont, the Brussels home of the interestingly named Madame du Porque. The last safe house in the vicinity of Brussels before the anticipated move across the River Somme into France, and to Paris. Hubert Casin was given the job of taking Jack to Madame du Porque's.

But first the parting from his favourite nun, and it was a tearful and memorable one. They promised to meet up again when the war was over. Jack asked her to give his best wishes to her brother, the monk, a mammoth of a man who was always laughing, and who waddled rather than walked. Jack recalled how her brother monk told him stories of meeting some of the Germans, how he had found the German airmen, the

Luftwaffe, more respectful than the soldiers; how he would nod and wave his hand courteously as he passed occupation troops, with the equivalent of a 'bless you, my son' as he did so. Turning the hand wave into a V-sign gesture behind their backs. A great character.

With a final wave, Jack set off, Hubert Casin leading the way. It was late afternoon and they had to reach their destination before the start of the curfew. That gave them about two hours, though less than one was probably enough to get across Brussels.

The journey by the ever-reliable, though horribly uncomfortable, tram was accomplished without incident. Apart from the German soldiers being so much in evidence, Jack told himself he could well be travelling through London. If only. Keeping Hubert in eyesight, Jack passed the time pretending to read his newspaper, until it was time to get off, with a bit of walking to do that took them across the bridge of the street address 'rue du Pont', before he found himself at number 51, another three-storey house. Yet another home with a huge, solid wood front door, so typical of Brussels. Awaiting was the warmest of welcomes from owner Madame du Porque.

Jack was shown into a first floor room, given a mug of coffee – this time all coffee – and invited to make himself comfortable. Madame P told him in stilted, but understandable, English that he was to meet some friends within the hour. 'Oh, no, surely not Langlois and Copley again!'

It was with some impatience that Jack passed the time to the anticipated second reunion with his old crewmates. Nobody had told him it was them, but it sounded as though it would be. He had barely slurped the last dregs of coffee from the bottom of his mug, when the door opened and in walked one of the Resistance guys with two escapees. No, they were not Langlois and Copley. These two introduced themselves as Larry Birk, an Australian sergeant pilot, and Albert Day – Al for short – a Canadian Air Force pilot.

'Phew. Hi fellas. Nice to meet you. Nice to meet people whose first language is English,' said Jack, showing how much their company meant to him. There was a lot of back slapping all round. More coffee was brought to the room by the accommodating Mme P, and the trio got down to the serious business of relating their incredible stories to each other by way of introduction. When the coffee had gone, Mme P was back again, this time with half-a-dozen wine glasses, and as many bottles of red wine. It was party time, a wow of an evening that was stretched well into the night and the early hours. Two rooms were made available for the airmen, one was the bedroom, and the other where they could relax. The rest of the house had to be off-limits most of the day, but could be used by the men in the evenings, if they wished. And for one very good reason, it was very much their wish because a prostitute lived across the road and entertained high-ranking German officers there overnight. The main entertainment of the evening was sitting in the dark in the front room, a glass of wine in their hands, a bottle on the table waiting to be emptied, and looking through a chink in the heavy curtains, as the customers turned up in their fancy German staff cars. More about that in a moment.

But getting to know each other was their first priority.

Larry was about four feet nothing. Even shorter than Tich Copley, so he was really short. He was from Melbourne, son of a vicar, and – like Jack – lucky to get out of a downed Wellington. What Larry lacked in height he certainly made up for in his sense of humour. He soon had both Jack and Al Day rocking with almost uncontrollable laughter as he described how he managed to keep himself out of the hands of the enemy. He said that somehow he got himself a priest's black cloak, black habit, a cross and a huge broad brimmed black hat with cantilever ribbons, as worn by priests. Al hinted he thought he probably nicked it from a Catholic church, or a priest's outhouse . . .

It was the perfect disguise. Larry said he was able to walk wherever he wanted, through towns, villages, along main routes, without fear of questioning. The German soldiers simply saw him as an object of curiosity, and certainly not one to be messed with. After all, what spy or escaping airman would be so foolish as to dress himself up like some joker drawing so much attention to himself? Larry was proved correct in believing that it was this Teutonic way of thinking that ensured he would get away with his priest drag act.

He told his new pals how he covered quite a few kilometres as a priest. How, when it looked as though he was about to be approached by an inquisitive soldier on at least two occasions to be asked for his papers, he fobbed them off with a wave of his hand, and a mumbling form of 'bless you, my son'. In fact, just as Antoinette's brother, a monk, was able to do, though, in his case, with perhaps rather more panache! Even so, with Larry it worked, and he was still free to prove it. He wouldn't hear, or understand, their request for his papers, but would carry on walking just as he had seen his father do when his parishioners tried to corner him, perhaps to complain about one of his sermons!

Larry told how another time when he was making his way through Belgium, he had to get from one village to another some twenty kilometres away. But how was he to do it without arousing suspicion? His solution was simple, and cheap. He turned himself into a labourer. He acquired (meaning nicked) a wheelbarrow, filled it with sand with a borrowed shovel, found himself an old cloth cap, roughed up his clothes a bit . . . and set off down the main road pushing the wheelbarrow full of sand.

As far as anyone else was concerned, he was a labourer making his way home, and he wasn't stopped once. He arrived exhausted, but safe.

'Dear old Larry. He was a tonic for all of us, and I had the pleasure of his company from that point on. We were to be the first three so-called Allied airmen "packages" to be delivered by the Comète Line, to freedom. Though, at the time, we had no idea how they planned to do it,' said Jack.

As for Roy Langlois and Tich Copley, they were eventually hunted down and captured in the Brussels sewers. It was a bitter blow for Jack. Now he really was on his own, and he wasn't far off being arrested himself in the same incident. A sudden rendezvous between the three airmen was set up by the Resistance, although it remained unclear for what reason. Jack and his Resistance guide, Langlois and Copley, with their guide, were to meet at 2200 hours close to the Hôtel de Ville, in Brussels. Jack was there at the arranged time, but the other two didn't make it. Later Jack was told his pals had already been caught, arrested, beaten up and incarcerated in the city prison. Copley recalled the drama.

Roy and I were taken to the house of Jean Vandenhove, 66 rue Washington, in Brussels, where we stayed several days in a room on the third floor. Early one morning we were awakened by the sound of jackboots, shouts and banging on the front door. We looked out of the window to see the street was lined with armed Germans, two of them were working on the very heavy front door with their rifle butts.

'This is it,' I told myself. 'We've been caught.' But that wasn't the way our host Jean saw it at all. He led us down the stairs three at a time into the cellar. He lifted a huge paving slab and told us to drop through it – into the sewer under rue Washington!

Ugh! We hadn't a clue where we were going, and it was far from fun wading around waist high in effluent. Being so small, with me it was nearly shoulder high. Anyway, Roy and I got lost. Then we found a manhole and Roy helped me to climb the manhole walls to try and open the cover – but I couldn't do it. Perhaps there was a car parked on it above. After seven hours we were forced to return to the cellar where we'd first entered the sewers. Two German armed guards looked so pleased with themselves when we finally emerged, disillusioned, dirty and smelling to high heaven. Within seconds we were surrounded by many more. As for poor Jean, he must have known what his fate would be because we could see him age in front of our eyes. I was never told what happened to him.

We were all taken off to the prison of St Gilles where we were put in solitary confinement. Sitting there with all my thoughts, I began to be seriously worried about my chances of surviving, having been captured wearing civilian clothes. The guard wouldn't tell me what was happening to the other two. All he kept telling me was that I would be shot as a spy. I was very concerned that my parents wouldn't know what had happened to me.

Over the next ten days I was questioned a number of times, some of it quite physically, although it was more to try and frighten me. They did a good job!

Then, on the tenth day of solitary confinement I heard jackboots marching along the corridor, my cell door opened and two soldiers and an officer escorted me upstairs where Langlois was waiting. We were taken out of the prison, to the railway station where we were both put aboard a train for Frankfurt.

From Frankfurt we were sent by another train to Lamsdorf V111B, a large army camp in Poland, which had a small compound for Royal Air Force prisoners. I was issued with a Polish prisoner's uniform and clogs. The movements from one camp to another continued. Next it was to Stalagluft III, where we were reunited with McLarnon, Burrell and Porteous, then on to Sagan, to Torun, in Poland, and to Memel (aka *Klaipede*-Lithuanian). When the Russians started advancing west we were shipped off, yet again, this time to Stalag 357, far to the west. Early in April 1945 we were marched out of this camp and abandoned on Lüneburg Heath to find British tanks in possession of nearby Wendische-Evern village. Two days later Roy and I were flown back to England by Dakota – free men again.

But in Brussels the Resistance was now concerned that Al Day might prove an easy victim of the Nazis.

In the few days spent at Madame du Porque's he became progressively more ill with an infection he had caught sleeping rough whilst on the run. The infection rapidly turned into bronchitis, and a Resistance doctor called every other day to treat him.

'When it was time for us to move on,' said Jack, 'the Resistance decided Albert Day would have to stay behind until his health had improved, so he stayed at Mme du Porque's for another fortnight under the medical care of the friendly doctor. Al's delay was a pity because if the three of us had escaped together, we would have been the first airmen from Canada, from Australia and from Britain to make it. Now we had to hope I'd be the first British airman to get home, and Larry the first Australian.'

But for the time being, for Larry the highlight of each evening continued to be the 'cabaret' across the road from Madame du Porque's house.

Their evening meal in their stomachs, each of them warmed up with a glass of Madame P's best brandy, the three boys took their seats in her unlit front room, and well back from the window for what they came to call 'the cabaret'. Soon after dark, a little German staff car drew up outside the house opposite. Its driver leapt out, ran round to the rear passenger door, dutifully opened the door and gave a snappy salute as the officer, immaculate in full uniform, stepped out. As this horny son of the German Wermacht nonchalantly pressed onwards up the path to the woman's front door, the little driver ran back, jumped into the staff car and sped off.

Madame opened her front door and tonight's client stepped inside for his passion-packed, overnight stay. Spot on time, no more than a minute before or after eight o'clock the following morning, the same little staff car was back again. Parked outside the hooker's house. The front door opened, and now as immaculately dressed as he was when he entered through it the previous evening, the German officer strode down the path back to his car. The door was opened for him, he received another snappy salute, and stepped into the rear seat. But first there was one more ceremony for the humble driver to perform. The goodies. Hans, if that was his name, delivered a large box, filled to the brim with all the things it was so hard to come by in Belgium even on the black market. Ground coffee, lots of butter, milk, eggs, tomatoes, fish, chicken, confectionary, silk stockings, shampoo, and more. Hans, his hands more than full, struggled with the box up the front path, and handed it over to the very grateful lady waiting at her front door. No words were exchanged. Just a nod of gratitude by both parties. Only she knew she had earned every single item!

Hans hurried back to the staff car, and drove off, presumably back to the officer's quarters, where his charge could continue to do his bit to keep the people of Belgium in their place. If only the horny little Hun knew his mischievous outings in his pursuit of sex provided such wonderful entertainment for escaping Allied airmen! If only that same officer knew that the goodies box he so slimily provided was later shared by his lady of pleasure with so many of her neighbours! If only he knew his eggs, the fish, the meat, the chocolates brought comfort, too, to Allied escapers in the house opposite! They were the ones who had the last laugh. And they laughed heartily.

Jack was left wondering if the lady of pleasure was giving her services for the love of her country, rather than for the love of German officers. It was a thought.

Jack and Larry knew that Al Day would not be moving out with them. The day before they actually left for what they thought would be the next stage to France, a new man came to Madame du Porque's to take Al Day's place. He was a Polish non-commissioned officer air gunner Jurek Budinsky. All three were then told that before leaving Belgium they would be taken to another safe house nearby where they would be given their identity papers, and their cover story.

But almost more important than any of this, they were about to meet a young woman who was going to make an indelible mark on all their lives. Especially, on the life of Jack Newton.

CHAPTER 5

Train Trip Trouble

Poor Al Day. He is going to feel very left out being left behind at Madame du Porque's. But as he is quite sick, it is best for him to get back to good health. The stress of shadow boxing one's way through an enemy-occupied country is difficult enough, let alone trying to do it with lungs overloaded with bronchitis. No, the Resistance have made the right decision, even if Al is not altogether happy with it. At least, he can see more of the 'cabaret' across the road!

There is even a certain amount of frustration felt by Messrs Newton, Birk and Budinsky. They believe they are on their way to France from Madame du Porque's, instead of in for a further stay in yet another Brussels safe house, but they appreciate they cannot survive in Paris – even for a short time – without identity papers. They know the city is crawling with troops and Gestapo. One foot out of place in Paris and that will be it. None of them has yet worked out how they will get back to Britain, still believing that it will be by the direct route, in a rowing boat across the Channel. When they are given their new identities they will find out just how wrong they have been, and why.

'The next safe house was meant to be a short stopover. Less than one day, we were told, but it was extended,' says Jack. 'The first day was partly spent at the local Bon Marché store. Our false papers had to bear our photo and the store had an automatic picture-taking machine. They were like the old PolyPhoto snaps. I sat there, and out popped some 48 different pictures. Quite amazing.'

Each of the airmen goes to the store with a different Resistance worker. Jack's agent gives him money to put in the machine, then waits the ten minutes for the pictures to be automatically processed. When they are ready and popped out into the delivery slot, the guide collects the sheets of prints, rolls them up and they leave the shop in sight of each other, but separately. The usual system. To Jack's surprise he is led back to yet another house, not the one he had left that same morning. When he realises what is happening it makes him smile; the Resistance boys have got things well organised. Jack, Larry and Jurek Budinsky are in Brussels for another three days waiting for their documentation to be completed, at which point they change identities. They are told who they now are, where they come from, and their business.

Jack is handed his papers and notes his home address is given as Des Landes, in the Arrondissement de Dax, which he is told is in the south of France. 'Surely that cannot be right. What would I be doing trying to get to the English Channel if I live in the south of France?' he asks. 'But you are not going to your English Channel. You are going to travel back to your home in the south!' was the reply.

'But, but . . . well, so I am not going back to Britain?'

'Yes, you are, but through France, across the Pyrénées, into Spain and down to Gibraltar,' says the Resistance man, smiling happily at Jack's innocent confusion.

It is a clever, well thought-out plan by the Resistance. At this stage of the war, the Gestapo believe any British airmen on the run in France will attempt to get home by the most direct route, across the Channel. So they set up two demarcation lines extending inland from the Channel. The first is five miles and the second ten miles. Anyone travelling within these two demarcation lines needs two quite separate sets of passes. And even then the checks are rigorous.

So the Resistance give their escaping Allied servicemen south of France addresses, and names. If they are stopped in Paris and have their papers checked, it is quite normal for them to be boarding a southbound express. How can they possibly be British if they are travelling in the wrong direction? Also, few Germans are fluent in French so are less inclined to try to cross-question those Frenchmen whose papers are in order. Likewise, if the Germans stop them in northern France it creates less suspicion if they are travelling south to Paris.

Clever stuff.

But the sudden realisation that he has many more weeks evading capture in occupied Europe makes Jack very edgy. There are now so many people in Comète who have already helped him, and probably many more still to come. He will be a real catch if the Gestapo get their hands on him. With their notorious torture techniques Jack is worried sick that he may not be able to hold out if he is arrested.

On the other hand, Jack reasons that the Resistance know the risks. He has to hope good luck will remain with him, so he continues to put his faith in Psalm 107 on the page torn out of Antoinette Becquet's Penguin paperback. He reads it regularly.

The other worry is that he must now think of himself as Monsieur Jacques Dumonceau, a French commercial traveller, and not Jack Newton, a Royal Air Force rear gunner. He even has a certificate to prove he is M. Dumonceau! Certificat de Domicile Numéro 138 attests that he has been living in Saint Geours de Maremne for more than three months. It is approved, signed and stamped at the town hall office in Des Landes, and is dated 12 November 1941. On the reverse side is the Bon Marché head and shoulders picture of Jack Newton – or rather, Monsieur Dumonceau! He certainly looks smart in the oversize grey suit so generously given him by M. de Voeght, the farmer in Bouchout, and his village friends.

Fascinated, Jack watches the forger at work. He uses a surgical knife to cut the rubber stamp obtained from a rubber doorstop in the second safe house.

The evening before the three airmen are due to leave for the Somme river crossing, they are told to expect a very special visitor. No less than the head of the Comète Line. The person who will take them to Paris, through France and over the Pyrénées.

'Must be quite a guy,' says Larry. Jack and Jurek agree. 'He'll have a few stories to tell,' says Jurek.

Within the hour, Jack, Larry and Jurek hear people approaching their room where they are sitting in line on the one bed, swapping more personal war stories. The door opens, and in walks a slip of a girl who cannot be more than 23. She smiles, then moves slowly towards the bed where the three airmen look as though they have suddenly become set in stone. Silent. Bewildered.

'Hello. It is Jack, Larry and Jurek, isn't it?' she says softly.

'Hmmm. Yes, that's right, Ma'am,' says Jack.

'Hi, I'm Larry. Australian.'

'I'm Jurek. Polish.'

'My name is Andrée,' says the girl, but I would like you to call me by my code name which is "Dédée". That means "Little Mother". From here on I will be your "Little Mother" and therefore you will be my "Little Children". It will be my job to get my little children safely to Spain. And to freedom.'

'Excuse me, you are taking us to Spain?' asks Larry, smiling disbelievingly.

'That is correct,' says Dédée. 'I will see you all early tomorrow when we will leave for Corbie and the Somme crossing into France. Goodnight.'

Dédée closes the door gently behind her, leaving the three young airmen lost for words. They had expected the person taking them on this very dangerous part of their escape route through France would be a big, tough, macho Frenchmen, bristling with Colt 45s, and quite prepared to use them. 'A bit like Friar Tuck,' says Jack. 'Friar . . . who?' asks Larry. 'Oh, just someone I met a few safe houses back,' says Jack.

'Yes, and our lives depend on a schoolgirl,' adds Larry, a little sourly.

Simply dressed, in a light blue floral patterned dress, a little dark blue jumper and white ankle socks, her thick, dark hair, cut well off her shoulders, Dédée does look even younger than her 23 years. It is a bitter blow. At first the airmen lower their odds of making it home, but the more they discuss the virtues of such a young woman being the head of an established escape line, the more they feel they may have underestimated Dédée. Perhaps they should give her the benefit of their doubt. They agree to sleep on it, and come to a conclusion the following morning. It is not a restful night.

Over breakfast Dédée makes a point of getting to know her new friends a little better. She tells them they will be called 'packages'. Jack is number one package, Larry is number two package and Jurek number three package. Dédée says a fourth package will join them before they reach Paris. His name Gérard Waucquez, who Jack eventually finds out is a hotshot Belgian skilled at blowing up bridges. The Special Operations Executive in London is eager to get him back to Britain so that he can be trained and involved in their numerous covert field operations across the Channel. On the journey south he has very little to say about himself and his wartime ambitions, but it proves useful that he and Dédée, both Belgians, can travel and converse naturally as a couple. Waucquez turns out to be quite a surprise little 'package', as Jack Newton is to find out.

In the meantime, Jack is still unsure about his ability to get across the Pyrénées, and Dédée's ability to ensure he does. Is this really what she intends?

'Yes, Jack, this is your way home. You will do it, you'll see,' says Dédée confidently. 'But first we must cross the Belgian border into France, which means getting ourselves wet wading crossing the River Somme. We will do that tomorrow.'

Dédée makes it quite clear to the three young airmen that they must do what she asks of them. From here on they are her responsibility, and she will not let them down. They must not let her down. If they all work together, she will get them safely to Spain.

'It will be tough and dangerous, but you are tough and brave boys. You can do it,' says Dédée, showing her excellent command of English, as well as her leadership qualities, and a touch of motherliness.

Jack, Larry and Jurek are impressed, not only by her spoken English, but by her dedication and decisiveness. She has made it quite clear to them that she is the boss. But maybe a boss with kid gloves.

'Within a short time we all feel very humbled by this young Belgian girl. We were flying bombers over Germany, and crashing or coming down in Belgium, yet here is this girl saying, "I will help you get home", and she was prepared to risk her life to do so. As were those friends of hers also helping us. Frankly, I didn't give Dédée much chance of being around at the end of the war. What she was doing, helped by her beloved father, Frédéric (agent code name "Paul") was far more dangerous than anything I was doing. If I got caught I would see the war out in a prisoner-of-war camp; if Dédée was caught she would probably be shot,' reflects Jack.

Unperturbed, Dédée begins coaching her 'children' in cloak and dagger tactics. At breakfast, in their room, and whenever she has a few moments, she chivvies them, pushes them, encourages them to see the danger and the risk in everything they do when they are under the eyes of the German occupiers. They must not be complacent. She explains the importance of being able to remain silent, and the need to overcome the instinctive need to talk. It must become instinctive NOT to talk.

All conversation must be considered. She tells them that if the Gestapo are suspicious they will try and trick a suspect into giving himself away. A favourite is to ask in English: 'Can you tell me the time, please?' The instinct is for that person to immediately look at his watch, straightaway blowing his cover.

Instead of chatting over breakfast Dédée asks the three airmen to practise being silent. And she tells them to try not speaking for periods when they are relaxing together in their room. It is not easy. But by the time the four of them set off for the border crossing and the Somme their silence is already golden!

The journey to the river crossing is about a ninety-minute train ride from Brussels to the French/Belgian border, leaving the train at the border point called Quievrain. Then two more train journeys to the Somme crossing at Corbie.

There is excellent protection here, woodland, bushes, and high river weed providing good cover should a German army cycle patrol make one of its regular passes along the towpath. This is Dédée's preferred crossing of the Somme, one she has tested a few months earlier with a group of ten Belgian escapees wanted by the Gestapo, plus a rather plump, middle-aged English woman named Miss Richards, who insisted on bringing luggage and wearing her Panama hat on the trip. Miss Richards seemed to think she was on a holiday excursion rather than a flight for her life! Luckily for her, the Germans hadn't quite got their act together at this stage of the war, nor were they too successful at apprehending those eager to escape their clutches. Nevertheless, it had proved difficult to persuade the group to ford the swollen river, waist high in water, suitcases and all. A boat had been tethered nearby to ferry the travellers across, but campers had pitched their tent so close to it that this plan had to be abandoned. On top of everything else, because six of the escapees, including the extrovert Miss Richards, couldn't swim, a rubber tyre and rope found in a nearby farm had to be used to haul the non-swimmers across one-by-one. The crossing took ninety minutes, much longer than had been anticipated. But largely due to the natural camouflage the site afforded, the crossing was eventually successfully accomplished. As a result, Dédée picked it as her first choice for future secret crossings, though she hoped there would be no need for the rubber tyre.

Now it is the turn of Jack Newton, Larry Birk, Jurek Budinsky, and Dédée. They expect to pick up the fourth 'package', Gérard Waucquez, across the river in the farmhouse of a Resistance contact named Nenette. The Belgian explosives expert, Waucquez, should be waiting there.

From La Corbie station, they walk into the town to a small café and have a meal. Then they head off in the direction of the Somme, hoping they look like office workers returning home. The sun is dropping below the horizon on a clear, but chilly evening as they make their way in single file to the river. None is looking forward to getting wet, wading perhaps waist high in ice-cold water.

Dédée leads the men to a small copse where they can hide until it is dark. For a good hour they huddle on a patch of damp grass, hoping they are well out of sight of the towpath and any German bicycle patrols. Larry's teeth start chattering. Jurek has to stifle a sneeze and Jack complains he needs a pee. 'Oh, Jack, is it really necessary?' asks Dédée. 'I am afraid it is,' he tells her. 'Then you had better go and find yourself a private place to do what you have to do,' she suggests. 'But look out for German patrols.'

Jack creeps off on all fours. He has moved about twenty feet when they all hear someone whistling. Instinctively, they spread themselves face down on the ground. It's a German, his gun across his shoulders, pedalling happily along the towpath straight towards them, but he doesn't see a thing. He passes by none-the-wiser and is soon pedalling out of sight. There are no more interruptions, and Dédée decides it is time to move off across the river. 'No talking,' she whispers to each of them, as she tells Jack to lead the way. He is to wade out into the water and just keep going until he reaches the far bank, some one hundred yards away.

'You next, Larry,' says Dédée. Then it's Jurek. And Dédée follows on last. The cold water takes Jack's breath away. The farther he goes the higher the water rises up his body until he begins to think it won't be long before he'll be needing a snorkel! In some fifteen minutes he is across and can see the shadowy figure of a woman coming to meet him. It's farmer's wife, Nenette, Dédée's contact. The others wade ashore, soaked to the skin, and shivering with the cold. They are taken to Nenette's farmhouse, not too far from the river, to dry off and to make themselves comfortable before they catch a country train from Amiens the next morning to Paris. Timing is all-important from here on. They must arrive in Paris with enough time to get to Austerlitz station to catch the southbound express to Bayonne, but not so much time that they have to hang around. Jack is in no hurry to leave the farmhouse. After his soaking in the Somme, he is more worried that he could end up with a dose of bronchitis like poor old Al Day. But, fortunately, he is spared.

La Corbie is the northernmost limit of the occupation at this time, so the concentration of German troops preparing to push on still farther north is considerable. This doesn't make life easy for the party but by now Jack is something of an old hand at being a Belgian, or a Frenchman. As is Larry, the playful priest! The trucks, tanks, heavy guns on the move through the streets, are no longer objects of curiosity. The airmen see them as a part of the country's way of life at this time, as does the French population. En masse, their spirit has been crushed. There is little they can do as a nation and it shows in their faces and in their resignation to their fate. It would not do for the airmen to be chipper, gung-ho, even curious. The lower their profile, the more chance they will get by unnoticed.

The local train journey from Amiens into the heart of Paris is uneventful. But for some reason, perhaps the movement of military equipment, they discover that their express from Austerlitz to Bayonne is delayed a couple of hours. This means they have a good three hours to kill. Dédée decides the best place to while away the time is in a news theatre just outside the station. As they both speak French, Dédée and Waucquez walk together as a couple; the other three know they must appear to be on their own, but keep Dédée in sight. Do everything Dédée does. Go everywhere she goes. So it is with some amusement to them when she takes them to the pictures – into a Paris news theatre. Dédée and Waucquez collect the tickets as the other three wait in the foyer, then they all walk in as individuals, and sit near each other.

Jack cannot help suffering a touch of the giggles as he sits back and gets a hammering of German patriotic propaganda. So boring. Hardly the stuff patriotic Frenchmen are going to want to sit through. But one person is soon joining in the spirit of the occasion – Larry. Loud military music, along with stirring images of German troops marching into Paris, has the clearly German-orientated audience standing up screaming with patriotic fervour. 'Heil Hitler' they scream. 'Heil Hitler, Heil Hitler . . .'.

Jack looks across at Larry, who is standing up too, screaming at the top of his voice, 'Heil Hitler . . . Heil Hitler . . .' and thrusting his right hand into the Nazi salute as he does so! What an extraordinary sight, mutters Jack. Just the sort of thing you'd expect from Larry, who continues to cheer and shout, and even catcall when the images call for it.

The celebration of the German army over, the five leave the news theatre and take the five-minute walk round the corner to the railway station, avoiding cars and bustling people as they cross the busy road. 'Imbecile,' shouts a swarthy-looking cyclist, his black beret perched on his head, as Larry, still on a high after his interactive film session, gets in the way and nearly has the poor bloke off his machine. There are people sitting on sidewalk cafes drinking coffee, doing what they always do in France, talking and looking at other people in more of a hurry than they are. A truck full of soldiers races by, followed by a sleek black Citroen. Someone's in trouble, thinks Jack, as he reaches the station side of the street. All five walk into the railway station like seasoned travellers. They walk past guards, posted at regular intervals. Past mothers and fathers with crying children. On to the ticket office where Dédée, accompanied by Waucquez, buys the five tickets, discreetly passing them over to the three airmen when they reach the concourse. They join the flow of people moving towards the barrier where two soldiers and two ticket collectors are checking people through. Jack braces himself. This is it. He can see Dédée and Waucquez arm-in-arm up-front like a married couple. He is next, with Larry and Jurek a little back in the queue from him.

They all know that if one of them is stopped and questioned, he is on his own. The others will not come to his assistance. This is the rule, and it is accepted. The party as a whole cannot be jeopardised by the difficulties of any of the others, but Lady Luck continues to bless each of them. Jack is more preoccupied with a shabby little Frenchman in front of him, puffing away on a smelly pipe filled with what he can only believe must be dried horse manure. It is foul and there is no way he can avoid the clouds of smoke billowing from the glowing bowl. A woman behind Jack coughs and splutters, but the hint goes unnoticed by the culprit.

'Billet?' snaps the ticket collector. Jack hands over his ticket, which the collector then clips and passes on to the soldier, who hands it straight back to Jack with a courteous 'Danke'. Well, that was painless, thinks Jack as he moves on down the platform, spotting Dédée and Waucquez ahead, talking and waiting for the other three to catch up.

Now Jack hopes Larry doesn't get carried away, and shouts . . . 'Yeeees' as he passes through the barrier. Or thinks he is back in his priest's disguise and, with a flourish of his hand, says, 'God bless you, my son' – in French, of course.

Somehow, he resists.

Dédée selects a carriage near the rear of the train. Jack, Larry and Jurek know they are to enter the same carriage. In the corridor they see Dédée up-front. With a sweep of her eyes she indicates to Jack it is the compartment she wants for him. He has already been briefed to sit by the window, well away from the door. By the window he is less likely to be asked for a light, or for directions by passengers passing along the corridor. Dédée and Waucquez enter the same compartment, with Dédée taking the seat just inside the door; Larry is seated next to Dédée. She seems to want to keep an eye on him perhaps because he is inclined to be the most unpredictable of the three airmen! Jurek is next to Waucquez. The only other occupants in the compartment are two elderly ladies. One positions herself in the window seat opposite Jack. He just hopes she doesn't want to chat. He has his newspaper ready, and he makes sure he doesn't catch her eye. A passenger with his head buried in a newspaper is usually left alone. Besides, Dédée has another anti-social weapon – oranges. Dédée has given Jack two oranges which she wants him to peel and eat on the fourteen-hour train journey. He has instructions to start the first one an hour out of Austerlitz so the other travellers can see he is the passenger they should all ignore. 'People hate other passengers who suck oranges on trains,' says Dédée. And if that doesn't work, then he, and the others, must pretend to be mute!

As it gets nearer the departure time of 1600 hours, the surge of passengers of all ages, shapes, sizes and political persuasion are joining the train. Mothers with children, elderly men with their elderly wives, German officers, full of their own self-importance, and ordinary young Wermacht soldiers in their drab uniforms whose faces bear tired, humourless expressions. Noticeable by their absence are young lovers, most probably because France's young girls are finding it increasingly difficult to meet eligible young French men. The German occupiers have plans for them elsewhere . . . back in Germany.

God help us, if the Germans ever get to England, Jack tells himself as he looks at so many sad people.

Suddenly, there are several shrill whistles. A guard runs past the window waving a flag, there is a jolt and the train starts to pull away smoothly. A good few people who are not travelling are still standing on the platform and excitedly waving their farewells to friends who are. In a moment, the platform is left behind and the rhythm of the accelerating train takes over. Sensing the lady opposite is about to make some remark to him, probably about the weather or her reasons for being on the train, Jack decides it is time to bury his head in his newspaper. He pulls his beret from his head and stuffs it into his pocket, pulling *Le Figaro* from his coat pocket as he does so. Then he settles back into his seat, which is quite comfortable, and opens out the paper to its fullest in front of him. Wonderful, it has all the merits of a hospital bedside curtain. Nobody can see over it, round it, or even under it. Whilst the paper is in place he knows he is in a little world of his own, just as long as he has the strength to hold it there. Madame opposite will have got the message. She will see her fellow traveller as boring and unsociable. She will want nothing to do with him, a view she will no doubt confirm a little later on when he starts peeling his first orange!

Unnoticed by Jack, Dédée is looking on from her corridor side corner seat with considerable satisfaction, even with a little friendly affection at the way her number one package is handling the situation. She knows she doesn't need to worry about her Englishman. Centuries of national indoctrination ensure the required aloofness and reserve that comes so naturally to the English!

As the express speeds through the Paris suburbs, from behind his raised newspaper Jack can see the intense military activity of occupation. Many hundreds of tanks, vehicles, machines in sidings on rail transporters. Stations bear the fluttering swastika, as do some buildings. Uniformed German military are everywhere. Then the Bayonne express moves out of the suburbs into open countryside, and the scene is suddenly more tranquil. There are cows, sheep and horses dotting the fields. The trees are beginning to loose their leaves to the fast approaching winter, and gardens bordering the line have lost their colour. This could be rural England.

He is beginning to feel very comfortable and very relaxed. A glance across at Larry and Jurek shows they are, too. In fact, they appear to be asleep, but this could be their cover, their way of passing the time.

Jack hears noises coming from the corridor. Something's going on. Heads turn as a smartly dressed ticket inspector accompanied by a not-so-smartly uniformed soldier appear, sliding open the door. 'Your tickets, please,' asks the inspector. 'Your papers,' snaps the soldier.

Dédée smiles charmingly. And quickly presents her ticket and papers to the inspector, making some comment about it being a lovely day, as she does so. The soldier takes her identity papers and gives them a cursory glance, handing them back with a polite smile. Thankfully, he doesn't seem too interested so maybe the two began their ticket and papers inspection from the front end of the train, rather than from the back end. He has probably had enough. In turn, the passengers present their tickets and papers. It is a routine check, and there are no problems. The inspector says 'Merci', the German 'Danke' as they both move on to the next compartment. Jack returns to his newspaper. The elderly lady opposite must think he is trying to learn its contents off by heart!

As they speed through stations, Jack tries to read the place names but without much success. They are going too fast. So he starts counting the stations . . . whoom. One . . . two . . . three, excluding the ones in the Paris suburbs. Just as station ten zips into view, and out of view in a matter of seconds, a man in a trilby appears at the compartment door. As he pulls it open Jack can see he has a cigarette in his right hand. The man leans in and asks Larry for a light. But, of course, no way can Larry react even, if has understood what was being said – which he has not. But Dédée is there in an instant. 'Oh, darling,' she says. 'You must be daydreaming. The gentleman wants a light. Here give me your lighter . . .'. She takes it from Larry's hand, and lights the man's cigarette. Larry looks up, half nods his head at the man in the doorway, and smiles. Then he sits back and gazes at the compartment ceiling. Even Jack is fooled. Larry really did look as though he had been daydreaming! 'In the States, they'd give you an Oscar for that performance,' shouts Jack telepathically to Larry. Larry's smile broadens. Maybe he picked it up!

Back to his newspaper, and Jack notices a small story that seems to tell how Spitfires over northern France have shot up a passenger train on its way from Lille to Paris. Not something he thought Spitfire pilots would normally do for fear of killing innocent civilians. Then he reads that the train was made up of passenger coaches and tank transporters. Fair dos, they were obviously after the tanks, thinks Jack. He lowers his newspaper, looks out of the window and up at the cloudy sky to check they haven't a Spitfire escort. No, they haven't. In any case, the Spits won't come this far south unless they are escorting bombers.

Now for that first orange, a good two hours late! Dédée won't be pleased. And from her expression, nor is the lady opposite, who openly huffs her disapproval as the peeling begins. Jack doesn't bat an eyelid, but carries on stripping his orange of its fur-lined jacket. Juice squirts everywhere, and the strong essence of orange pervades all corners of the compartment. However, Jack can see that Dédée now looks well pleased!

Before the train finally pulls into Bayonne there is one more ticket and identity paper check, although Jack is not quite sure why because the train hasn't stopped anywhere en route. Once again Dédée's party's papers are seen to be in order so the Resistance forger must have done a good job back in Schaerbeek, which reminds Jack that this is the same district where Dédée's father, Frédéric, has his family home.

The thought encourages Jack to look up at Dédée who is sitting diagonally across the compartment from him. She is slim, she has an almost angelic face, and she is certainly fanciable. But not in a blonde bombshell way. Besides, Dédée isn't blonde. She is dark-haired, with deep brown eyes and the cutest little elfin shaped face. In the short time he has known her there has been no overt sign of affection from Dédée, no caressing or cuddling; barely any touching. Just an occasional brush of his arm, or pat on his back. And yet, Jack feels a curious kind of bonding with the delicate young girl on this trip of a lifetime with him. The young girl who literally has his life in her hands. But there is something in her eyes, when she looks at him, that makes him feel just a little bit more special to her than the others. And yet it is not something he would say to Dédée, and especially not to the other two. It would embarrass Dédée and probably upset Larry and Jurek!

The inspector is back again. He pokes his head in through the sliding door. 'We arrive at Bayonne in ten minutes,' he says.

CHAPTER 6

'Little Mother'

To Andrée de Jongh, the task was simple. All she wanted to do was walk over the Pyrénées from France into Spain, and back again. Not once. Not twice, but many times. And yet she was finding it difficult to convince guide Thomas that she was serious; that he should take her. His answer was, 'No! I will not go with a woman; women cannot walk'. But by the end of the same day he was forced to change his mind!

Thomas's refusal was like a red rag to a bull. 'What are you doing today?' asked Andrée. 'I am going into the mountains to see my family,' Thomas told her gruffly. 'May I go with you?' asked Andrée. Thomas said she could join him if she wished.

'So I followed him across the mountain all day, and kept up a constant stream of chatter,' said the Belgian former nurse. 'By the end of the day Thomas was very tired, and I was not. He got the message. 'OK, I will take you across the mountain with me tomorrow,' he promised. The next day, at dawn, Andrée – better known by her code name Dédée – and Thomas, met at a farm at the foot of the Pyrénées from where they would set off. She had three 'friends' with her. But Dédée was not suitably dressed for climbing. She was told: 'You cannot cross the mountains wearing a skirt and ordinary shoes', so she was given a pair of blue trousers borrowed from one of the servants, and a pair of canvas shoes. The three men who joined the party were given more appropriate clothes too.

Dédée wanted to get to San Sebastian . . . across the mountains, across the Franco/Spanish border, and into Spain. But this was 1941; France was occupied by the Germans, and Spain remained neutral. The Spanish border guards shot any escapees they spotted illegally entering their country. Yet the young Belgian girl was not dissuaded. She had a mission to fulfil – to save Allied airmen from German prisoner-of-war camps. This was the route she intended to use to take them to freedom.

It was the beginning of a remarkable story, about a remarkable woman.

The next day was a hot afternoon in August 1941 when 'Dédée' – the nickname was often given to Belgian girls called Andrée – breezed into the British Consulate in San Sebastian, only to be referred on to the consulate in Bilbao where she met the Vice-Consul, Michael Cresswell. She told him

81

how she had travelled through German occupied Belgium and France, then across the Pyrénées to get to the consulate. Cresswell was polite, but not convinced. Such a mission would be impossible, he believed.

He asked what she wanted from the consulate. 'Money,' she said, so that she could finance her escape line, and bring many more Allied airmen and Belgians to Spain, and freedom. But he continued to doubt her story, and even considered the possibility she might be part of a German plot to embarrass the British government.

Dédée was finally able to discuss her plans with the top man, the Consul.

The Consul asked more penetrating questions. He told Dédée that he also found it difficult to believe she was capable of such a mission. That such a young girl, in white ankle socks, had crossed the hostile Pyrénées, and had set up an escape line through Belgium and France to rescue crashed airmen.

Dédée told the Consul she had three escapees with her to prove it, two Belgians who wanted to fight for the Allies, and a Scottish soldier left behind at Dunkirk. She had borrowed money from friends to pay for their journey. 'We left Brussels last week and crossed the Pyrénées two nights ago,' she said quietly. The Consul got up out of his chair, and walked to his office window that looked out across the busy streets of Bilbao. 'How long did you say the journey took?'

'I told you – a week,' said Dédée.

'And how did you get across the Pyrénées?'

'With a Basque guide. There were no problems,' she answered, believing she was slowly winning him over. Time to press home her advantage . . . 'There are many British soldiers and airmen hidden in Brussels. I can bring them through to you if you will help me do so.'

Dédée explained how she had set up the Comète Line from the home she shared with her father Frédéric, her mother and sister at 73 avenue Emile Verhaeren, in the Schaerbeek district of Brussels.

'Mmmm,' mumbled the Consul, returning to his seat. He was beginning to realise he was in the presence of a quite remarkable young woman. A woman who would allow nothing to deflect her from her mission. 'And you would be prepared to cross the Pyrénées again?' he asked.

'Yes, as many times as it takes, if you will help fund us. We will need money to pay for food, for clothes, for guides . . .'

'We are, of course, more interested in British servicemen,' said the Consul.

'Of course,' said Dédée, a huge grin on her face. She had done it. The Comète Line was in business. Dédée told the Consul that she would need 6,000 Belgian francs to get a man from Brussels to St Jean de Luz, near the border, and 1,400 pesetas to pay for a guide to take them across the Pyrénées.

1. Sergeant Jack Newton, aged 21, air gunner in Wellington bomber 'G for George'.

2. Leaflets like this one were dropped in their thousands over France in May 1941 by Jack Newton and his crewmates. 'Propaganda designed to help break the will of the enemy'.

3. Jack and Mary on their honeymoon in the Cotswolds two days after their wedding in London on 19 April 1941.

4. The ill-fated Wellington bomber 'G for George' that crash landed in Belgium after its starboard engine caught fire on its first bombing raid over Aachen.

5. "We need a miracle". This was the terrifying view the crew of 'G for George' had of Antwerp Cathedral as they headed for a crash landing into the Scheldt estuary, which can clearly be seen here. Less than two hundred feet from the spire, and level with the clocks, the stricken bomber looked doomed – until the miracle Jack Newton called for happened. From the front gun turret Jack suddenly spotted Deurne airfield, and skipper Langlois made a near-perfect landing on it. (By kind permission of Daniel Philippe)

6. Antwerp International Airport as it is today. In 1941, crippled 'G for George' made an emergency landing on its main runway when it was known as Deurne airfield. (By kind permission of Daniel Philippe)

7. All that was left of the Wellington after it safely crash-landed on Deurne airfield, fired by its crew to stop it falling into enemy hands. These amazing pictures were taken by a German military photographer. (By kind permission of the Jean-Louis Roba Collection)

8. The front door of 66 rue Washington, Brussels, Belgium. (Taken by John Clinch, August 2001)

9. Brave nun Antoinette Becquet, who made life as pleasant and as comfortable for Jack as she could in her Brussels 'safe house'.

10. The little dog that hated Germans, in the arms of its owners, courageous members of the Belgian Resistance, Max and Céline Evrard. But the dog loved Jack, and when it got the chance it snuggled up to him on his bed.

11. A safe house in Spa, on the outskirts of Liége, where Jack was hidden for several days. It was here that Jack first met Emile Witmeur – the Resistance chief who thought he might be a German!

12. Emile Witmeur interrogated the three British aircrew believing they might be German infiltrators. He was prepared to shoot them had they not been able to prove they were Allied airmen.

13. It was the last safe house before the mountain crossing. The south of France home of Mme Elvire de Greef, seen here with her equally brave daughter, Janine, was 'open house' to escapees.

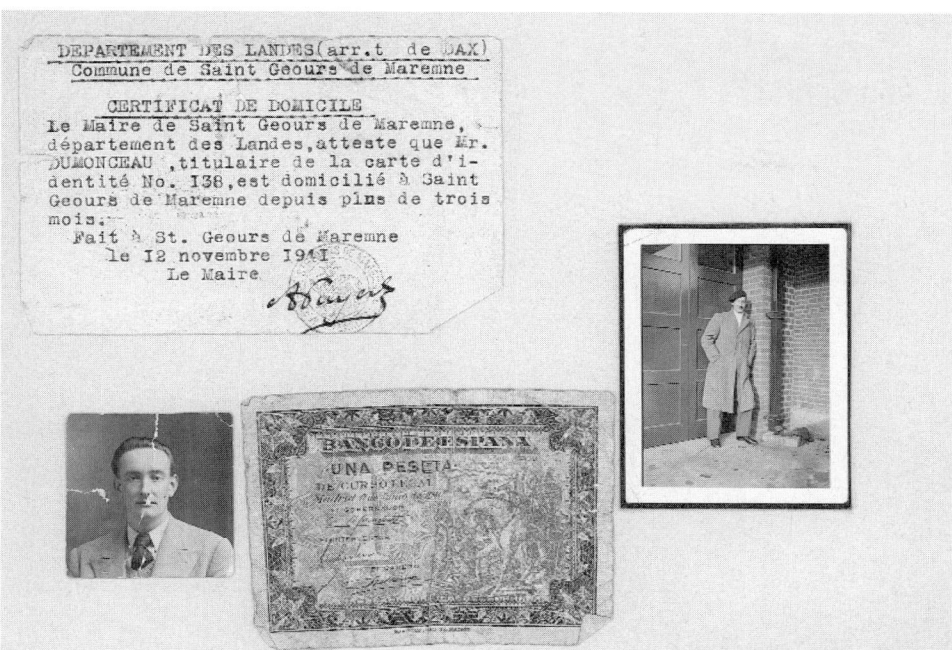

14. Four interesting reminders of Jack's shadowy life on-the-run from the Germans in Europe. His false identity paper, the Poly Photo taken in a Bon Marché shop, dressed to look like one of the locals, and the one peseta note given to him by Dédée to pay for his tram ride in San Sebastian after he had crossed the Pyrenees. 'I forgot to pay!' says Jack.

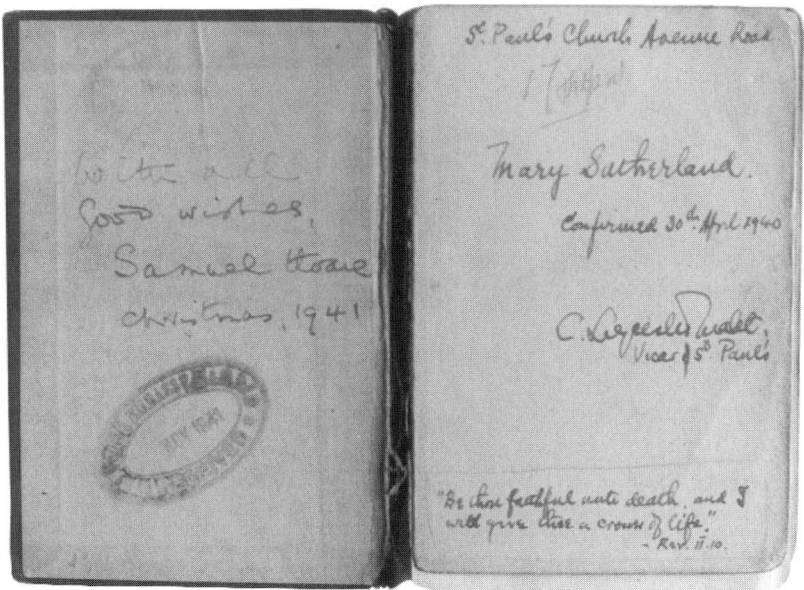

15. The first one out of Europe! The prayer book that became a receipt from the British Ambassador in 1941 neutral Madrid. It was to acknowledge Jack Newton as the first British airman successfully to use the one thousand miles long Comète Escape Line.

17. Explosives expert Gérard Waucquez joined the escapers so that he could get back to Britain to join the Special Operations Executive, be trained and return to France to blow up bridges and buildings.

16. The young Richard Copley shortly after his return from Germany, where he was held for four years in a prisoner-of-war camp.

18. It remains a mystery how a Spanish artist was able to produce this spectacular poster. 'It was a new specification Wellington, so I don't know how the artist was able to paint it so accurately. Anyway, this picture showed he did not have much sympathy for the Germans' says Jack, who found the poster on the wall of his basement internment room in the Madrid British Embassy – and took it home with him!

19. One for the album… at a Brussels reunion of some of those involved in the Comète Line and some of those who used it. In RAF uniform are (left) Skipper Roy Langlois, Jack Newton and in front of him, Richard 'Tich' Copley. Liége resistance leader, Emile Witmeur, is third from the left, standing next to Langlois. Front row (r-l): Witmeur's wife, Jeanne Vereecke, Betty Barlen, who became Copley's wife, and Marie, Langlois' wife.

20. Nadine, second in command to Dédée, with two of her 'boys', evaders Al Day (centre right) and Jack Newton (right), at a Brussels reunion.

21. Jack Newton and his wife Mary, in the garden of their Brede, East Sussex, home.

22. An emotional meeting between Jack and Dédée in 1946 in London, there to receive the George Medal from King George VI. The last time Jack and Dédée had seen each other was in the British Embassy in San Sebastian after they had successfully crossed the Pyrenees.

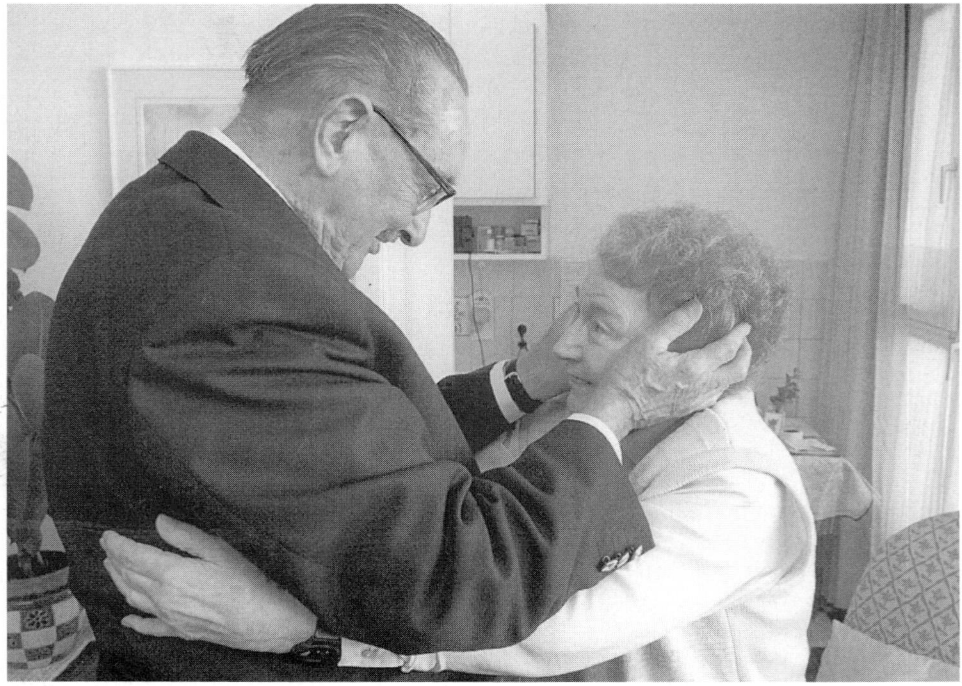

23. Another emotional moment for Jack and Dédée. Fifty-four years on in Dédée's Brussels flat. They keep in monthly contact by letter and with regular telephone calls.

The Consul made notes, and asked: 'When do you think you could return with another party?' In three or four weeks, she told him.

Dédée, nicknamed 'Little Cyclone' by her father, walked confidently from the Consul's room, down the stairs to her first 'packages', Private Colin Cromar, of the 1st Gordons, a survivor of St Valery, and the two Belgians. They were now in good hands, under the protection of the British Embassy. And free. Dédée said her goodbyes to the three men, turned to give them a quick wave, and she was gone. On the tram back to San Sebastian Dédée thought over her vital meeting with the Consul. Why had he seemed so unimpressed? Did he believe her story? Did he think she was being used to bring enemy agents into neutral Spain? She reasoned that if he had, then she would not have been allowed to return to France. In fact, Dédée had already won over the hearts of the British Embassy officials by her story and bravery. The Consul had already decided to obtain the support of the British Foreign Office for Dédée's plan.

Now Dédée's priority was to get back to Brussels to tell her father what she had achieved. To let him know that the Comète Line was up and running, financed largely by the British government. Over the following months it quickly became the most successful escape route out of German-occupied Europe.

Back at 73 avenue Emile Verhaeren, in Brussels, Andrée's father Frédéric was thrilled at her news. None of the neighbours in this modest and respectable little street ever imagined it harboured a family whose daughter was so dedicated to setting up an escape route that was to become so effective, even famous. From this house Dédée masterminded the line of safe houses that was to extend over one thousand miles through Belgium and France, to the Pyrénées. It was an amazing achievement. No. 73 was the hub of Belgian resistance to Hitler, and later Frédéric de Jongh was to become involved, too, taking the codename 'Paul'. Few knew that this respected headmaster, who walked to school each day in the Place Gauchard, was leading such a dangerous double life. His schoolchildren were aged 7 to 11, and the school nestled in a maze of grimy warehouses in a working class district of the city. Its concealed situation lent itself to the nefarious activities Paul and Dédée were engaged in. The man who specialised in teaching geography began holding secret meetings with Resistance contacts in his school study which adjoined the main school hall, and when lessons were over he would pull down the blinds for privacy. There was even a door from his study that led to the back of the building, a very handy escape route if the Gestapo turned up unannounced. Aged 56 at the time, he was a scholarly looking man with thick, horn-rimmed glasses who was deeply shocked by his country's surrender in 1940. Once the Comète Line was in place, set up by Dédée, he wanted to fight back and persuaded his daughter to let him become involved.

By the end of the year he had made contact with a number of British survivors of Dunkirk in hiding in Brussels, and with his daughter, Andrée, and friends, started raising money to set up their resistance organisation.

Dédée told how the Gestapo paid a call on their home one evening in 1941, trying to find her.

Two Germans drew up outside No. 73 in a grey coloured Opal, the bigger one with a briefcase tucked under his left arm, and pressed the bell firmly a number of times. Paul was inside, but couldn't answer the door until he had concealed some blank identity cards and money that had been spread out on his kitchen table. The Gestapo didn't ask to be invited in, they invited themselves, stamped their way up the stairs to a front room, where the man with the briefcase opened it, and prepared to make notes. 'Where is your daughter?' the other one snapped. Paul told them she had left home months ago, as daughters tended to do. He didn't know where she was. But from the less than adequate interrogation that followed, it was clear the Germans didn't know about the Comète Line, nor that Paul was linked to the Resistance. And they had few details about Dédée. Paul believed it likely they had obtained their information from someone they had arrested. It was the first time the Gestapo had taken any interest in a house in avenue Emile Verhaeren. which made the neighbours very jittery! Not Paul, however.

One of Paul's earliest trusted helpers was Jean Ingels, known as 'Jean de Gand'. Paul told him he had decided to make his school office the Comète Line's headquarters for the time being. He believed they were safer operating from the school than from a private house. Ingels said he knew of at least ten English airmen in hiding in the city. But they had to be sure the line was properly set up before testing it with real 'packages'. Paul, however, was keen to start passing escapees and evaders down the line because it was dangerous to hold them for too long in safe houses. In any case, he argued, people would lose confidence in them unless they got results.

Another enthusiastic helper in those early days was Andrée Dumont, known as 'Nadine'. She was a young looking, slim figured 19-year-old, with a tendency to be rather shy. Paul called her Nadine to avoid confusion with his own daughter, also called Andrée. She began by carrying messages for Paul in Brussels, but later acted as guide to Valenciennes and Paris

Now it was Dédée's turn to make the Comète Line a force to be reckoned with. One of her first big successes was to take Royal Air Force air gunner Sergeant Jack Newton along the line from Brussels, through France and over the Pyrénées, into Spain. It was another milestone. Newton was officially acknowledged as the first British airman to evade from German-occupied Europe in World War II. 'Evade' as opposed to 'escape' because Newton was never captured and, therefore, was not classed as an escapee. An important difference at the time.

From her early days training as a nurse in a Belgian hospital tending wounded British soldiers, Andrée showed great compassion for her fellow human beings. She was driven by the example of Edith Cavell, the English nurse executed in Brussels by the Germans in the First World War for helping British, French and Belgian soldiers to escape captivity. But she felt the need for more stimulation, the need to make more impact, so when war came to Belgium in 1940 it offered her the excitement and involvement that had been missing in her young life. As the Germans poured into her country, she saw a way of ridding herself of what she had felt was her tedious lifestyle. Here, at last, was a chance to do something really worthwhile. Really exciting.

Along with her father, towards the end of 1940, Dédée began sharing her concerns and her ideals with close friends. She secretly gathered round her those who would provide safe houses, and feed and care for young Belgians and Allied servicemen wanting to escape to England. With her father, Frédéric de Jongh, concentrating on the Belgium end, and under the noses of their German occupiers, Dédée set up a string of safe houses, and helpers, from Brussels, through France, to a farmhouse at the foot of the Pyrénées. It was a dangerous, and complex operation.

Guinea pigs for the escape line were the two Belgians and Private Colin Cromar, Dédée's first three 'packages' delivered safely to the British Consulate in San Sebastian following her first mountain crossing. Two soldiers named Bobby and Alan, from the ill-fated Highland Division, became Dédée's next packages safely delivered into Spain. Then came the line's first big test, a party of eleven, which included ten Belgians fleeing from the Gestapo and the flamboyant English woman, Miss Richards, whose residence in Belgium was similarly compromised.

The buzz this gave Dédée told her that she was doing the right thing for her country – and for herself.

At the San Sebastian British Embassy, now her Spanish point of contact, they gave Dédée a new name – The Postman. They took delivery of her 'packages' then smuggled them by diplomatic car out of Spain and into Gibraltar. For many months it worked a treat because the Germans hadn't yet clicked on to what was happening, and much of the important but routine work was undertaken by women in the Resistance organisation – young women such as Dédée who, initially, were not seen by the Germans as suspect. It was to be this understanding of the German psychology that gave the Comète Line such a huge early advantage. German women were largely brought up to run their homes, bring up their children, and look after the needs of their husbands. Getting involved in the skullduggery of resistance work, espionage and the like was not their scene at all. So their husbands serving in the military in Belgium and France preferred to believe the women there were similarly inclined. They were not! Belgian women were not afraid of danger, nor were they afraid of the Germans. Or, if they did fear the Germans and their tyrannical methods of interrogation, then they overcame it for the love of their country and its citizens. Dédée was to comment that sometimes she had more women volunteers for her dangerous work than she needed.

As the Comète Line became more successful, and was getting more Allied servicemen through to Spain, so the Gestapo piled on the pressure to infiltrate the escape line and break it. Dédée was told not to go back to Brussels, to her schoolmaster father's house in Schaerbeek, because the Gestapo were closing in. They arranged to meet and Frédéric – code name 'Paul' – insisted he would run the Brussels section of Comète from his school. 'Nobody will think of looking for the Resistance there in the headmaster's office,' he told Dédée. She was loath to involve her father so heavily in her activities, but agreed to it for the time being until he could find a replacement for himself, and a new home in Brussels for Comète.

The new arrangement ran well for several months until the day 'Paul' was identified by the Gestapo. He had no option but to flee Belgium, like his daughter, and re-establish himself in Paris. Frédéric's assistant, an Italian named Henri Mitchelli, took over in Brussels. He moved the Comète Line's headquarters to his own home in rue de la Loi. Henri became involved after Frédéric sought his help with a loan to fund 'some secret work'. Mitchelli asked how much he wanted, to which Frédéric replied: 'Well, 50,000 francs ideally, but anything less would be gratefully received.' Mitchelli generously handed over the 50,000 and didn't even ask what it was for. Some months later, Mitchelli was arrested.

Long after Jack Newton was back home in Britain, Dédée continued to put her life at risk as many more airmen were shot down, and needed to get to Spain. They needed to be given civilian clothes, forged papers, food and accommodation. Their fares had to be paid. The logistics were enormous, but the Comète Line was so well organised that, even when parts of it were infiltrated and broken up, it grew a new limb, and continued virtually uninterrupted. People like M. and Mme Maréchal provided short-term lodgings for airmen. Their 18-year-old daughter often collected them from a pick-up point in a local church, where Elsie used her fluency in English to question the airmen and judge if they were genuine, questions that had been prepared by Michael Cresswell at the San Sebastian embassy. The object being to prevent the infiltration of the net by German agents. But on occasions they failed, as was the case when two phoney 'Americans' were put in touch with the Maréchals, claiming to have been shot down in their Halifax. Apart from the fact that they both wore khaki shirts and said it was part of their uniform, they also claimed there had been four men on board their bomber. This was fewer than usual and Elsie knew airmen wore blue shirts. Her suspicions were rightly aroused. When she went to question them further at a house in rue Ducale, the Gestapo were waiting and Elsie was arrested. In another incident, a Resistance agent was shot dead by three Gestapo agents. In two days more than one hundred people were arrested. The situation was desperate, and many replacements were needed. But before they were recruited, new Resistance workers were told they could expect to be captured in less than six months, and probably tortured. If they cracked under interrogation and informed, many more people would be arrested, and probably die. Even so, very few changed their minds.

Faking German identity documents became a challenge the Resistance men took on with a passion.

Said Dédée: 'We discovered the Germans *"Passier Schein"*, an "admit bearer" pass printed on orange paper. This allowed people to move freely anywhere in occupied countries. But it was extremely difficult to reproduce because it was printed on very strong paper bearing a faint green and complicated watermark written in a gothic text.

'But we had a man skilled enough to do a good job. We provided the orange paper and our man, Pirard, copied the green watermark and the gothic text. It was impeccable. The fake *Passier Schein* was then printed and we filled it in and signed it ourselves, generally for Flemish-speaking Belgians who worked on the airfield under construction near Biarritz. They left Paris as Parisians and arrived at St Jean de Luz as Basques, with no possessions.'

One of the safe houses just outside Bayonne was the home of the family Dassie. Lucienne Dassie, known as 'Lulu', and her mother provided a safe house for airmen waiting to cross the Pyrénées. They were well looked after, too. Two would sleep downstairs, another two upstairs in the bedroom. At around 0530 they were woken and while they washed, Lulu's mother warmed up the kitchen. Then they had breakfast in the kitchen with food mostly collected from black market sources.

Another safe house, much used by Dédée and her escaping airmen, was the home of Elvire de Greef, whose agent's name was 'Tante Go', and her husband, Fernand. The strange pseudonym was derived from the original password used by visitors to her villa at Anglet, and her pet dog called Gogo. Tante Go was in charge of the south-west region of the Comète Line, and she ran it with disciplined efficiency. Dédée and Elvire were great friends, and very protective of each other. The de Greefs had two teenage children, Freddy, who was about 18, and Janine, 17, both of them very active in the Comète Line running messages and accompanying escaping airmen into the foothills of the Pyrénées. Janine, a very pretty girl, often skipped lessons at the local Lycée to go on such trips.

On the road between St Jean de Luz and Bayonne was Anglet. A narrow lane led to the rather drab grey village with a distant view of the mountains and below them the clear blue waters of the Bay of St Jean de

Luz. It was where Dédée had soaked up some of the warm south of France sun before she set out on her first crossing of the Pyrénées, returning to the de Greefs some three weeks later jubilant after her memorable first visit to the British Embassy in San Sebastian, then afterwards in Bilbao. It was to this house that only six weeks earlier she had brought Miss Richards and the ten Belgians on their epic journey from Belgium, across the Somme to Paris and by express train to Bayonne. Fortunately, there was not another party like that one!

Dédée revealed details of the deal she had clinched with the British, telling Elvire that no written agreement had been made because she accepted that an Englishman's word was his bond. She was never to regret that trust in her new partners. However, at first it worried Dédée that she might have to take her escaping airmen all the way to the consulate in Bilbao, much preferring to pass them over to the British in San Sebastian, which was much closer to the border. That was not to prove a problem, either.

Tante Go was the focal point at this bottom end of the line, the last safe house before the mountain climb into Spain. She was ruthless and energetic. She had prominent features and fierce grey eyes tinged with green. Her slight build and pleasant round face belied her strong character and disarming charm. This was a woman, like Dédée, who knew precisely where she was going. And got there! Guesses were that she was at most aged 35.

Elvire quickly learned the tricks of dealing on the black market, ensuring she had all she needed to feed and keep her young airmen in the best condition possible. She reasoned they needed good food to keep up their spirits, and to give them the strength to get over the mountain. Regularly she jumped on her bicycle and rode off to do the rounds of local cafes and bistros to pick up smuggled goods from well-wishers. It proved a sound policy.

Fernand was tall, dark and young looking, and was perfectly happy to accept that Elvire, his wife, ran the Comète Line operation in the south. And as an interpreter in the *Kommandantur*, the local German HQ at Anglet, he was well placed to help his wife build her escape organisation. He had access and obtained blank identity cards essential to travellers in occupied France. He could get his hands on special passes, *Certificats de Domicil*, issued to visitors to the restricted zone established by the Germans along the Atlantic coastline. Sometimes he slipped a couple of blank passes into his pocket on his way home at the end of the day. His German employers had no idea what he was up to, and they didn't miss the blank passes. Fernand saw to that because it was his job to account for them.

Ingeniously, Fernand took the code name 'L'Oncle' (the Uncle). It was the perfect match with his wife's code name 'Aunt'.

One of Uncle's daily tasks was billeting enemy troops, and there were several thousand in the area. Undertaking these duties gave Fernand the opportunity to visit the headquarters of many German units so he didn't miss the chance to steal the occasional official rubber stamp. In no time at all, he had amassed quite a collection of identity documents, forms, stamps, and official papers which were then distributed to branches of the Comète Line in Paris and Brussels.

And by virtue of working in the *Kommandantur* he had authority to pass freely through the streets of Anglet and the surrounding towns, often on vital missions for Tante Go.

But one of the most amazing 'rescue' stories of the war in this part of France concerned the bravery of Elvire and Fernand.

Their favourite Basque mountain guide was an extraordinary character named Florentino. Dédée recruited him to take her airmen to safety, and she accompanied him on more than thirty crossings. But on his last trip, one month after D-Day, Florentino was returning to France, having successfully delivered important written messages for Allied intelligence (rather than airmen, on this particular occasion). He was descending the French side of the mountain in the early hours of the morning when he was hit in the leg by a burst of automatic gunfire. He fell with his leg badly shattered and was picked up by the Germans. Taken back to the police headquarters at Hendaye, Florentino had nothing to say. In great pain, he was then transferred to a civilian hospital, run by nuns at Bayonne, where he received treatment.

Word got back to Tante Go that Florentino was in big trouble. He was in bed, in hospital, not talking to anyone and pretending to be near to unconsciousness – his way of avoiding further interrogation. So Tante Go went to the hospital on the pretext of visiting another patient hurt in bombing, who was in the next bed. On her way out she dropped her bag alongside Florentino's bed and whispered to the apparently lifeless Comète Line man, 'Two o'clock'.

Precisely at two o'clock there was a disturbance at one end of the ward. German voices were shouting and frightening the patients. Three big men – clearly Gestapo because they had not removed their hats, as was customary with them – stood arguing with one of the nuns, who pleaded: 'He must not be moved. It could be dangerous. But the men ignored the nun's pleas, brushing her aside as they strode on down the ward looking for their man. One waved an official looking paper. They came to Florentino's bed and in German informed him that he was being transferred to another hospital.

Although Florentino understood every word they said, he didn't respond. Nor did he protest, appearing to accept his fate. He was bundled onto a stretcher and unceremoniously wheeled out to a waiting ambulance which drove off at great speed, leaving the nuns standing on the hospital steps waving their fists and threatening the Gestapo men with eternal retribution.

Even by Gestapo standards, the men's handling of the situation was a bit excessive.

But inside the speeding ambulance, Florentino was now laughing uncontrollably. The Gestapo men removed their hats, hugged Florentino and handed him a large glass of cognac, which he downed in a single gulp. Then they all discussed their little ruse – in French. Leading the 'Gestapo' ambulance crew was 'L'Oncle' (Fernand), who, along with friends, had set up Florentino's rescue. Fernand had used his influence as an interpreter working with the Germans to arrange the 'transfer'. The snatch was all over in twenty minutes.

Florentino was soon hidden in a safe house on the outskirts of Anglet. But a few weeks later, France was liberated by the Allies whom Florentino had served so well, and he was able to return to his home in the mountains a free man again.

By the end of 1942 Dédée had crossed the Pyrénées thirty-two times, having taken out 118 people, but she began to feel the Germans closing in on her. Suddenly 'If I am arrested' became 'When I am arrested'. Then on 15 January 1943 she made her thirty-third crossing and the weather was at its worst. At the farm in Urrugne, the last stop before the walk to the foothills, her guide, the irrepressible Florentino, said it was not possible to leave that night. They would have to wait until the following day, when the heavy rain had eased. The lady farmer agreed the three airmen, Dédée and Florentino could stay overnight.

But treachery was in the air.

One of the trusted farm labourers went to the German authorities and for the promise of 50,000 francs per person he named and betrayed the three airmen, Dédée and Florentino. Fortunately, Florentino left earlier than the rest, but the others never caught up with him. They were taken away and interrogated. It was the end of the line for Dédée. The Comète Line had been beheaded.

Ironically, though, the Germans had no idea they had just caught the woman who masterminded its creation, a woman whose exploits throughout France were as well recounted as those of the Scarlet Pimpernel a century or so before. They didn't even know her name. Dédée was transferred to the Château Neuf prison, in Bayonne, where the Gestapo hoped they would make more progress. Dédée's distraught father, hearing of her capture, and the arrest of the three airmen, considered a plan to spring the four from prison.

In the meantime, Dédée, not knowing of her father's deep distress, underwent her first interrogation. The Germans were convinced her father headed the escape line. There were more interrogations with five men firing questions at her, but she avoided revealing her real name because she realised they would know the Gestapo had been seeking her since 1941. Besides, if they knew her real name it would lead the enemy to her father.

'Tante Go' conceived another rescue plan, which involved a key maker responsible for the locks and doors in the new prison, the Villa Chagrin where Dédée had now been transferred. But that had to be abandoned, too, as it was being carried out.

It began to look very bad for Dédée. She passed her time in her cell singing opera much to the annoyance of her guards, until the hunger and cold sapped her strength. A German officer questioned her again, asked if she had been thinking of her mother, if she was going to tell him where he could find her father. Dédée said 'no'. That if she did, her mother would condemn her for it.

'Then he said I would be tortured and that that would make me talk. I replied that as I had never been tortured I didn't know if it would,' said Dédée. She told him she would resist as best she could. Dédée recalled eighteen interrogations, each one building on the other, so she just kept making up new stories, even though each 'truth' was as false as the previous one! Lie followed lie until the Germans were as confused as Dédée.

In the end, she told the Gestapo at the huge villa in Bayonne where the interrogations took place, that she was, in fact, the head of the net that interested them. They asked her why she wanted them to believe she was its head. Why did she pretend? 'Because it was true,' she said. But by this time they couldn't tell what was truth and what were lies. They continued to believe that she was protecting her father.

By admitting she was the chief of the escape organisation, she hoped it would take attention away from her father. They wouldn't believe her because in their view, a woman was not capable of such a thing.

In Bayonne the situation became critical. The Dassie family was arrested, others left for England, and 'Tante Go' had to cut back her activities. Unable to help, Dédée's father returned to Paris, as the Germans decided to transfer Dédée, the Dassies, and the young airmen to Fresnes prison, in Paris. Another important Comète Line man, named 'Franco' and unknown to the Gestapo, happened to be catching the same train to Paris, when he spotted Dédée and the airman waiting on the platform under armed guard. He made a point of passing Dédée, though neither of them showed any signs of recognition.

On arrival at Austerlitz, Franco made a point of passing the front carriage where he again saw Dédée through the window, and she gave him a wink to show that she had seen him. The prisoners were taken to a police wagon outside the station, and on to Fresnes.

Franco headed for Dédée's father's flat to tell him his daughter had been transferred to Paris.

Over the days following the prisoners in Fresnes were regularly taken in a prison van to the Gestapo headquarters in rue des Saussaies for questioning, including Dédée who day after day found herself in the company of an interrogator named Obersturmführer Arnold Schneider. A strange bond formed between the two. Said Dédée: 'He was a very special German. Essentially a remarkable man.'

Their sessions were like a game of chess between two grandmasters. Two very intelligent human beings, one the tiger, the other the mouse. Each shadow boxing the other, but each soon recognising the strengths of the other which, in the end, created a kind of stalemate. Even a bond.

According to Dédée, the interrogation went along the following lines:

Schneider: Do you know that we have had almost the same job?

Dédée: I would be surprised!

Schneider: Not now, but before the war you worked in the decorating business.

Dédée: Yes.

Schneider: You worked for the Artistic Cooperation. Well, I delivered to the Cooperation. I was an agent for the Faber paints.

Dédée: That's good, they are good paints.

Schneider: Perhaps we met, or have seen each other?

Dédée: I don't know.

Schneider: Good. Do you know what is going to happen now?

Dédée: Oh, yes. You want me to talk!

Schneider: Tell me where your father is, and we will say no more about it.

Dédée: My father has nothing to do with this.

Schneider: So you say, but I find that unbelievable. I've never met anyone so obstinate. Is a dark cell not enough? Do I have to ask you in Spanish, in Italian, or perhaps in Flemish?

Dédée: Why, do you speak Flemish? [Dédée's interrogator asked her if she was frightened of being tortured.]

Dédée: Yes, I am scared to death! Wouldn't you be in my place? But that's the way it is. It changes nothing. I would rather die.

Dédée described her experience as 'very strange'. She said:

Very soon there was a sort of understanding between this man and me, because he was essentially a very strange man. At that time the big joke was to say that one cannot be intelligent, sincere and a Nazi

92

all at the same time. But this man was intelligent, he was sincere, and he was a Nazi.

Schneider went on to ask Dédée if she thought Germany would win the war, then he interrupted himself by commenting that surely they could exchange views.

Dédée's response was, that certainly they could talk but not as equals. She said she could tell him what she thought of Hitler and if he listened and she told another German he had listened to her, then he could be sent to the Russian front. 'So you see, we are not equals,' said Dédée!

Schneider asked if she liked the English.

'Yes . . .'

'And do you like the Germans?'

'Not at all . . . !'

In the end, deciding they could learn nothing more from Dédée she was sent back to Brussels, to the Saint Gilles prison. She had not been in her home city for months, and now here she was back again, and in handcuffs.

Frédéric de Jongh made a last attempt to free his daughter. He was told it could be achieved with the payment of one million French francs, raised through the British government and brought across the Pyrénées from San Sebastian. But it was a trick. The money did not buy Dédée's freedom, and she remained in Saint Gilles.

In June 1943 there was more heartache, when a traitor was found within the organisation. He was Jean Masson, a Gestapo agent, who attempted to arrest other agents. Jacques Cartier, the new head of Comète in Brussels, was exposed and had to flee to the south. On the night of 23 December, as he attempted to across the Pyrénées, there was shooting as the party tried to cross the Bidassoa river. Cartier was killed, though it was not clear whether he died from a heavy fall in the fast flowing river, or by a bullet. His body was found the following day by a German patrol.

On 6 June 1944 the Allies landed in Normandy, and the Comète Line became a part of Operation 'Marathon' in which the aim was to keep bailed out airmen under cover to await the liberation. Two camps were set up in France between Orléans and Chartres, as well as in Belgium. Many airmen were hidden in the Ardennes forest, helped by people who lived in the area.

On 3 September Brussels was liberated, and a few days later all Belgium was freed of its German occupiers. But over 150 agents of the organisation were not around to celebrate the victory which they paid for with their lives. That included the extraordinary Frédéric de Jongh, who was executed by firing squad at Mont-Valérien prison, in Paris, on 28 March 1944. He was 58.

For three years the Comète Line, set up by Paul (Frédéric de Jongh) and his courageous daughter, Dédée (Andrée de Jongh), returned over 300

Allied servicemen to freedom. The job done, its members who survived slowly picked up the threads of their former lives.

In their own way, and often at great self sacrifice, they had written their place in the history of Belgium and France during World War II.

It was a very personal testament.

CHAPTER 7
Mary's Love Diary

Jack and Mary had barely tied the marital knot. With his first serious operational flight coming up immediately after the August Bank Holiday, Jack decided the best way to spend those precious few days together was to have another honeymoon! He rented a small cottage not far from RAF Binbrook, 12 Squadron's home station in Lincolnshire, and Mary caught the train up from London to join him there. It was a blissful three-day extension of their first Cotswold honeymoon that had been cut short in April.

But as Mary made her way back to London the following morning, unknown to her, overnight Jack had already flown out on his first bombing raid over Germany. That afternoon Mary received a telegram informing her that her husband was missing. The Wellington and its crew of six, which included front gunner Jack Newton, had failed to return, and none of the crews on board the other 12 Squadron Wellingtons on the same raid had seen what happened to 'G for George'. Had Mary said her last 'goodbye' to the childhood sweetheart she had just married? It was to be nearly five months before she had the answer. Said Mary:

> They were the hardest five months I have ever lived through. It was just so unfair. One moment I was on cloud nine, three months into marriage to the man who had been my sweetheart since I was 14, and the next I didn't know whether I was suddenly widowed. Whether Jack was alive or dead, killed in his first bombing raid. For the following two weeks I was off work and in turmoil. Then, on the advice of my family, I went back to work at the Post Office in London's Cannon Street to try and occupy my mind with other thoughts. It seemed to work. Suddenly I had this very strong feeling that Jack was very much alive. And that I would see him again, even if I didn't know when. Not once after that did I doubt that Jack would come back to me.

Mary was 22 and very much in love. Her Royal Air Force air gunner was eight months younger, but the age difference wasn't a problem for either of them. Since that moment when they first set on eyes on each other outside their homes in Townshend Road, St John's Wood, they had eyes only for one another. It was an instant love match. Then war came and Jack couldn't wait to get involved. Recalled Mary:

It never even occurred to me to try to stop him signing on. Nobody at the time worried that things might get nasty, even dangerous. There was excitement in the air, and I totally understood that Jack wanted to be right in the thick of the war effort as a flyer. I just accepted the risks, as he did. Besides, it never even occurred to us in 1939/40 that we might be heavily bombed, and even be under the threat of invasion. We just got on with our lives.

We were married at St Stephen's Church, in Avenue Road, St John's Wood on 19 April 1941, Primrose Day. Because of bomb damage, the little restaurant in the high street where the reception was held was better ventilated than usual. All its windows were blown out. But it didn't matter. Some thirty of us celebrated, seemingly without a care in the world. Hitler wasn't going to spoil this wedding celebration.

But the food rationing did mean our wedding cake was not quite what it seemed. No icing sugar was available, so a white cardboard case represented the icing; the cake itself was under the case lid. When the reception was over, Jack drove me away in his little MG for four days honeymoon in the Cotswold home of some Royal Air Force friends, Kath and Lionel. In fact, they were newly married themselves, and hadn't long been in their new home in Bourton-on-the-Water, not far from RAF Little Rissington where Lionel maintained the planes.

Mary never asked Jack where he was flying because she knew he was not allowed to tell her. Operational flights were secret. And although she knew he was flying on that fateful Sunday night, she had no idea it was on his first bombing raid over Germany. As she left by train for London on the Monday morning, Jack and his crewmates were already on Belgian soil doing their best to evade capture, sitting out the daylight hours of Monday in the cornfield, waiting for the Resistance boy on his bicycle to take them to the safe farmhouse that same evening. Recalled Mary:

Then I got the telegram from the Binbrook station commandant advising me Jack was missing. I just could hardly believe it. I was devastated.

My one horror was that his plane had crashed into the sea. Jack cannot swim so if that had happened, I knew he would likely be drowned. As I say, that was my one big fear. Then word came through that two of the other crew had been picked up and had been made prisoners-of-war, so I then knew that Jack was over there somewhere roaming around! At least he was alive, and I thought it wouldn't be long before I'd get word that he was in a prisoner-of-war camp, too. But I never did.

By this time, more than a month had passed and Mary decided to start a diary so that when Jack eventually returned home he would know how much she had been thinking of him, and worrying about him.

I bought the book from Alfred Woodcock & Co, general stationers at 47 Bow Lane, Cheapside, for four shillings and sixpence, and on Friday 26 September 1941 wrote my first entry. It read:

I would have started this diary to you sooner darling, but I just couldn't take any interest in things for a while, so please forgive, Sweet, and I'll start now. I have a few days leave until next Wednesday, so Kath has invited me to stay with her (By the way, dear, Li went overseas three weeks ago, so poor Kath is also down in the dumps.) I was off early today, so caught the 4.45pm for dear old Bourton and when I arrived at Kingham, found Kath waiting there with a car. I was so grateful because it would have meant waiting for an hour. She was just as sweet as always, and when I saw '24 Springvale' again I thought of the glorious memories we have there. It may be a long wait until I'm in your arms again, darling, but I'll wait. I wouldn't be with anyone else for the world, as I love you with all my heart and there will never be anyone else. I discovered that Kath had an airman and his wife living with her, who have a six month old baby, Dorian. He is a flight mechanic at Little Rissy. We sat talking until very late, and then both slept together in our 'honeymoon bed'. I lay thinking about you, sweetheart, wondering where you are, and how you must be worrying about me. Goodnight, dearest, and God bless you and bring you safely back to me.

The significance of Jack's absence hit his wife still harder when she received a letter from the Royal Air Force Central Depository in Colnbrook, Buckinghamshire, listing Jack's personal effects. The letter, sent to 39a Pope's Grove Mansions, Heath Road, Twickenham, in Middlesex, the home of Jack's sister, Babs, and where Mary was staying at the time, told Mary these personal effects would be held at the depository for safe keeping until such time as more specific information was received.

Every day Mary wrote down her private thoughts in her diary. Then on Saturday 4 October she included in her diary a printed message of happiness which read:

Till we come to that day when our partings are over
Till our hopes and our wishes come true,
I shall carry the thrill of those days spent together
and a future – all centred in You.
Till the things that divide us for ever are ended
and these troublesome days all depart,
In my thoughts your dear face will be always beside me
your Love ever locked in my heart.

Mary received another letter from the Royal Air Force records office in Gloucester. It was dated 30 October 1941:

Dear Madam,
With reference to my letter of 9 August 1941 I regret to inform you that nothing further has been heard of your husband No. 742570 Sergeant Jack Lamport Newton of No. 12 Squadron, Royal Air Force, since he was reported missing.

According to further information received, the aircraft took off from base at 10.48 pm on the 5th August 1941, detailed to bomb a target in Gachan [though this should have read 'Aachen']. *Information has been received that Sergeants Burrell and Porteous are interned in the south of France. Nothing further has been heard, so far, of your husband or of the three remaining members of the crew.*

With renewed expressions of the sympathy of the Royal Air Force with you in your great anxiety.

I am, Dear Madam, Your Obedient Servant.

Mary noted receipt of this letter in her diary entry on 3 November 1941:

When I got home, there was a letter from the Air Ministry telling me that two of your crew, Sgt Porteous and Burrell are both interned in 'unoccupied' France, and nothing has been heard of you or the others. I bet you're all hiding somewhere. Oh, I do hope so, darling. I keep wondering where you are, and what you are doing.

Three days later, on 6 November, Mary's diary entry read:

What a day!!! Yippee! I feel years younger and so happy. I've been crying with relief. Mrs Brewer has written to us to say that her mother had written to Sgt Burrell and he has cabled back to her to say, 'Dick and other members of crew safe and well and in good hands – not prisoners.' I knew it, I knew it. You'll be walking in before Christmas. What a difference in me now. I shall say a special prayer tonight. I have something to live for now . . . YOU, and gosh won't I be good to you. I'll be your devoted wife and helpmate. Night, night sweetheart. I pray we will be reunited soon.

On 17 November 1941 Mary noted:

I had an answer from Mrs McCave, Flt Lt Langlois's sister this morning to say that he is a prisoner of war and she has had a letter from the German prison camp. That only leaves Sgt McLarnon and you now. Darling, I'm still worrying and wondering where you are.

The next day Mary wrote:

Had a shock today, though dear as Mrs McLarnon, Jack's mother, has replied to my letter and says he is interned with Doug and Burrell, so now five out of the crew of six are internees and prisoners. Gosh! I wonder if you are still at large. I mustn't give up hope, though. That would never do.

On Wednesday 26 November Mary revealed in her diary that she went to her doctor, who confirmed that she had mumps. She wrote that she left Twickenham to go and see out her mumps at her mother's home in the New Forest, Hampshire. She caught the train from Waterloo the same afternoon.

Mary's diary entry on 5 December hinted at a little desperation at Jack's fate:

No news of you, darling. I do wonder when I shall hear something. This waiting is awful, but I suppose it could be worse, as some poor girls have definitely lost their husbands altogether, and I know that you must be alive somewhere because of that cable.

On 14 December, Mary scribbled:

How I keep thinking of you, darling, wondering where you are on a day like this. If only I could hear you are alive, it would make such a whole world of difference to me. I get so miserable some days, but things must come right again one day.

Mary's diary entry on Monday 22 December revealed she had new hope:

A letter from Doug's aunty with a telegram enclosed from Doug. It says, 'Newton and other two OK' so darling I feel a lot easier now, as it's certainly better than not hearing anything at all. It seems strange to me all this silence, but I must have faith and be patient.

Mary spent Christmas Day at her friend Kath's, in Bourton-on-the-Water. She wrote in her diary:

> *Christmas Day again, but darling what a difference from last year when you were with me. We spent it very quietly, as Kath and René felt miserable, too. I'll celebrate my Xmas when you come home darling. I do miss you so much at times like these, but I will never give up hope. I know I shall hear something soon.*

Then came the news that Mary says showed God had answered her prayers. On Tuesday 30 December 1941 she wrote in her diary:

> *After five months of anxious waiting I've had the most marvellous news. I got home, there was an extremely nice gentleman who told me he had been with you since 6 August. He is a Belgian, and I just sat there in a daze. I just can't realise you are alive and well. I really feel as if I am living again, darling and when he told me you would be home in a month's time, I nearly collapsed. God has answered my prayers, sweetheart. I love you dearly and now I know I shall be able to live my life with you. Nothing else matters.*

The following day, she recorded:

> *Well, dear, I don't know what's up with this world, but now 'Records' report you interned in Madrid, Spain. Something must have gone wrong. Oh, what a disappointment. I did think I was going to see you soon.*

Then, on Wednesday 7 January 1942 came the news Mary had been so anxiously awaiting for five months. Her diary records the occasion:

> *Darling, today has been the grandest day of my life. I've had a cable from YOU. It was such relief to get it. I couldn't help crying . Also 'Records' report you are safe at Gibraltar. What a wonderful ending. I am just counting the hours until I'm in your arms again, sweetheart. I sent a cable back to you from Twickenham. I put 'Darling, received cable. Am overjoyed you are safe. Am longing for our reunion. Take care of yourself. Tons of love, Mary'. Hurry back, dear, you've got such a reception awaiting you. Especially from your little wifey.*

And on Thursday 8 January Mary wrote:

> *I am busy getting my 'second honeymoon' things together. I feel more excited than when I was married. God bless you, sweetheart. I don't know how to keep my mind on my work. I'm so very, very happy because you're coming home to me.*

With Jack's arrival back into Britain, at Pembroke Dock aboard the Sunderland flying boat, imminent, Mary could hardly contain herself. On Monday 12 January she wrote:

Another lovely day for me, sweet. One cable and another letter from you. It seems you will soon be leaving Gibraltar. I'm so glad you have received my cable, darling, cos now you know your 'little deadbeat' is alright. You've no idea and never will know my dear how completely life has changed for me since hearing from you. I love you (in capital letters!!). Goodnight, Jack, dear, look after yourself for me, cos I want every little bit of you.

And the last entry on Tuesday 13 January 1942 read:

Sent you a cable today, dear. Nothing else of importance has happened.

At their neat, little two-bedroomed retirement bungalow in Broad Oak, East Sussex, Mary and Jack are surrounded by memorabilia of their sixty years of married life together. And of Jack's extraordinary flight from captivity through Belgium and France, into Spain.

Did Mary ever worry that Jack might fall in love whilst 'on the run' and be unfaithful?

'It doesn't do to be too self-assured, but I believed it would have been very uncharacteristic of him had he done so. In the same way that it would have been uncharacteristic of me to have had an affair in Jack's absence. We have always only been for each other, and that is the way it was, and the way it still is,' said Mary. 'Our love was bonded still stronger by the pressures of those war years and separation, not weakened by them.'

Mary said that in their years together, Jack had always been loving and thoughtful. She paused for a moment, then added with a smile: 'Sometimes he's a bit too thoughtful. He can be ahead of me. He thinks of everything. And he hasn't changed. I continue to be so lucky.'

CHAPTER 8
Walking with the Enemy

As the express slowly pulled into Bayonne station, Dédée turned to Gérard Waucquez and, in French, told him they needed to get their things together, ready to disembark. Dédée gave the three airmen a nod to let them know they had arrived. She took a quick look in the compartment mirror, as if to straighten her beret, but also to reassure herself that her three 'brave boys' were preparing to leave too. Jack stood up, used the same mirror to adjust his black beret, giving it just a trace of a rakish left side tilt. As he liked it. He folded his paper and slipped it into his coat pocket as he followed the others out of the compartment, leaving just the two elderly ladies still in their seats.

Other passengers were already spilling out into the corridor, and shuffling their way towards the front end, to a door that opened out onto the platform. A German soldier brushed by, quickly followed by another. They seemed to be in a hurry. But Jack showed no interest or concern, other than that he knew he must keep Dédée and Waucquez in sight. It was early morning, with the sun still struggling over the horizon. And there was a chill in the air. Jack appreciated the warmth and comfort of his heavy overcoat as he stepped down from the train. He took a quick glance left and right to get his bearings and to see who was about. There was not a lot he needed to know; just a half-dozen uniformed soldiers, a couple of gendarmes, and no doubt a handful of the usual beady-eyed secret police who liked to melt into the shadows, and who posed the biggest threat to escapees. But maybe they weren't up yet.

It was barely six o'clock, and it showed on the passengers' faces as they shuffled along the platform in a steady stream to the exit barrier, trying hard to stifle disturbed sleep yawns! Bayonne was normally the favourite destination for thousands of French holidaymakers in early August; the region the Parisians in particular loved to bring their families to, to relax in the southern sun. But this was wartime occupation and the French had little heart for such pleasures any more. Many of the travellers on this train were returning from business trips to northern France, in fact, just like Monsieur Jacques Dumonceau (Jack), whose home address was north of Bayonne, in the nearby region of Dax.

Dédée didn't go to the exit but, instead, led the men to the station refreshment room. Janine, the attractive, blonde-haired teenage daughter of Tante Go, was there to meet them. Dédée and Janine kissed. Janine nodded shyly to the three airmen. Then it was time for the secret way out of Bayonne station which avoided any complications that might arise passing through the ticket barrier, and the lurking secret police. The three airmen were each told to follow either Dédée or Janine out to the station lavatories where there was a door leading out onto the street. The guides had a duplicate key to the door, and each would be met outside. It worked a treat. All were quickly outside the station, and into a nearby café.

Dédée and Gérard sat at one table, and the three airmen at an adjoining table. Dédée was able to tell them quietly that they had a short tram journey ahead to Anglet. Gérard Waucquez ordered coffees, Dédée paid and when everyone had emptied their cups, they set off for the last part of their journey to Anglet, and to the villa of Madame de Greef on the outskirts of the town.

They were now so tantalizingly close to freedom, and yet so dangerously close to capture. Anglet town hall was the local German military headquarters, and Fernand de Greef, husband of Elvire de Greef, one of its most trusted employees, as well as one of its most courageous enemies. The sheep was truly in the fox's lair, and every bit a match for the fox's reputed cunning!

The de Greefs' house, quite drab looking from the outside, was on the road between Bayonne and St Jean de Luz, but the view from it across the sparkling blue bay was spectacular. The Pyrénées, rising at their highest to just over 11,000 feet, though rather less on the western end towards Hendaye, provided a naturally magnificent backdrop. It was as though God had had second thoughts about making Spain and France such close neighbours and had shovelled the rocky Pyrénées into place to keep the two countries apart. It has to be said He did a pretty good job because even at their lowest point the Pyrénées were still considered impregnable to all but the hardiest of climbers. One of nature's natural barriers. And yet this was to be the route to freedom for so many Allied airmen, and others escaping from German tyranny.

The de Greef family was an extraordinary one by any standard. Elvire ran the south-west region of the Comète Line, secretly and efficiently. Those who came into contact with her never questioned her authority because she was so clearly in charge and felt answerable to only one person – Comète's chief, Dédée. Even Fernand happily accepted the situation, and gave Elvire his unstinting support in everything she did.

They had two children, Frédéric, who was 18, and Janine, 17. Both were deeply involved in saving Allied airmen, and their mother's dedication to this cause.

Jack recalls:

As the five of us made our way along the last stretches of the country road to Tante Go's safe house, I remember thinking how many people had put their lives at risk to get me this far. An enormous number, probably by this time at least thirty-five. And there were still a good few more to come, too, the de Greefs at the head of them. I just didn't dare think of the consequences if I was caught now, and tortured. The Jerries and their thumbscrews would have had a field day with me! I had come into contact with so many Resistance helpers, and the Germans would have done their best to squeeze every last name out of me. I am not sure I would have been brave enough, or strong enough to have held out – unlike Dédée and so many of those who worked with her to get airmen like me back to England. My admiration for every one of them has never diminished.

As we hurried up the path to the de Greefs' front door, the house looked large and quite overbearing. Not at all light, and attractive, as I imagined it would in this mostly sunny part of southern France. Thick shrubbery filled the spacious front garden, including five or six large, shaped bushy trees which seemed oddly out-of-place. I had to take three steps up to the large front door with Tante Go just inside giving each of us a warm embrace, French style, as we entered. What a relief it was to be off the streets again. After such a long journey, feeling so vulnerable, it was so relaxing to be with friends once more. Be able to speak some English. No more charades . . . for the time being.

Within fiteen minutes Tante Go had served coffee all round. None of the ground acorn stuff. This was the real McCoy. And later I was to find out how it came to be in relatively plentiful supply in the de Greef household . . . Elvire was one of the best at working the black market to the advantage of her family and her house guests. They didn't want for much at the Comète Line's south-west headquarters!

As I have said, every few days, Tante Go would hitch up her skirt, jump on her bike and go peddling off in the direction of Anglet to do the rounds of the town's cafes and restaurants, shops and selected friends, to scrounge whatever she needed to oil the wheels of her secret operation. None of them knew, or asked, nor were they told, where their 'contributions' ended up, but they probably guessed it was something illegal. Tante Go operated quite unashamedly with the black market, believing that it was necessary for us escapees to eat well. She said we needed good food to give us courage and strength to face the ordeal of the mountain crossing. It was sound reasoning. We even had steaks on one occasion, cooked by her mother-in-law whose name was Bobonne.

The house may have looked a bit gloomy on the outside, but inside it was quite spacious and very comfortable. Not many rooms, but large, nicely furnished ones, and very well looked after.

In fact, the de Greefs didn't own the villa. It became their home by chance and by necessity.

When the Germans invaded Belgium, Brussels businessman Fernand, and his wife, Elvire, decided to make a run for it with their two children to Bordeaux. They hoped to board a ship from Bordeaux bound for England, but in the panic and turmoil at the port caused by the quick collapse of France, there was no room on the last ship out. The de Greefs were trapped. For nearly a week they wandered around not knowing what to do. Escape was impossible, but they didn't even have a home until they came across the empty villa and agreed it was their only solution. That was where they would settle. From 1940, for the duration of the war, they made this their home; it was where they became a vital link in the chain that helped some 300 Allied servicemen get back to England.

And when fellow Resistance agent Arnold de Pé, mutual friend of Dédée and the de Greefs, asked Fernand and Elvire to be that important link, they accepted without hesitation, as they also agreed to help Dédée find suitable guides to lead escapees across the mountains.

Son Freddy and daughter Janine continued their studies in Bayonne; Fernand became an interpreter in the German headquarters in Anglet, leaving Tante Go to develop her organisation right under the noses of the occupiers. What better cover?

'I didn't really see much of Fernand when I was there. He seemed to work very long hours,' continued Jack.

But we did see a lot of Elvire, as well as Freddy and Janine. She was a very pretty girl, and Al Day, who passed through this house a month later, became quite besotted with her. Janine used to skip school sometimes so that she could accompany airmen to the foot of the Pyrénées. She and Freddy used to run Resistance errands for their mother, and act as 'lookouts' when it was necessary.

Freddy was a very brave boy, very much like his father in looks. He'd put on a German uniform and run urgent messages after dark. But in 1943 Freddy had to use the escape route across the mountains himself, when it became unsafe for him to remain in France. He went to England. But Janine saw the war out in Anglet, along with her mother and father, until the last days of the occupation.

It was while Jack was at the de Greefs' that he was able to get to know Dédée a little better. They would sit and chat about their lives. Jack liked to talk about his wife, Mary, and Dédée encouraged it, whereas it was difficult to persuade Dédée to talk about herself. It was as if she had closed the book on her life for the duration of the war, preferring to put all her memories on hold until the day came when they could be unlocked and enjoyed once more. Dédée did not want those precious memories tainted by the German occupation of her beloved country. She hated the Nazis with a passion. And she worried a great deal about her father, Frédéric, whose work for the Resistance frequently put his life under great threat. Dédée hoped he would slowly withdraw from the organisation, and lead a much lower profile way of life, but he was as stubborn as his daughter. They preferred to worry about each other, and continue their fight against the Germans, agreeing not to blame each other if any disaster overtook them. Jack recalls:

> Dédée was a most attractive and gentle young girl. I became very fond of her in my own sort of way, although I wouldn't have done anything to compromise my marriage to Mary.
>
> When you are thrown together in such a life-threatening situation, you become very protective towards each other. The same goes for your pals, too. It is what brings people together in wartime, but being on the run in an enemy-occupied country, the need for fellow human comfort becomes all-consuming. It is perfectly natural.
>
> When the five of us arrived at the de Greef villa, there was only one bedroom available so that was where we had to sleep. The first night we were all exhausted and keen to get our heads down, but what were we going to do with Dédée? The only woman among four men!
>
> The bed was huge, with decorative brass knobs on the headboard and the mattress looked very inviting. Should we men sleep on the floor and let Dédée have the bed all to herself?
>
> No, she wouldn't hear of it. 'We will all sleep on the bed,' she told us. 'But, I will sleep in the middle. The two married men – Jack and Gérard – will sleep either side of me, and the two single men, Larry and Jurek, will sleep on the outside.'
>
> So all five of us piled on the bed, fully dressed. I seem to recall that none of us slept very well that first night, though I think it was better the following night. So, that's how I came to sleep with a lady who was to become a countess!

There was not much for the airmen to do at the de Greef villa, other than to sit in their room and discuss what was going to be perhaps the most difficult part of their bid for freedom. They weren't even allowed out into the garden. Dédée had made the crossing several times, and warned the young flyers what to expect . . . very difficult, craggy, climbing conditions, narrow, steep paths, dense fog preventing climbers seeing anything more than a few feet in front of them, and heavy rain, even snow that can suddenly come from nowhere. It was hardly a picnic trip into the hills! At the same time, there was always the risk of running into a German patrol so there was to be no talking.

Jack soon began to seriously doubt that he was capable of such a physical feat. Dédée reassured him that he should put his faith in his determination to succeed, and in the guide who would lead them safely across. Florentino was no ordinary man, as Jack and the others were to find out. 'And if you run out of steam, then Florentino is capable of carrying you across his shoulders,' added Dédée, smiling. The thought of getting a piggyback over the Pyrénées brought a smile to Jack's face. It was going to be an interesting experience!

CHAPTER 9
Can I Cross the Pyrénées?

Many people came to Tante Go's home. Her friends, various members of the Resistance, often from the far corners of Belgium and France; Spanish guides – the first being Thomas, followed by Florentino, and, of course, the Allied servicemen on their way home to England. This was the last safe house on the Comète Line trail, the regional Resistance headquarters, and sometimes it was so busy it was more like Grand Central Station than a hideout in an enemy-occupied country! The only unwelcome visitors were the Germans, but such was the effectiveness of the de Greef family resistance cover, that on the few occasions when a German staff car drew up outside, it was to deliver Fernand de Greef home after his day's work in the German military headquarters in nearby Anglet!

Not long before the arrival of Jack, Larry, Gérard and Jurek, the de Greefs had given house space to one party of no fewer than eleven escapees, including the extrovert Miss Richards. Jack couldn't work out how they had all been packed in and prepared for the mountain crossing, until he was told that some of them had been distributed in the area to Tante Go's friends. Unfortunately, although the party made it over the Pyrénées – which gave heart to Jack Newton – they didn't make it down to Gibraltar, or to Lisbon, in Portugal. Basque guide Thomas, a smuggler and likeable rogue, revealed that all eleven were picked up by the *carabineros* as soon as they arrived in Spain and were taken to the concentration camp in Miranda. This was much to the chagrin of Dédée, who asked Tante Go bitterly: 'What is the point of raising money to buy food and to risk so many lives, if the escapees are only to end up in Spanish concentration camps?' She had a good point, and it was this that had triggered her resolve to enlist the help of the British.

Dédée had since come to an agreement with the British Consul in Bilbao, and arranged for consulate officials to pick up her 'packages' from the nearer consulate in San Sebastian. It was the perfect deal. The British would get back their airmen, and the Comète Line would be paid so it could continue its work.

When Jack's Wellington was forced to land in Belgium, it was a relatively rare occurrence because there were few raids over the country at this stage of the war. But an increasing number of Allied aircraft, like Jack's, were crashing onto Belgian territory on their way back to England after bombing raids over Germany. Survivors were difficult to find because ordinary Belgians who gave them refuge were loath to pass over their airmen until they knew that Paul and his friends could be trusted. To inspire confidence, Dédée persuaded the British to broadcast messages over the BBC, knowing all patriots tuned in each night. One such coded message was *'La plume de ma Tante est noire'*, and when that was broadcast just before the nine o'clock news it showed any Belgian doubters that the Comète Line and its friends were genuine. The broadcasting of coded messages worked well; Paul and Dédée would arrange for different messages to be put out for any sceptics to hear over their radios. Very soon many more Allied escapers and evaders were being passed on to the two of them.

Now Jack Newton, the last of the six evaders from the Wellington 'G for George', was at the end of the line due largely to the bravery of over forty Belgian and French families, and especially the unselfish dedication of the Comète's mastermind herself, Dédée. After all he had been through, he found it hard to believe that he was only a mountain and the neutral country of Spain away from getting out of the scary hell he had lived through for the past few months. It would be so cruel if he was caught now.

Sensing Jack's stress, both Dédée and Tante Go did their best to reassure him that he and his friends were in good hands at the de Greefs'. And as for his doubts that he had the ability, and was fit enough, to climb the mighty Pyrénées, Tante Go would jokingly point to Dédée and say to him: 'If this young girl can do it, so can you. Don't worry.' But Jack knew that Dédée was tough in both spirit and body. There was nothing she couldn't do if she turned her mind to it. And if that still left Jack looking a bit glum, then Dédée and Tante Go together told him the story of Miss Richards. If the ebullient Miss Richards could get across – as she did – then so could anyone else in France and Belgium. Or the world, for that matter! It was reassuring for all three young airmen.

Jack had heard stories of the mountain guide, Thomas. Like all the Pyrénées mountain men, he was rough, tough and feared very little. If he feared anything, it was the unpredictability of the weather which ruled the Pyrénées and which he feared far more than the Germans who patrolled it with their dogs and guns. Thomas never attempted to out-smart the mountains, but many times he outsmarted the Germans on their rocky slopes in pursuit of his numerous smuggling activities. After successfully taking Dédée and three evaders across in August 1941, an even more dedicated 'Man of the Mountains' came the way of Dédée and Tante Go, so it was decided they would use his services in future, rather than the wildly expensive services of Thomas. Florentino, a Basque who knew the Pyrénées like the back of his hand, was to become a legend as a Comète Line guide. And about as unlikely a partner of the diminutive Dédée as anyone was likely to find. Perhaps that was an important part of their successful working relationship. Nobody, not even the Germans, would have given it credence!

And yet both Dédée and Florentino had the greatest respect for each other. They each earned it in the eyes of the other. Though Florentino always accepted Dédée as 'la patronne'. She was the boss, and always had the last word when difficult decisions had to be taken, but she always based such decisions on the good advice of Florentino when they involved the Pyrénées. None knew them better than he did.

The four days spent at the de Greefs' were quite difficult for Jack and his fellow evaders. Although they were given the freedom of the house, they were not allowed outside or near the windows, but because of the heavy shrubbery that surrounded the building there wasn't much risk of being spotted from outside. Most of the time, Jack, Larry, Gérard and Jurek chatted together, reminiscing about experiences, and what they would do when they got home. Gérard had money of his own, and said that once he was across the Pyrénées and into Spain he intended making his own way to Portugal to pay for a flight back to Britain. He hadn't finished with the Germans, yet, and wanted to get back to Belgium through the SOE so he could use his skills as an explosive expert to sabotage a bridge or two, railway lines, industrial premises, in fact, anything that might hinder the Nazi war effort. Larry wasn't sure what would happen to him. It rather depended on the attitude of the Australian Air Force. Jurek, the Pole, had little to say because of the language difficulty. Whereas, Jack just wanted to get back home to his wife, Mary, and to carry on where he had left off when the war so rudely interrupted his marital plans!

For Jack the quiet life at the de Greefs' was a time to reflect on many things, and right now, perhaps more than anything else after all they had come through together, his admiration for Dédée. Maybe it amounted to rather more than simple admiration. Perhaps it was love for someone who had put everything on the line – including her own life – to try and save him from the tyranny of Nazi occupation? Jack said:

She was an extremely good looking girl. Not all that tactile. She would occasionally tap me on my arm, or brush her hand across my cheek if she was feeling really demonstrative. She didn't flirt, but just teased a little if she was feeling very relaxed, as she was at Tante Go's home.

But I do think I was a bit special to Dédée, as she was to me. I was her first English airman to be passed through the organisation, so this must have counted for something in her eyes.

And speaking of eyes, the way she always looked at me, so deeply as though into my very soul, was how I knew I was special to her. It was quite extraordinary and many people remarked on it, too, even just seeing us together in photographs.

Apart from being a very charming girl, she also spoke pretty good English. Dédée was always talking about her homeland, and what a dreadful thing it was that Belgium had to capitulate, emphasising that her countrymen had little option. They were overpowered.

I have had two girlfriends since 1941, and they both know about each other. But I married young and have never wanted to do anything silly, like have an affair. I have always remained true to Mary, my wife, and to Dédée to whom I owe my life. It will remain that way until I die.

Early in 1941 Arnold de Pé visited the de Greefs on behalf of Dédée and her father, Frédéric, who wanted them to find mountain guides prepared to take rescued young airmen over the Pyrénées into Spain. Tante Go jumped at the chance. Life in their 'occupied' villa had become a bit boring. The two children, Freddy and Janine, were at school in Bayonne, and with husband Fernand settled into his interpreter's job at the German military headquarters in nearby Anglet, that left Elvire trying to busy herself around the house when the others were out. The only real excitement that came her way was what other members of the family thought was her rather risky involvement with black market racketeers. Though even that was to have life saving consequences in due course.

In the meantime, here was Elvire's opportunity to do something meaningful for herself and for her onetime Brussels friends. Elvire took on the codename Tante Go and, with Arnold, began the task of finding a guide prepared to make the mountain trip into Spain. Thomas was no angel, but if the money was right he would take the job. Well pleased, Arnold returned to Brussels to give the good news to Dédée and her father. The safe house at St Jean de Luz was up and running, with a mountain guide organised too. Tante Go spent each day cycling around the area setting up more safe houses and helpers to cope with the overflow of arrivals who would soon be passing her way. Within a short time everything was in place.

The new setup was given its first big test in mid-August when Dédée's party of Belgians and the English woman, Miss Richards, successfully reached the end of the line. Even Miss Richards wanted for very little because Tante Go was already tapping black market sources for the little luxuries that made life more pleasurable. In fact, the Resistance movement and the black market worked hand-in-hand, being largely dependent on each other. Even the German sentries and some officials who should have known better were open to a spot of harmless corruption, as they saw it, exchanging certain favours for little delicacies that came their way through unofficial channels of distribution! Tante Go knew all the smugglers, such as Thomas, as petty criminals with an eye for business, and with access to the otherwise unobtainable luxuries everyone wanted.

Sometimes, early on in the Comète Line's existence, its members fell victim to the many dangers they faced each day in their resistance work. Arnold de Pé was one such casualty. Dédée and Arnold were bringing airmen and fleeing Belgians from Belgium through to Bayonne. At Brussels they split into two separate groups, Arnold's group travelling by train via Lille to La Corbie, and Dédée taking her two Belgians and a Scottish soldier by train from Brussels to Valenciennes, over the Somme, to La Corbie. They were due to rendezvous in the Corbie café, but Arnold never showed up. Dédée left her three escapees with helper Nenette and went to Lille to try to find Arnold, but without success. She told Tante Go that at Lille railway station there were an unusually large number of gendarmes on duty, as though something had happened there earlier. She feared Arnold had been arrested. Dédée then returned to La Corbie to take her own three escapees south via Paris – her first three 'packages' which she safely delivered to the British Embassy in Bilbao. It was later confirmed that, as feared, Arnold de Pé had been arrested along with his airmen at Lille railway station. This triggered the Gestapo search for Dédée which prevented her returning to Brussels.

At times like this, it was good for Dédée to have Tante Go's shoulder to cry on. Someone close to open up to; to be reminded of the dangerous business they were in, and that many lives were at stake every step of the way. That, of course, included Dédée's own father running the Belgian end of the Comète Line from their Brussels home. She always worried about his involvement, and feared the Gestapo would catch up with him sooner or later. Many times, Dédée tried to persuade him to 'retire' as a Resistance agent, but he would not hear of it. Because they worried about each other, they eventually agreed that they were both involved because it was their choice to be involved and that if anything was to happen to either of them – however serious – then the other must not feel any guilt. It was the risk both chose to take, and it created an incredible bond between this father and his daughter. Sadly though, its tragic conclusion was the death by firing squad of Frédéric de Jongh in a Paris prison only a few months before Belgium was liberated in 1945. Sad as she was, Dédée was to abide by that agreement with her father and count the blessings that he ultimately gave his life for the cause to which they were both so dedicated.

From his upstairs room at the de Greefs', Jack would sometimes catch sight of Dédée and Tante Go strolling round the rear garden in the warm sun, often arm-in-arm. Deep in conversation, no doubt making plans, discussing the successes and the problems of their south-west Resistance organisation. At least, it was now being funded by the British government in exchange for safely returned English airmen. That would help enormously. More black market food could be bought, train fares funded, essential clothing paid for, safe house lodging expenses covered in Belgium and in France. Life was going to be just a little bit easier, at least in this direction. In establishing Comète it had been necessary for Dédée and her father to approach wealthy friends to ask for substantial 'no question' loans, and these had largely been generously given. But it had been risky. Now that element of risk could be removed. It was a big weight off the minds of Dédée and Tante Go, and those back in Belgium where the larger costs of running the organisation had to be borne.

For three days, the four escapees had very little to do at the de Greefs' villa. The weather over the mountains had suddenly taken a turn for the worse, heavy rain having moved in from the Atlantic to make the crossing potentially treacherous. It looked a distinct possibility they might have to stay a little longer. Then, on the fourth day the four men woke to find shafts of sunlight piercing their darkened room through the shuttered windows. Dédée, in consultation with Florentino, decided the group would leave that evening on the first leg of the mountain crossing, to the isolated farmhouse of Bidegain Beri, in Urrugne, where they would spend a few hours changing from their lightweight summer clothes into heavier mountain climbing gear. There they would be briefed by both Dédée and Florentino about the hazards ahead, as they supped Franchia's hot soup that would see them through the night-long hike. Franchia lived at the farm with her three children, and provided the last brief refuge before airmen tackled the mountains.

It was the moment Jack had probably feared more than any other. He believed that pitting his strength, his skills, his endurance against the mighty Pyrénées – nature in the raw – was going to be a far bigger personal test than walking the streets of Brussels under the eyes and noses of the Germans. And in his heart-of-hearts he doubted he was going to have the strength to do it, though he didn't even hint at this inner pessimism to any of the others. He must not think of failure. Only success. He had got this far, now he had to overcome the last big hurdle. Although none of them discussed their own self doubts, Jack knew that Larry, Jurek and Gérard all had similar worries about the trek ahead. Whether they were up to the demands it would make on them. This was a trip into the unknown, and they all knew it was going to be every bit as difficult as they imagined.

Tante Go made sure the boys ate well as they sat at the large farmhouse kitchen table. Freddy cut up chunks of bread and handed it round. But pretty young Janine, sensing the turmoil going on in their heads, laughed and chatted with them, her bubbly personality a much-needed distraction. 'You will all promise me that when the war is over you will come back and see me,' she told the four men, and they each happily gave her their promise.

One month later, another evading airman – and good friend of Jack Newton – made a similar promise to pretty, young Janine. In the short time they were together Al Day lost his heart to her. And after the war, he did go back to see her . . . many times.

CHAPTER 10
Bitterness of Failure

It is time to go. Jack's heart is pounding with excitement as he slips on his heavy overcoat, giving Tante Go an embrace and whispering a softly spoken 'thank you for all you have done' to her as he turns to join the other three now on their way out into the back garden where the bikes are kept. Janine is already astride hers. Frédéric has gone on ahead to make sure the late afternoon roads are free of patrolling Germans. Fernand (*l'Oncle*) goes to the road to see them away.

Then they are off, following in stretched single file behind Janine. Dédée and Gérard Waucquez ride on together a few minutes later. They all go into St Jean de Luz, across the bridge to Ciboure, then on to the farmhouse near Urrugne. Heavy rain and strong winds over the past twenty-four hours have left the roads littered with debris fallen from overhanging trees; the country cart tracks are muddy and almost impassable. Not the weather for a cycle ride, but at least it keeps the pro-German gendarmerie inside and out of the way. There is a temporary respite in the weather, so for a while the driving rain eases a little.

Janine turns off the lane, and waits for the others to catch up. The sight of Franchia's farmhouse is a welcome one as it comes into view round a bend in the road. Two barns to one side rise eerily into the evening darkness, but their roofs are seemingly decapitated by the heavy mist now descending over the countryside. Franchia must have been looking out for her expected guests because she comes out to welcome them, her three young children alongside clutching at her skirt. 'The puddles, mind the puddles,' she is heard warning them.

In no time at all, all six cyclists have parked their bikes under cover alongside the front door, and are quickly inside the kitchen where it is cosy and warm, lit by two small glowing lamps. The smell of Franchia's vegetable soup, simmering gently on the stove, wafts across the room, prompting Jack to say, 'Ummm. Something smells good!'

But the banter between the three women – Franchia, Dédée and Janine – is in a frenzy of French. The men congregate in one corner, and discuss in English – what else – the filthy weather! Maybe they would prefer another distraction? 'Would you like to hear the BBC?' Franchia asks them through Dédée acting as interpreter. 'Yes, I think they would,' Dédée decides, as she leans across Jack to switch on the small radio that is set into the dresser. Everyone is happy. The boys with their radio, the women catching up on local gossip. Forgotten for these few joyous moments are the angry mountains, towering high into the sky less than four miles away, lurking there like some hungry, hunch-backed ogre expectantly awaiting his next feast.

The door opens and in walks Florentino looking a bit like an ogre himself! His broad shoulders and hugely muscular arms are covered by a beige-coloured, open-necked shirt that is surely an extra extra large! He quickly looks around the room at his new charges, sees Dédée and envelops her in a huge embrace. For a moment she is out of sight in the giant's warm, yet gentle, bear hug. Then it is Janine's turn, and she squeals with girlish delight. Finally, Florentino settles for pumping bone shattering handshakes with Jack, Larry, Gérard and Jurek. Larry described the experience as like putting his hand into a car-crusher and being unable to switch off the power! 'Yes, this is Florentino,' laughs Dédée, as if everyone hasn't guessed. He nods, and a huge grin spreads across his weather-chiseled face that is framed in a mop of unruly black hair. Here, indeed, is a mountain of a man, who is a man of the mountains. The airmen sense they are in good hands.

The wet clothes having been dumped on the stone floor away from the table and seeing that time is creeping on, Franchia asks if they are ready for their soup. She begins pouring it into deep-bottomed plates. Janine hands round chunks of bread, as conversation gives way to the serious business of filling stomachs. The clatter of spoons against the plates, and the slurp of soup as it is drawn into hungry open mouths brings a contented smile to the face of Franchia seeing it so appreciated. Janine fills each glass with freshly opened red wine.

'*Salut!*' says Dédée. 'I wish you all good luck, whether you are crossing the mountain, or staying behind. Good luck everybody.' Glasses clink. The conversation picks up again, and more soup is offered round. A happy three hours pass all too quickly. It is soon time for the party to leave. Janine and brother Freddy decide they will walk a little way to keep the group company. Jack recalls:

> I sense that Florentino is a bit worried about the weather. He seems to be quieter than I was told he was likely to be, and he seems concerned about the previous twenty-four hours of heavy rain. He warns us that the descent to the Bidassoa river is going to be the trickiest bit, especially after the rain. The four of us begin to get a bit nervous.

There is talk that Florentino's engine is driven by ample quantities of cognac; that on narrow tracks in the thickest of mountain mists it is still easy to follow this Basque because his body is nourished with a mixture of goat's cheese and rough red wine that it has an explosive effect on his digestive system. It is said that he conceals bottles of cognac in the forked branches of mountain trees; that he knows where every bottle is hidden and that he only stop for breaks if he is close to one of his special trees! He hides spare pairs of espadrilles in rock crevices along the route, and he knows precisely where every bottle of cognac and every pair of espadrilles is located.

Everyone wants Florentino. The Comète Line wants him because he is the best mountain guide around. But he is wanted on both sides of the frontier for very different reasons. The Spanish because he slips in and out of their country with such ease on his numerous illegal activities that it makes the Spanish authorities look as though they have issued him with his own personal free pass. Whereas, in France the douane and the Gestapo correctly believe he is working against them for Allied intelligence. If ever a man needs to keep a low profile, it is Florentino, but his enemies are determined and he never underestimates their chances of getting lucky one day.

Franchia leaves the room for a moment and returns, her arms filled with coats and warm underclothing. Florentino brings in espadrilles, rope-soled shoes, that give the best grip on the craggy mountain tracks. He gives out three pairs to each person, two spare pairs per person. And he hands out a stout walking stick to each of the mountain walkers. Florentino demonstrates how the sticks should be used . . . from behind, as a brake, when descending. Dédée points out that if the walking stick is used in front, as a blind person would use a white stick, then it is more likely to be a hindrance rather than a help. Even cause a serious fall.

The four airmen wrap up, slip on their new footwear, adjust their black berets and stand together near the door, ready to go. Dédée, a large pack on her back containing a few necessities such as a skirt, blouse and shoes, issues her last orders to the airmen, and hands each one a light backpack with a bottle of wine, and small snacks that will sustain them on their journey. Florentino, who has an even larger pack on his back, will lead the way, followed by Dédée, and then the airmen, all in single file. There must be no talking until they reach the mountains. And they must do everything the guide tells them. Florentino inspects each man, to check that his espadrilles are a good fit. Ill-fitting espadrilles cause blisters and blisters slow up the walkers. There must be no laggards on the twenty-hour crossing!

Florentino takes a last long swig of cognac, slips the bottle into his backpack, and with a sweep of his hand moves out of the kitchen door into the evening air. It is still murky, and quite chilly. Janine and Freddy follow on at the rear, behind the airmen. It is only Florentino's second crossing with Dédée, though between 1941 and 1944 they are to share the dangers of more than twenty-five crossings with parties of Allied airmen.

The farther the group walk, the more the mist lifts until it is suddenly gone, leaving the walkers under a clear, starlit sky. The farmhouse has long since been out of sight. Up ahead the airmen can see the hills merge in with the outline of the mountains. 'But the mountains just don't seem to be getting any nearer. It is like we are on one of those exercise machines – getting nowhere fast,' says Jack. 'But we keep on going. Frankly, I don't think I can talk even if I want to. I need every breath in my body to keep me going.'

For some six or seven miles, the going is not too difficult. The terrain is damp, but quite firm. And mostly flat. In the summer, these same foothills are awash with yellow gentians, and the wild strawberries that sweeten the meadows with their liquid red berries and lace-like leaves. Wild boar roam the pine woods that stand like bastions on the sides of the ever-precipitously rising peaks. The summer sun brings forth pockets of deep red azaleas and broom, its golden flowers trying hard to out-colour the azaleas. Only a few months before, wild geraniums and mountain lilies peppered the sloping and winding track. But the changing seasons turn these slopes of the Pyrénées from a playful pussycat to a snarling and vicious panther. Nature's gentleness, brought on by the summer sun, turns to what can only be described as a hell on earth as the days draw shorter and colder and wintry. As if within the time span of a single blink, even the relative tranquility of the earlier ever-upward walk towards Spain, suddenly becomes more challenging, more depressing, more gruelling. The track, until now gentle and defined, begins to narrow quite noticeably. Starts to steepen. The fertile soil that could nurture a world of wildflowers suddenly turns to grey, unstable scree. The mountain closes in on those who dare to enter its sacred domain. Jack has vivid memories of the trek:

> We seem to have been walking forever. Janine and Freddy had said their goodbyes and turned back to the farmhouse, leaving just the six of us. Florentino leads the way, Dédée is behind him, then it's me, Larry, Gérard, and Jurek.
>
> I am pleased to be wearing the grey woollen pullover knitted for me by my mother, and which I have worn over my battledress since I flew out of Binbrook on 5 August. There is no way the cold mountain air is going to penetrate that!
>
> Dédée drops back every so often, to make sure we are all OK, though she seems a little concerned about Jurek, who has dropped back a bit too far. But I think everything seems to be mostly all right.
>
> This walk . . . march . . . call it what you will, is nothing like I have ever encountered before. I have trodden the Fells fairly regularly, and parts of the Scottish Highlands, but none of it really compares to this. The tracks are very narrow, craggy with loose scree that makes firm

footsteps virtually impossible. One moment I am making good progress, the next I am on my backside grabbing at brushwood to stop myself sliding downhill most ungraciously. We all have falls, a good few of them. But none is serious. We drag ourselves up again, and carry on.

It is after one such fall that I am alarmed by a bright light that suddenly sweeps across the hillside where we are walking. My immediate thought is that it is a German mountain patrol, but Dédée is quick to reassure us. 'It is the lighthouse at Irun. It will light our path for a little way.'

Ah, yes, the Bidassoa. Irun is the town at the mouth of the river, which is the one we must wade across to get into Spain. Once I know what it is, it is kind of reassuring to see the light sweep across the mountain, momentarily casting its eerie glow across the rocky slopes.

Several falls and the thinner mountain air begin to make me feel queasy. I sense myself slowing down, and holding up Gérard. Dédée realises I need a break, and if I do, the other two probably do, too. But Florentino won't hear of it. We must press on farther. This is not a good place to stop and rest, he tells Dédée. Obviously it's not where Florentino has hidden one of his bottles of cognac! After another thirty minutes, thankfully Florentino thinks it is safe to stop, so we all collapse on our backs and look up at the stars. There is even time for one of Franchia's snacks, and a swig of wine. I can feel it warming my inside as it washes round my stomach. And the ten minutes rest allows my blood to reach parts of my body – like my feet – where it seems to have stopped flowing for quite a while. Dédée sits down beside me, and says that Florentino worries about coming across a German patrol on the French side of the mountain. This is a serious risk. But sometimes what can be mistaken for Germans is really mountain sheep. The sheep wear small bells that tinkle their where-abouts. 'We've even thought about fitting sheep bells to ourselves, so if the Germans are around we fool them into thinking we are sheep,' says Dédée, unable to withhold a little giggle at the thought of it.

But there are no sheep bells attached to members of this group!

Florentino takes another swig from his cognac bottle, and gets to his feet again. It's the sign for the rest to follow, which they do. 'Doucement,' says Florentino, using one of the few words in his French vocabulary. He wants the party to be careful because of loose rock on the path, which is now noticeably wending downhill.

They have passed the highest point, around 8,000 feet. Now it is the still more hazardous downhill stretch to the river valley, and the equally hazardous crossing into Spain. The tension is almost palpable. But their luck is holding. The rain is keeping off, even though the wind is brisk from the mountain sides. And there are no signs of German patrols. It won't be too long now before they are across the river and getting their first taste of a qualified freedom. Olé!

Jack realises the need to use his stick as a brake, on the steep down slopes. It saves him from tumbling many times.

As they come over one small hill, Jack believes he can hear what sounds like an express train. He catches up with Dédée and asks her if she can hear the noise. 'Yes, it is the river. It is not good news that we can hear it from here,' she says cautiously. Though Jack isn't quite sure what she means, and feels it is not the time or the place to ask her to explain.

The more they walk, the louder the noise becomes. It now sounds like an express train or, as Jack prefers to describe it, like some mountain giant emptying his lungs with one continuous rush of air! By the time they have descended to a hiding place not far from the river bank, the torrent of water hurrying its way towards Irun and the open sea is almost deafening. 'And we have to get across that?' asks Jack. He can see the river in full flow, about one hundred feet across to a narrow meadow leading up to an embankment on which there is a railway line. Another rocky embankment leads from the railway line to the road, and a customs post can be seen a few hundred yards away to the left. Frontier guards can be seen patrolling the road.

Florentino and Dédée are huddled together some twenty feet away in deep conversation, looking hard at the raging torrent. They return to the others, their heads held low. 'It is not good. We cannot cross the river. There is too much water. I am sorry, but we must go back to the farm,' says Dédée.

'Go back?' exclaims Jack, alarmed and frustrated by the thought that they had all spent nearly seventeen hours slogging their way over the Pyrénées, now to be told it has all been a waste of time. That they must go back to where they started.

'Yes, I am afraid so, dear Jack,' says Dédée, fully understanding his frustration, and the frustration of the other three.

Florentino and Dédée face the four men, and Dédée explains that it is the current which is so destructive. There is no boat, there are no ropes. It is necessary to wade across, or swim across. At this moment, the river is in flood and the current is too strong to even contemplate swimming. Nor is it possible to ford the river for the same reason. If one was to fall, or be knocked over by the sheer force of the current, then that person would die. Be drowned. They have only one alternative, and that is go back to the farmhouse and in a few days' time, return to the Pyrénées, and take the five-hour diversion to the alternative crossing over a wooden bridge, alongside a Spanish customs building. Even so, this alternative Spanish border crossing is considered still more dangerous, even if it has been used successfully by Florentino several times.

It is not the news Jack wants to hear. He is so near to freedom and to seeing his darling Mary again that the disappointment of being told there is no alternative but to go back to the Urrugne farmhouse is just too much to bear. Another twenty-hour climb, and another five hours on top of that to get to the alternative border crossing, isn't fair. 'I will never make it,' splutters Jack.

He turns and spits. 'I spit on this soil,' snaps Jack, angrily.

Her eyes bulging, her nostrils flared, Dédée shouts back at Jack: 'Don't you spit on this beloved country. You must not do that.'

For a moment the conflict of interests, and split patriotic passions, get the better of both of them.

But as quickly as it happens, it is over and deeply regretted.

Jack and Dédée hold each other in their arms. Jack, close to tears seeing how he has so deeply upset the 'Little Cyclone' . . . his 'Little Mother' . . . he immediately and emotionally reassures her that it is not his intention to spit on French soil, but on the Germans he holds responsible for compromising this country and those Dédée loves, as well as his Mary, whom he loves.

'I ask Dédée to, please, accept my apology if what I had done had been taken any other way,' says Jack. 'I am pleased to say that she did . . .'

Their heads bowed, their spirits low, the six begin the return to the farmhouse, arriving back at around 10pm on the third day after they set out.

It is a very alarmed and surprised Franchia who opens the door to the tired and exhausted airmen she believes are now safely in the sanctuary and protection of the British consulate in San Sebastian.

Franchia believes that Florentino and Dédée have returned on their own, their mission successfully accomplished. Over more hot soup, and wine, they tell her their story.

They will try again in a few days' time.

CHAPTER 11
Rickety Rope Bridge

The prospect of facing more days at the Urrugne farmhouse is not easy for the four escapees to bear. The disappointment shows on their faces. One attempt at crossing into Spain has failed, even though the Pyrénées were successfully negotiated. And now that it has been decided the Bidassoa river cannot be crossed on foot, but only by a largely unused rickety floodlit rope bridge another five hours farther upstream, morale is naturally a bit flat. So near, and yet so far. Jack Newton is beginning to think that maybe he won't get home after all. Beaten by a river!

In any case, crossing by the old footbridge is fraught with danger. Even Florentino hasn't used it for a long time and he isn't sure it is even passable, but back at the farm he checks this out with some Basque friends who tell him it is still in use. There is a possibility the bridge itself is unprotected, though it is believed Spanish guards occupy the nearby customs post building and patrol the road that runs parallel to the river. He will only find out for certain when he gets there! Dédée has only crossed the border by fording the river. Never over the rope bridge under the noses of the Spanish *carabineros*, in their green uniforms and cocked hats. Trigger happy guards along the frontier have a reputation for shooting to kill at anyone trying to cross illegally. Is it too risky?

The decision is already made by Florentino and Dédée. The rope bridge it is, and by the end of the third day back at the farm the six are setting off to try again. Only this time they will go straight to the western crossing and hope the guards don't surprise them.

The weather is more settled so the trek to the foothills is quick and trouble free. Having walked the same track only a few days before, and being familiar with the route, good progress is made. There is actually a bit more time to admire the view having left in daylight hours to take into account the five more hours they must walk. Along the coast from St Jean de Luz, they look across at the Fuenterrabia lighthouse which, after dark, sweeps the surrounding bay and hillsides. As they climb higher, Jack and his party can see a few specks of light from across the Spanish border, but just pitch blackness behind them in France. A gloom as impenetrable as the misery nurtured there under Nazi rule.

The young men think they will find it easier this time, knowing what to expect and having at least a little knowledge of the kind of terrain they will be crossing. Besides, their bellies are again full with good food, and a glass or two of French plonk. In their packs, some cheese, a little fruit, and wine. They know that Florentino is generous with his cognac if they need something a bit stronger.

But as the climb becomes steeper, a damp, thick mist descends on the group, enveloping it like a blanket of cotton wool, and just as smothering. Dédée drops back to each of the airmen to tell them to keep much closer, always to keep the man in front in sight. She points out that in such conditions it is very easy to get lost, to walk off the track and to lose sight of the person in front.

Jack cannot help smiling at Dédée, this young girl, as he watches her slim legs carry her svelte body with such agility across the boulder-strewn ground, brushing aside overhanging branches as she goes with no more effort than she would use to flick a fallen fringe of hair out of her eyes. And always smiling. What an amazing woman! Just for a moment he forgets the uneven climb is making him desperately out of breath until he takes another tumble. He knows he is collecting a colourful choice of bruises on his legs and backside, but it doesn't stop him slipping and sliding onwards, and upwards. Maybe Florentino will soon find one of his bottles . . . and stop for a drink! He must be reading Jack's mind. '*Dos cien metros*' he calls back to let the rest of the party know they will be stopping for a break very shortly. But another half-hour goes by, and they are all still climbing. Does this mountain range have a peak? '*Dos cien metros*' calls out Florentino yet again.

'Dos cien metros,' mumbles Jack to himself. 'How many more dos cien metros before we can rest our aching bodies?'

Florentino must have picked up Jack's vibes. He stops, turns and holds up his big, sledgehammer-shaped right hand. 'We stop here for a little while,' announces Dédée. The four men puffing and panting, coming up behind, collapse onto the ground and begin to fish around in their packs for something to nibble, and a swig of the wine given to each of them by Franchia.

'You are all doing very well, my brave boys,' Dédée tells the young men encouragingly. With Dédée as his interpreter, Florentino uses the break to tell the four what to expect when they get near to the rope bridge crossing. How there is quite a steep descent to the entrance to the bridge, that they must stay under cover and go over one at a time. He will go first, followed by Jack, Larry, Jurek, Gérard and finally Dédée. Florentino tells them that he will wave when each person has safely reached his side, and it is time for the next one to move off to the bridge. Successively, until they are all over.

He warns them that the trickiest part will be going past the customs post, assuming it is occupied. They must be sure to duck down low as they pass the window, though, with a little luck, the guards will be tucked up in their beds and be fast asleep. Because this is such an isolated post, at the time of the crossing it is unlikely any of the guards will be awake, let alone patrolling.

Jack says maybe they should all pray the guards have lots to drink during the evening, and get an undisturbed night's sleep.

Time to go again.

Florentino is quickly up on his feet. He takes one last swig at the cognac bottle, dispenses a little flatulence, and strides off on the last leg of what is now largely the downhill run to the river gorge. Jack says:

> I had been on many walks over the Lake District, and some quite dramatic ones, too, but none of them is a match for this one over the Pyrénées. Going up is bad enough, but coming down towards the river and frontier is even worse. The track is so narrow, covered with a rocky scree. At times it is impossible to say it is even a track, and yet Florentino knows precisely where he is going. We just literally follow in his footsteps when we can keep up with him and Dédée – the two mountain goats. I do as I am told to do, use my stick as a brake behind me. Not in front. But I still take several tumbles, as do the others.
>
> Then I hear the rushing water noise again. Faintly at first, but as we descend down the zigzagging sides of the gorge so the noise grows louder.

They can now see the Bidassoa river ahead of them and it is again a forbidding sight, as its water spills downstream in one great plunging torrent, throwing up plumes of foam as it crashes across rocks and swirls around boulders. There is the bridge. The party stop high up on the gorge concealed behind rocks and a thicket that gives them a good view of the scene below. They can make their plans, see if the customs post is manned. Look out for any border guards patrolling the road.

It is late evening, and they don't want to risk using the bridge until the early hours of the morning. They can already see there are two guards in the customs post, although the men don't seem very interested in guarding or patrolling. During the following hours, a vehicle comes along the road, and stops at the customs post. Two men get out, the other two get in. It's the change to the night shift. Florentino seems pleased to know there are only two guards, probably because he also knows they will sleep the night away. They won't expect any illegal immigrants from France! Jack continues:

> We find our safe hideaway about two hundred yards from the bridge, so I can see it clearly. It looks very rickety, supported by two lengths

of rope parallel top and bottom and slats of wood about two feet wide on which to walk. One or two of the slats across the one hundred feet width of the bridge are missing.

I suppose it is about midnight when Florentino decides the two guards are now in the land of nod, and will not bother us. The bridge itself is floodlit, as is the area around the building. Florentino briefs us all again. Once across the bridge, we have to crawl below the window level of the customs office before crossing the road farther up, then get ourselves up a small incline onto an old disused railway track that leads into the mountain tunnel.

Florentino goes first. This huge man makes his way down the slope to the rope bridge like a young gazelle, his head turning left and right all the time. But the noise of the water is so loud it drowns out any other noise. Nobody would hear us even if we had been wearing jackboots!

Now this is going to be the interesting bit, as Florentino takes his first tentative steps onto the swaying bridge . . .

If anyone is going to fall in, it is surely Florentino. If the bridge takes his weight, then the rest of the group can feel reassured. It is not a problem. Florentino is quickly across, and weaving his way towards the building, getting down on his hands and knees as he passes underneath the level of the window that faces out to the road. There is only one small light, and the room appears to be empty, but this is no time to take chances.

Florentino is across, over the road, up the embankment and along the rail track where he can now be seen by the others. He waves Jack to cross.

One down, five to go!

I take a big gulp, adjust my beret and slowly feel my way down the slope to the bridge. My God, it does look flimsy. Surely, it cannot possibly take my weight? But I quickly remind myself that it has taken Florentino, so it will certainly cope with me. Then I look down. The water is a good one hundred feet below, thundering down the gorge. There will be no chance if I fall off the bridge into the Bidassoa. It'll be curtains. What if a plank breaks? So many doubts come into my mind, but I know I have to just hold my breath and start the walk across. After all, on the far bank I am out of German-occupied France and into neutral Spain. That thought is the incentive I need, and I begin to walk.

In any other situation and in daylight, this will have been a beautiful holiday location. Certainly one to record with pictures. But this is no time to get dreamy. I focus on the far bank, and keep walking very carefully!

Phew. What a relief it is when my feet touch down on the far bank.

Still no movement or sign of life from the customs building. I approach it cautiously, duck, slide by under the front window as Florentino has done, then over the road, up the embankment, and join our guide a little way along the rail track. 'Bravo,' he says, slapping me heartily on my back.

Florentino is now waving furiously again to encourage Larry to make his move. Larry is away. He crosses the bridge, creeps like a hunting lion along the roadside to the customs building, under the window . . . and stands up, by the door! What is he doing? Joker Larry looks across at Florentino and me as we urge him on . . . he grins like a Cheshire cat, then he appears to knock on the door! Fortunately, it is his sense of fun getting the better of him again. Moments later he is up on the rail track with the other two, and still beaming from ear to ear. Jurek and Gérard cross safely, too.

Then last, but not least, it is Dédée's turn. She descends the slope to the bridge as though she is running an egg and spoon race. She moves with the lightness of a windblown feather, seeming to tiptoe across the wooden slats of the bridge with the eloquence of a prima ballerina. She moves along the road as though borne by a puff of wind, stoops down and crawls carefully past the building, and in no time is standing alongside the rest. She is not even breathless.

'Bravo my brave boys,' Dédée says to us all softly, as she gives my hand a gentle squeeze.

With the river crossing now safely behind them, the six move off down the track which takes them into the mountainside tunnel, and deeper into Spain.

'What were you doing at the customs place?' Jack asks Larry.

'I was going to knock on the door and ask them if I could use their toilet. That bridge crossing scared the shit out of me!' he quips.

Everyone laughs. Trust Larry. At least, it eases the tension. They can all relax a little now they are really on their way to freedom.

Florentino leads the forty-yard walk through what remains of the dirty old railway tunnel, out onto the other side of the hill into open country-side. The tunnel isn't wide enough for a car to pass through, and is just about high enough for people to walk along it. The tunnel has probably been some kind of mining link to the main centre of San Sebastian that can be seen along the coast about an hour's ride away, although even Florentino isn't really sure what purpose the rail line once served. Right now it is the road to freedom for the four men. And, in fact, the end of the road for Gérard Waucquez and his escape companions because he is about to take off on his own – destination Portugal, where he plans to catch a flight back to London as soon as one is scheduled.

Jack Newton, Larry Birk and Jurek Budinsky are warned they are still at risk in Spain because the Spanish are more pro-German than pro-British, and will not hesitate to throw them into one of their concentration camps if they have a mind to. Or, they might return them to the French border, and hand them back to the Germans. The Spanish like to keep their options open. So, it's not much of a choice for the airmen. They agree it is best to maintain their low profile and hope to get to the sanctuary of the British Consulate in San Sebastian.

Gérard is eager to get on his way, and the isolation of the countryside they have now reached is a good place for the Belgian explosives expert and the rest of the party to say their goodbyes. Gérard promises Jack that as soon as he gets back to London he will call on Jack's parents in St John's Wood to tell them their son is safe; that he will be home soon. He gets Jack to pen his signature on a scrap of paper just in case they ask for some proof. Jack happily obliges. He thanks Gérard and says he hopes they will meet up again when the war is over. Similar sentiments are expressed between the others before Gérard sets off on foot in the direction of Renteria, the nearest Spanish village.

Florentino takes the opportunity to leave, too. He wants to get back over the mountain, to the farmhouse where he may be needed to bring over another party. The farewells to Florentino are especially meaningful, and praise for him is generous to the point of embarrassment to the gentle giant.

For Jack Newton, Larry Birk and Budinsky life can surely only get better, or can it?

Dédée gives each of them a one peseta note, their tram fare to the San Sebastian British Consulate. They must only get off the tram if there are no Spanish guards on duty outside the Consulate. If the airmen attempt to get into the Consulate without papers they will be either turned away or, more likely, be arrested.

'Do not risk it,' Dédée warns them.

But first they must hole up until daylight.

'Where?' asks Jack.

'Over there, in that water tower!' says Dédée, a big smile on her face. In fact, there are a good few strangely shaped water towers across the landscape. Similar to three telegraph poles coming together at the top like a tripod. This structure supports an open top container, encased in a wooden jacket. The containers collect rainwater, which is then fed through a pipe to a tap near the ground.

Dédée tells them it is not as bad as it probably sounds. The container, which is some ten feet in diameter and a little over six feet high, is wrapped in a jacket of straw, and that is where the three of them will safely see out the night. In the space between the wooden jacket and the container. It is dry, warm and safe. Nobody will find them.

Dédée must go into San Sebastian to let the Consulate know she has three packages to deliver. Then she will return for the men and lead them to the popular Spanish seaside resort on a tram. They have the peseta note to buy their own ticket.

Dédée has her official papers for Spain as well as her pass to the British Consulate, so she will meet the boys inside the Consulate later that same morning. If they cannot get into the Consulate, blocked by the Spanish guard on duty outside, then they are to meet her in a nearby café.

They all say their goodbyes, then Dédée, Florentino and Waucquez leave for the walk down into the valley, across fields where sheep with tinkling bells graze contentedly, onwards and into the small town of Renteria. From there, it is just a short tram ride into San Sebastian and the British Consulate. Waucquez will then continue his journey to Portugal.

But Jack and his pals have time to kill. They walk over to their water tower hideaway, well out of sight from prying eyes, and await Dédée's return.

'This is going to be the first time I've slept in a water tank,' says Jack, none too sure it really is such a good idea. But Dédée says it is, so they agree it is probably all right. They climb the ladder and crawl through the small entranceway. Inside, the restricted space is packed with straw, though this is easily pushed aside to give just enough room for the three men to stretch out on the wooden floor.

'Does anyone mind if I don't slip into my pyjamas?' says Larry, impishly, 'and I'll not bother to shower.'

'All right, go to bed smelling like a Spanish bull,' says Jack.

There is excitement in the air. They are in Spain, and they can sense freedom for the first time in months. And it feels good. They cannot wait for Dédée's return later that day. What will it be like in the embassy? How will they be received? Will they let those at home know they are safe at last? So many questions are on their lips, but for the time being there are still no answers.

The airmen are tired. Their 'digs', though hardly palatial, are surprisingly warm, even cosy. And the numerous insects that had laid first claim to the accommodation are none too pleased to be sharing it, and show their displeasure accordingly! A few bites are not going to drive them out, and in no time at all, the zzzzzzzzzz are flowing thick and fast from the occupants of this bizarre Spanish dwelling.

They hardly stir until Dédée returns and her soft voice awakens them from their pleasant dreams.

'Come, my brave children. Time for you to meet the British . . .'

CHAPTER 12

Safely Delivered

They look an odd lot as they walk down the steep, sloping fields with obvious difficulty, wrapped up in heavy coats fit for a mountain, but so out of place on the sunny slopes of Spain. Cows stop chewing and stare with intense curiosity as the three men and Dédée pass by. Grazing animals are not used to seeing people on these largely deserted, hilly pastures. The novelty interests them. 'What do we say if we are stopped by an equally curious Spanish farmer?' asks Larry. 'That we collect butterflies?' Even Dédée allows herself a smile at this one. 'No, we tell them we have come across the mountain from France. Most of the Spanish peasants haven't too much time for the Germans. They know they could be next,' she tells Larry.

It is early in the day, and the sun has a way to go before it heats the still fresh air to a point where it becomes uncomfortable. But the huge stretch of sea that is the Bay of Biscay reflects the deep blue of the cloudless sky. What a wonderful day to get back your freedom. Their sticks, cut by Florentino before they left St Jean de Luz, are still a big help and the men have mostly got the knack of using them behind as a break, rather than in front to stop them falling forward. Seeing how skilfully they are now using these sticks, Dédée says, 'Well, we've taught you something on the way! You will be experts next time.' Jack is not so sure he wants there to be a 'next time'.

After an hour, they have covered a couple of miles, and the mountains are beginning to recede behind them into more of a backdrop. A small hamlet seems to be coming into view as Dédée leads the men out of the fields and onto a country lane that snakes its way downhill, round big boulders and the few trees that reach up to the sky on these higher slopes.

An old man, with a large straw hat covering most of his heavily lined and tanned face, goes by on his way up the lane, stabbing his thick gnarled walking stick firmly into the road with each step he takes. He nods in the direction of Dédée, who smiles back.

In less than half-an-hour they have made Renteria, and a café where they can sit and enjoy a coffee and small snack before their tram ride into San Sebastian. Jack is now starting to get very excited. The gloom of occupied France well behind him, he takes Mary's prayer book out of his inside top pocket and looks at it, deep in thought. 'Not long now, my darling,' he says quietly. 'I will be home soon.'

'Yes, you will Jack. We all will,' adds Larry. Jurek nods. Dédée is pleased for her 'boys', but her own struggle must go on, and she is becoming seriously concerned for her father's safety. He is taking too many risks, and Dédée would prefer him to keep a much lower profile, or drop out of the Comète Line altogether so that she can concentrate on the work she must do.

Dédée cannot begin to know the difficulties about to beset herself, Florentino, the de Greefs, nearly two hundred Comète Line helpers – and especially her father, Frédéric de Jongh. If only she could look ahead . . .

Towards the end of October, after Dédée has taken two Scottish soldiers safely over the mountains, and down to the British Consul's office, she is asked to bring through more airmen because of their more valuable contribution to the war effort. So the priority is given to Royal Air Force flyers shot down over Belgium, and 'Paul', her father, largely organises their collection and movement out of Belgium, initially in the care of Dédée. In fact, Jack Newton is her first British airman to successfully evade capture, and find himself with this young heroine across the Franco/Spanish border, heading for San Sebastian.

Others who will follow will not be so lucky.

Already, in the trail of Newton's success, problems are building because the Gestapo realise that Resistance help is now becoming well organised. They are determined to infiltrate it and break it up.

The first cracks in the Comète Line's operation show in February 1942, barely one month after Newton arrives safely back in Britain. The secret police of the Luftwaffe call at Paul's home, 73 avenue Emile Verhaeren, in the Schaerbeek district of Brussels but he isn't there. He is in Valenciennes. Instead, Dédée's sister Suzanne Wittek is harshly questioned for about an hour in her front room. It is Dédée they are more interested in. Where is she? Then the Gestapo put a price of one million Belgian francs on Paul's head; he has to flee Brussels, and continue operating for the Comète Line in Paris, leaving his daughter Suzanne as the Brussels contact. A new man comes on the scene to rebuild the Belgian connections, Baron Jean Greindl, who takes the code name 'Nemo'. The Comète Line is again in good hands, the man who is director of a canteen run by the Swedish Red Cross, in Brussels. Known as the Cantine Suédoise, its headquarters is in the rue Ducale, in a partly furnished house of the early nineteenth century. Nemo works closely with Suzanne, picking up the threads of the scattered Comète Line helpers. It is a difficult and dangerous time, but they are successful. However, Nemo's one big regret is that he has never met Dédée, whose name is fast becoming a legend in Belgium and France. Then Dédée pays a daring visit to Brussels to see her sister, and Suzanne takes her to meet Nemo. It is a touching and exciting moment. They have both found good friends, good Resistance compatriots in each other, although they are to meet only three more times. From July through to October 1942, over fifty men are escorted by the Comète Line guides to Tante Go, in Anglet, and are successfully taken by Dédée and Florentino over the Pyrénées to Spain. But this happiness is tainted by the arrest of Suzanne in July. She spends the remainder of the war in the notorious Ravensbruck.

By the autumn of 1942, Dédée is crossing back and forth over the Pyrénées, accompanied by Florentino, like some hyperactive mountain goat, and probably just as nimble! A journey guaranteed to exhaust the fittest of men on just one trip, let alone the many return trips she is making. On top of that she has to run the gauntlet of gendarmes and Gestapo on the way to Anglet. Just how long can this feverish Resistance activity continue?

Not too long, as it happens, but through no fault of those who so bravely put their lives on the line – the Comète Line – to get airmen back home. Then comes the incident of the two pilots, claiming to be shot down American pilots serving in the Royal Air Force, who are brought to the Resistance safe house of the Maréchal family in the avenue Voltaire, Brussels. They are dressed in civilian clothes, but Madame Maréchal is uneasy about the two men, as is her daughter, Elsie. And when one of them asks the way to the cabinet, instead of the toilet, it arouses their suspicions still more. What a strange word for an American to use. They also wear khaki shirts, not the blue shirts worn by British airmen. The evidence indicating they are not Allied airmen, grows alarmingly. Finally, their fears are realised when Madame Maréchal is arrested in her home, and then Elsie, too, when one of the so-called Americans pushes a revolver into her stomach as she enters her front door. She is pushed into the dining room where more men are seated, drinking tea. They tell her the game is up. That because her mother wouldn't talk 'something happened to her in the kitchen'. She had been beaten to the floor, then arrested and taken off to the Luftwaffe's secret police headquarters. The Germans continue to occupy the Maréchal's home and arrest visitors, many of them Resistance contacts, as they call there. It is a sad, sad last week in November.

It soon transpires that the two phoney American flyers, both German agents, have wreaked havoc throughout the Comète Line. In two days almost one hundred people directly and indirectly involved with the organisation, are arrested. Many never to see their homes or their loved ones again. It is a high price to pay for the sixty airmen who had been saved over the past six months.

Dédée recalls how the desperate news reached her father, Paul, in Paris. He is now the Gestapo's number one enemy; chief of the Comète Line. And they increase the price they are prepared to pay for information that leads to his arrest. Dédée returns from her latest trip, her twenty-fourth having now escorted more than one hundred and eighty men over the Pyrénées, and she pleads with her father to flee to England. It is much too dangerous for him to stay in France any longer. He is bound to be caught. Finally, he agrees, and on 13 January 1943 Paul, Dédée, agent Franco and three pilots leave Paul's Paris flat in the rue Vaneau, arriving in Bayonne during one of the worst storms on record that has dragged on for several days.

At the rendezvous in the café, Tante Go breaks the news to Dédée and to Paul that the Bidassoa will be impassable for at least a week. Holding his hand, and looking into his sad eyes, she has to tell him that he will not be strong enough to cope with the five extra hours' march to the bridge crossing at Puicgerda. 'Your age is against you,' says Tante Go. 'You will not survive. Conditions are the worst they have ever been in the mountains.' Dédée and Florentino will have to take the men alone.

Paul knows Tante Go is right. Besides, he must not jeopardise the lives of the others by taking a chance, only to find he cannot make it. He just longs to go over the mountains with his beloved daughter, to say au revoir to her from the neutral country of Spain and be there for her when she brings over her airmen. But it is not to be this time. Paul takes Dédée's hand and leads her outside; under cover of the station he says goodbye. He hugs her, and tells her, 'I will be back, then we will cross together.' He stands and watches as they all set off on bicycles through the teeming rain for St Jean de Luz. Paul goes on to Tante Go's home in Anglet, before he plans to return to Paris.

At Franchia's farmhouse, Florentino expresses grave doubts about their crossing that night. He tells Dédée it cannot be done. It is agreed they will have to wait until the following day. Dédée and the airmen will stay in the farmhouse overnight. Florentino decides to go home to Ciboure and return in time for the crossing the following night. The more the wind tears at the building and the harder the rain beats on the windows, the more Dédée accepts they have made the right decision, both for themselves and for her father. She is confident it won't be long before she will be able to take her Papa to freedom, and have him taken on to Britain where he will be safe.

Up and about early the next morning, they all eat a good breakfast. There are many things to do on the farm, and Franchia hopes the others won't mind if she gets on with her work. They should make themselves comfortable, and perhaps the men won't mind washing up the breakfast plates? One of them puts on Franchia's apron and begins to do as she has asks.

Dédée looks around at the airmen having fun with Franchia's three children. Giving them piggybacks across the floor, swinging them in their arms. Laughing and chattering. The happiness is so heartwarming . . . but it is not to last for more than a couple of hours.

Later that morning, 15 January, someone hears the faint sound of an approaching car. Even Dédée is not alarmed. Cars sometimes do pass by, but this one is not passing. Its engine suddenly cuts, and the sound of men's voices are heard coming to the farm. 'Quickly, upstairs,' says Dédée, motioning the men to get out of sight. But before they have reached the first step, the door bursts open. Two gendarmes stand framed in the half light. Ten more come into the kitchen, most of them carrying guns. Their hands above their heads, Dédée, Franchia and the airmen are taken out into the yard while every corner of the farmhouse is searched. Floorboards are lifted and stored hay poked with bayonets.

'Where is Florentino?' one of the gendarmes asks coldly. But none answers, and they are taken off for questioning. The children, too. Dédée knows that someone has betrayed them. It is a betrayal that leaves the three young children without a mother, because Franchia Usandizanga dies in Ravensbruck on 12 April 1945.

After an hour, in increasingly heavy rain, the soaked and flimsily-dressed shivering women are escorted away on foot by two guards. Behind them, the three airmen, their hands behind their heads, are led in single file escorted by five oafish gendarmes either side, in the direction of St Jean de Luz. It is a strange sight as the party makes its way down the road, across the bridge, coming to a halt at the bureau de police. They are briefly interrogated, then locked in cells in the town prison.

Bad news travels fast, and Florentino is one of the first to hear that Dédée has been picked up, as is Tante Go. Florentino immediately sets off for Spain to warn the British in San Sebastian what has happened. Tante Go does her best to comfort Paul, who is grief stricken that Dédée is in the hands of the police, and will no doubt very quickly be passed over to the Gestapo at Anglet. The storm continues unabated, and Paul, heartbroken, his eyes filled with tears, is unable to take in the well-meaning condolences of those around him. He just wants to be with Dédée. So sad is he that he cannot think of anything else. This is the moment he has always dreaded. And it has finally come.

Events move swiftly. The following day Dédée is transported to the aptly named prison Villa Chagrin, in Bayonne, whilst the fiercely focused Tante Go begins conceiving plans to rescue her from captivity. It is too dangerous for Paul to remain at Tante Go's, so, for his own safety, he is sent into hiding in a friend's home, that of Jean Dassié. In his anguish, Paul has already made a senseless visit to the prison to establish for certain that Dédée is being held there. But when the initial shock has passed, and more rational decisions are taken, Paul is still determined that a dramatic rescue be made so that the two of them can escape into Spain.

A plan is hatched, but before it can be carried out Dédée is collected by the Gestapo under the very noses of Tante Go and two of her cohorts who are keeping watch on the prison gate. Are they too late? They see Dédée, still in her trousers and mountain climbing espadrilles her head held high, escorted to the waiting car and driven away to the German headquarters in the town. But it is for questioning; she is returned to prison later that same night under the cover of darkness.

Paul pesters Tante Go to organise a dramatic rescue attempt, but she continues to counsel caution in everyone's interests, including Dédée's. There is an attempt to scale the prison wall, but only after they have got over the first outer wall do they discover there is another similar inner prison wall. The plan has to be abandoned.

Before further efforts can be made to reconnoitre the inside of the prison to check if another rescue attempt can be undertaken, Dédée is transferred to a Gestapo interrogation centre in Bordeaux. It also becomes clear that one of the airmen has, under harsh interrogation, revealed the route which the party took from Bayonne to Franchia's farm. He is forced to accompany two Gestapo through the streets of Bayonne to reveal where he had been hidden. The Gestapo conclude that the headquarters of the Comète Line is, in fact, in the south of France, in Bordeaux. Dédée realises that not only do the Germans think Comète is a local organisation, her true identity is still not known to them. She doesn't enlighten them on either count!

Further plans are made to free Dédée from prison, but again the Gestapo, by their own good fortune, are one step ahead, having moved their captive from prison within hours of an attempt by the Resistance to spring her. It is bitterly disappointing for Tante Go and her helpers.

Towards the end of February, the Gestapo conclude their inquiries in Bayonne. Tante Go and her family can breathe again. But Dédée and Jean Dassié, given away through information forced from one of the airman who stayed at his safe house, are taken by train to Paris. Jean, his wife and their daughter are all deported to Germany where they suffer enormously.

Franco and Tante Go see Dédée and the Dassié family board the train at Bayonne in handcuffs. Fear for them is in everyone's heart. And Dédée's arrest looks like being the death knell for the Comète Line now that its most important flame has as good as snuffed out. But that flame is not so easily extinguished. There are many more all too eager to keep its inspirational light glowing bright.

In Paris a new guide is found to lead airmen from the marshalling points there to Bayonne. Her name – Madeline Bouteloupt. Aged 30, with big brown eyes, she exudes an innocence that fools many an en route gendarme and ticket inspector. From April 1943 she meets escapees from Brussels at the Gare Montparnasse, in Paris, and leads them, as Dédée had done, to the Gare d'Austerlitz for the journey south.

Most times such train journeys are routine, and incident free, but on occasions they are anything but. As is the case when Tante Go embarks on a local journey from Bayonne to the coastal town of Ustaritz to look for a new route over the frontier. A fellow agent, code named 'B', British by birth, accompanies her. Less than fifteen minutes into the trip the train is searched by Germans, a quite frequent happening, but this time one of the soldiers is suspicious of 'B'. His English appearance attracts the attention of an eagle-eyed soldier who accuses 'B' of being an escaping English airman and Tante Go is charged with being his guide. They are both taken off the train at the frontier town of St Jean de Port and put in a wooden hut for further interrogation, but the guards fail to lock the door! A fellow prisoner decides to make a run for it, and successfully gets across the border to safety. Tante Go urges 'B' to go next, but he will not because he thinks it will make things worse for her, saying he will stay to try to talk his way out of his problems. 'B' is taken away by four soldiers and left overnight in a cold, dank cell. The next morning the now angry Tante Go demands to know what the Germans plan to do with her and she threatens to report them to the Kreis Kommandant in Biarritz. She says she thinks he will be very upset to hear she has been arrested, and is being treated so badly! Asked if she knows the Kreis Kommandant, Tante Go points out that she knows a great deal about him, and those who supply him with black market luxuries. 'Ring him and ask him,' she challenges her interrogators, adding that it is her task to buy these black market items on his behalf.

As for 'B', she says she is taking him to a recommended doctor for treatment of tuberculosis.

After further checks, it is all too much for the German inquisitors. They decide discretion is the better part of valour – and release both 'B' and Tante Go.

By the spring of 1943 it is becoming increasingly dangerous for Paul to remain in Paris, and friends advise him that his arrest will be dangerous for Dédée too. Paul is grieving so deeply for Dédée, in custody in Paris, that his behaviour is becoming increasingly without a sense of caution which is so out of character for the schoolmaster. He even tries to buy her release, but that plan also fails. Then on 7 June, at 4.30pm on a platform of the Gare du Nord, Paul, his friend Jean Masson and some confused airmen are arrested and taken at gunpoint to a room where they are interrogated by railway police. The thought enters his head that in prison, which is where he will now be sent, he will be nearer his daughter. But first Paul is taken to the Gestapo offices in the rue des Saussaies. Then Jean Masson appears. He is without handcuffs, stands in front of Paul and spits on the floor. His contempt shows all over his face. But it is the worthless contempt of a traitor. For Paul many brutal interrogations are just about to begin. Dédée has now endured many weeks of torture and questioning, leaving the Gestapo in no doubt that she is no more than a guide rather than the architect and coordinator of one of World War II's greatest resistance organisations. It is just not conceivable that such a young girl can create such a web of mischief, is the way the Luftwaffe police and the Gestapo see it. They believe the true leaders are Paul and Nemo. This ignorance does much to give Dédée the strength to continue her bluff.

Nemo is to die on 7 September 1943 in an Allied bombing raid over Brussels. One bomb drops on the barracks of Etterbeek where Nemo is imprisoned, and he is killed instantly. Two weeks later, Berlin orders the execution of eight other heroes of the Cantine Suédoise, including George Maréchal, the father of Elsie. Frédéric de Jongh (Paul) is executed by firing squad at Mont-Valérien on 28 March 1944, along with two friends, Robert Aylé and the masseur Fouquerel. Paul dies with a smile on his face, knowing he has served his daughter well to the bitter end.

If only Dédée, on the Spanish hillside this day in January 1943, could see what the next eighteen months have in store for her. But even if it was possible, such was her dedication to her cause it is doubtful she would have changed very much.

It is just so good to be here right now, and it shows in every step they take. There is bounce in their stride, there is new life in each of them, a feeling of great joy and well-being that lifts their spirits as they laugh and chatter, half walking, half running towards what seems to be a small town spread out ahead. But the nearer they get, the more people there are in the streets, so the lighthearted banter among the airmen and Dédée has to stop. Spain is not yet a place to be too British, or the concentration camp at Miranda might become 'home', rather than soft centred internment in the British Consulate in San Sebastian, or Bilbao. The four airmen agree they prefer to check in at the Consulate!

Jack cannot get over the sight of so many apparently happy people going about their business. Children laughing, skipping along the street holding on to their mother's hand, asking the questions children ask. Pleading for the clothes children want from well-stocked shop windows. Men in black berets puffing on chewed cigarette butts. Women in summery dresses at pavement café tables enjoying morning coffee; discussing the day's plans. Or, maybe the war.

The bustle of town life increases around every corner as Dédée leads the way to the centre where trams start out for San Sebastian. Jack notices that the Spanish trams are more open, more inviting than ones he sometimes journeyed on in Brussels. It has to be something to do with the different climate, he concludes. But then a tram is a tram is a tram. For him they still make too much noise, heaving their passengers from one side of their seats to the other as they rumble over their rails through wary traffic. It is not a pleasant experience. Jack recalls that final journey to the safety of the consulate:

140

We three airmen follow Dédée onto the tram, but none of us sit together. We are still doing our best not to draw attention to ourselves because it is still too risky. I am now very suntanned, and with quite a thick, fancy moustache that makes me look like a Basque. But only if I keep my mouth shut. So that's what I do. Dédée is going to lead the way off the tram when we arrive outside the Consulate. If we see guards outside the building then we are to go to a nearby café and wait for her there. If the Spanish guards are not on duty, then we have to walk straight in. As luck will have it, the Consulate gates are unguarded. In all the excitement, I even forget to spend my peseta note to pay for my tram ticket.

I have kept it to this day, along with my false identity papers and other memorabilia from that time. Just looking at that note brings back so many memories.

Dédée, ahead of me, walks straight into the Consulate. I am not far behind her, and Larry and Jurek follow on behind me. We must look a shady bunch of characters, but probably no more so than most of the locals!

We create quite a stir once we are inside. The first man to see me is the Vice Consul. A guy named Arthur Dean, who is Dédée's contact in San Sebastian. The handshake welcomes with various people seem to go on forever. I feel like royalty paying a visit – not some smelly airman who is in desperate need of a good scrub down!

But before such necessities are seen to, I am taken to Dean's office where he and another man, presumably one of the 'funny men' from MI9 under cover in the Consulate visa section, have me run through my story. This is from the landing on Deurne airfield, and I have to empty my memory as best as I can. The tougher stuff is to come later when I am taken to a place called The British Seaman's Rest Home, along the coast just outside Bilbao. I am there for a couple of days and they want to know every little detail. It is hard work, and after all I have been through my mind is not at its most alert. But those asking the questions eventually seem satisfied.

They want to know why we had to make an emergency landing. Any details of enemy aircraft on the airfield, and whether we saw signs of the Germans after we had landed. They want to know how we were picked up by the Resistance, about the safe houses I stayed in. The fate of the rest of the crew. What Brussels was like. Concentration of troops; likewise in Paris. How I got to Bayonne, and over the Pyrénées. I had enough to keep them going for a good two days, information that will tell the authorities in Britain a great deal about the enemy. And those helping the British airmen.

But I am so looking forward to giving my brain a break from all the pressures put on me over the past four hellish months.

Then comes word that me, Larry and Jurek are to be taken to the British Embassy, in Madrid. That same afternoon we are shown to a large, black car, bearing CD plates, with darkened windows, and it takes us from the Seaman's Rest Home, south to Madrid and straight into the British Embassy building there.

I could never have guessed the kind of reception the three of us are to get. It is just unbelievable. So low key as though we'd simply got lost in the mountains on a ramble, and it was all proving a bit of a nuisance! That seems to be their attitude.

There are a couple of 'Well done, fellas', but that is about the depth of the welcome home.

On the other hand, when we get to the Embassy in Madrid, the Ambassador, Sir Samuel Hoare, does lay on a celebration reception. More about that in a moment. And he gives me a signed and stamped receipt to prove I have passed through!

At first nobody even thinks about me being the first British airman to successfully escape from German-occupied Europe, so the celebration isn't even about that. I think the Ambassador is just pleased to have pulled off my escape under the very noses of the Germans and the Spanish. Bit of British one-upmanship, if you like. But before I leave Madrid, Sir Samuel Hoare confirms I am the first British airman to come out of German-occupied Europe. He says to me: 'As you are the first, I think I had better give you a receipt,' which, as I say, he does. He signs the inside cover of Mary's prayer book, writing in it: 'With Good Wishes. Samuel Hoare, Christmas 1941'. Then he date stamps it – November 1941. I still have it among my collection.

After all, I've been through a great deal, my life continually under threat, to get to that Madrid Embassy. I may have felt like a hero, but I am certainly not treated like one. Even my accommodation is hardly fit for a hero – a palliasse spread out on the stone floor of the Embassy chapel! The three of us are locked inside, with an armed guard on duty outside. Cloak and dagger stuff, but it seems this is the only way we can be properly interned. It has to be within the Embassy and locked inside the chapel. I suppose it wouldn't have done for word to get out that the British are smuggling downed airmen across the Pyrénées, and home via their Madrid Embassy and the courtesy of the Ambassador's diplomatic car!

I am not at the Sailor's Rest Home for long, perhaps a couple of days at the most, then the diplomatic car – a Daimler 15 – takes me to Madrid. The vehicle is like a huge hearse. Just amazing. I am driven there on my own.

I am not really sure what happens initially to the other two guys, but for the time being I am separated from them, possibly because

Larry Birk is an Aussie and Jurek Budinsky is Polish. I sit in the back seat of this enormous car with its darkened windows, and its smart, uniformed chauffeur who doesn't have much to say. He is a bit more talkative when we stop for a glass or two of white wine. But hardly chatty. In the front seat, alongside the chauffeur, is an armed escort. The journey takes a good three to four hours, with a couple of stops well out of towns for those welcome glasses of wine. What with the wine, riding in the Ambassador's car, sitting alone in the back seat of the Daimler with its blacked out windows, I feel very much a VIP. For the first time in months I begin to feel relaxed. Free at last.

But I also miss Dédée. We have been through so much together. Her bravery has had such an incredible effect on me, now that she is no longer by my side it is unsettling. I turn to her to say something, and she isn't there.

But her sweet face, her funny little ways, her gutsy determination and dedication to what she is doing, are etched in my mind from that day forever. I only have to close my eyes and I can see her as clearly as if it is yesterday. As are memories of my wife, Mary.

How many men can truly say they have two eternal loves in their lifetime? For me, two women who have made that life so complete, in two very different ways? Well, I can.

Then, suddenly, I am in Madrid.

The Daimler glides smoothly through the guarded gates of the British Embassy in Madrid, and parks to the rear of the building well out of sight of the less private front entrance. The escort opens the car door for Jack, who steps out and takes barely ten paces into an Embassy side door being held open by one of the Embassy staff. Newton is led through darkened corridors, lined with paintings. Down some stairs, and into a huge, well-furnished room. A man is seated at a light-coloured polished desk, and as Jack walks in so this man gets up out of his seat and extends a welcoming hand. The handshake is firm, and quite brief. 'Do, please sit down,' he says. 'Tea?'

'Yes, sir, I'd like that. Thank you,' says Jack, thinking here we go again; another grilling!

The man at the desk, who still hasn't introduced himself, is there before Jack . . . 'No more questions, well not yet anyway. There are a few things which you may be able to help us with, but they can wait until tomorrow,' he says. Jack sits back in his seat. That's a relief.

'No, I just need to tell you about being here. And why we must treat you the way we will have to while you are in our custody,' says the anonymous one.

'Custody?'

'The Embassy cannot, of course, be seen to be harbouring illegal immigrants into Spain. The Spanish authorities won't like it, even though they know it is going on, and it is likely to get much worse before it gets better. No, you are here in the sanctuary of the Embassy as a British citizen, and in body only. No official record of your stay will be kept. In other words, you do not really exist!'

'Oh, that's nice. At least the Germans have been doing their best to track me down, make a note of my name. Now I'm with the British and they don't even want to acknowledge my existence!'

The anonymous one does his best to reassure Jack. That he is in good and safe hands. It won't be too long before they will secretly sneak him into Gibraltar. Until then, his 'home' is in the chapel. That is where he will be interned for his own safety and security. His bed is a palliasse. And if he feels like praying, then everything is on hand!

'At one point I take the opportunity to say a prayer for Dédée's safety. I am free, she was returning to the cauldron of hate and despair. When we parted at the San Sebastian Consulate, our goodbye was poignant, but quite brief,' says Jack.

She always said how sad she was that Belgium was forced to capitulate, and how thankful she was to the British for helping her country and its people. We hugged each other and kissed goodbye, which was a perfectly natural thing to do, but it all seemed so little for what she had done for me. And, in fact, would continue to do for so many other airmen in the months and years ahead. Then she turned, walked away, looking back just one last time to give me a final wave, and she was gone. I didn't see her again until 1946 when she came to London to receive the George Medal from King George VI.

CHAPTER 13
Smuggled into Gibraltar

It was the most bizarre party Jack had ever attended, and it was in the unlikeliest of venues. For a start it took place in the chapel of the British Embassy in Madrid. Secondly, it had been laid on by the Ambassador . . . for law breakers. And Jack was one of the law breakers, the other two being Larry and Jurek who had been reunited with the British airman. All three were illegal immigrants into Spain – and the party's 'guests of honour'. Loud music filled the holy shrine, wine flowed as though it was going out of fashion, and glasses were raised to celebrate the escape of the first British airman from German-occupied Europe – Jack Newton! There was drinking, there was dancing with the Embassy secretaries who joined in the fun, live music provided by a band formed from members of the Embassy staff, and a feast to enjoy, too. There could not have been more than thirty people present at this very special party, but what a night! Jack tells the story:

> It was the inspiration of Sir Samuel and Lady Hoare to celebrate my escape from occupied France, along with the Aussie Larry Birk and the Pole, Jurek Budinsky. Being the only Brit, I was treated like the star turn. As I have already recounted, at one point during the evening, Sir Samuel Hoare jokingly said to me: 'I suppose I should give you some kind of receipt to show you stayed here as guest of the British Ambassador, because something like this has never happened before.' I gave him my wife Mary's prayer book and asked him if he would please receipt that for me. He wrote: 'With Good Wishes', then with a flourish, stamped the page with the official embassy rubber date stamp, and signed it.
>
> But when the private celebration was over and the Embassy got back to normal, so did my presence there. Along with fellow escapers Larry and Jurek, we were again locked inside the chapel with a guard posted outside to make sure nobody discovered us. This was our place of internment and it was where we had to stay until plans could be made to smuggle us out of Spain and into Gibraltar. Frankly, they didn't really know what to do with us, because we were the first

Allied airmen to escape from the Germans and pass through the Embassy. Inside the chapel was the only reasonably safe place for us to be hidden. As I have already explained, it was little more than a sparsely furnished room with straw palliasses thrown down on the floor, alongside a small, rough wooden table and some chairs. At one end of this room – or chapel, as it was really called – was an altar, and a large cross. So we didn't have to go far to pray for something better!

We were not allowed to leave the chapel so we had to amuse ourselves as best we could by reading, talking, and exploring. We found a door that led down some steps into a kind of cellar, so the night after the party, Larry and I decided to go and take a look. It was filled with stacks of clothes hanging on rails, shirts and lots of pairs of shoes. Shelves were overflowing with tins of food, as well as many cartons and tins of cigarettes. We had discovered Aladdin's cave. We helped ourselves to a couple of new shirts, and several tins of cigarettes (I was a smoker at the time). We felt a bit upset that with all this stuff in the cellar nobody had thought to ask us if we would like a change of clothing, or a few cigarettes, so we had no qualms about helping ourselves. I wore one of the new shirts and stuffed several tins of fifty cigarettes into my new kitbag.

Another thing that caught my eye was a colour poster hanging on the chapel wall. It was signed by a Spanish artist and, incredibly, it showed a Wellington bomber (similar to the one I had put down in, in Belgium) over-flying and bombing a German industrial complex. Its bomb doors were open and buildings were on fire so the artist, who had signed his name VW Krockman, clearly depicted a successful raid on the so-called Fatherland. He was also obviously very pro-English, which was a bit unusual because at that stage of the war, even though Spain was meant to be neutral, it still showed a strong bias towards the Germans. Also, the Wellington on the poster was one of the latest versions, with Merlin engines, and my own squadron – 12 Squadron – was the first to put them into service, so the poster was recent. No. 1 Group were given the first four hundred new Wellingtons and they had only been operating from Binbrook since around July of that particular year, which was 1941. The poster's caption, in Spanish, read: 'By day and by night the aircraft of the RAF Bomber Command attacked the German targets.' Just how a Spanish artist was able to be so up-to-date, I never found out. Anyway, I knew I just had to have that poster so I carefully took it down it down from the wall, folded it neatly, and hid it in my kitbag. It was a fine souvenir of my stay in the chapel, and that same poster now hangs on a wall in my spare room at my home in Broad Oak, East Sussex.

The Air Attaché in Madrid interrogated me, and someone was sent up from Gibraltar, too. As I have said before, I think they just wanted to be one hundred percent sure I wasn't a German spy trying to infiltrate the escape route. The Germans had tried it before, and would no doubt keep trying. When the Embassy officials were sure I was air gunner Jack Newton, and that Larry and Jurek were genuine too, we were asked if we would take back to Britain with us several maps showing certain German fortifications, along with the positions of dummy haystacks concealing anti-aircraft guns. When there was an air raid, the haystacks fell apart to expose the anti-aircraft guns which then went into action. We had spotted them on our way down on the train from Paris. But the idea that I should carry such incriminating documents through Spain down to Gibraltar made me nervous. The three of us put our heads together and decided it was too risky. We declined, but promised to tell British intelligence what we knew immediately we got to Gibraltar.

The Air Attaché was quite a friendly guy. He had lots of gold braid and he knew about flying, so he was the real stuff. A man of about 40.

He even allowed me to send a telegram back home. I wanted to let my wife know I was safe so I just wrote 'Alive, safe and well. Interned'. The Air Attaché read it, approved it, and had it radioed to Mary.

After a couple more days in our chapel digs, the three of us were suddenly told it was time to leave Madrid. Our departure was all very low key. There was no line-up of staff outside the Embassy front gate, nor any waving of British, Australian or Polish flags as the three of us were driven away in the back of the Ambassador's own blacked out private car. No goodbyes. No fanfares. We were just uncere-moniously driven out. The diplomatic car made the journey from Madrid to La Linea and across the Spanish/Gibraltar border fairly regularly, so this particular trip was seen by the authorities as nothing out of the ordinary. If only they had known that three escapees from occupied France were on board, instead of Sir Samuel Hoare.

The car was very distinctive with its CD plates front and back, so the Spanish Guardia never intervened. And we had an armed escort on board, sitting alongside the chauffeur.

I suppose the nonstop journey from Madrid to the Spanish border post of La Linea took about five to six hours. When we arrived there was just a brief halt at the barrier, which was raised and we were waved across the border, into Gibraltar. Very routine. None of us left the vehicle until we were actually in Gib. Then the first thing we did was ask for three stiff drinks to help us unwind, and to celebrate our freedom. The adjutant who received us kindly obliged. His batman saw to it immediately.

Newton, Birk and Budinsky crossed into Gibraltar on 7 January 1942. It was a sunny afternoon, and the sight of the Rock rising from the clear blue waters of the Straits of Gibraltar, brought a lump to Jack Newton's throat. This was British soil, and at last he felt as good as home. All the traumas of the past four months behind him. Now for the last leg . . .

The trouble was, Newton was in a class of his own. Because he was the first airman to be brought by diplomatic car from Madrid to Gibraltar, nobody on the Rock really knew what to do with him. He wasn't a prisoner so they couldn't lock him up in a cell, and yet he was still officially 'missing'. On paper he didn't, as yet, officially exist! It was a bit of a dilemma for the Royal Air Force adjutant who accepted this first 'package' from across the Pyrénées, along with the Aussie and the Pole. Three little problem packages that had to be sorted out, and forwarded to their correct addresses.

There was no problem finding them temporary accommodation on Gibraltar, although it was hardly five star. A corporal military policeman was given the job of taking them to their assigned barrack block, where they were each allotted a white breeze-block room furnished with two iron beds, two chairs, and a writing desk. Very basic. There was no glass in the window frames, and the doors could not be secured. On the other hand, there was no one else around. And, at least, they did have the whole block to themselves, well away from the barrack blocks occupied by other station personnel.

That first meeting with the station adjutant was interesting.

'We are very pleased to welcome you to Royal Air Force Gibraltar. Unfortunately, we cannot let you loose, so there will be little chance of sightseeing while you are here!' he told them. 'For security reasons we want to keep you away from the main areas of the camp, which is why you will be billeted near the end of the runway. I hope you find it reasonably comfortable there. And we will do our best for you.'

This meant their meals were brought out to them. For breakfast it was porridge or cornflakes, and bacon and eggs. Sandwiches for lunch, and mostly fish of one kind or another for supper. Jugs of tea and orange juice were available at all times. Some chocolate was sent across, too, for mid-morning or midnight nibbles.

But one of the first tasks that had to be attended to was their delousing! Jack recalls:

And we probably needed it. I don't think I'd changed my underwear more than half a dozen times over the four months. It wasn't something that seemed too important when I was sleeping rough, ducking and diving from the attentions of German soldiers, the Gestapo, and secret police. So, it was great to get properly cleaned up for the first time in a good number of weeks. I received a change of underwear, new socks, but I kept my battledress top, though my RAF trousers had to go because they were getting a bit worn. But the suit, given to me at the de Voegts' was still fine, and I continued to wear it until I arrived back in Britain.

The treatment we received was good, but it seemed there was still some doubt about our true identities. A bit like it was with dear old Emile Witmeur, I suppose. Only he came very close to shooting us as German spies! The three of us discussed the situation among ourselves and agreed there was nothing we could do to help the British on Gibraltar, other than answer the many questions which continued to be put to us. They would have to make up their own minds, and it wouldn't do any good us trying to pressure them. Or to complain.

Maybe, it was more curiosity than doubt. Whatever it was, we were told not to speak to anyone, other than to our interrogators.

Finally, I was allowed to send cablegrams home to Mary and to my mum and dad, and my sister, so I knew that any doubts about me had now been resolved. I had cablegrams back from them, too, saying how wonderful it was that I was alive. Possibly, for me, the understatement of my lifetime!

For nearly a week, Jack Newton and his two pals had very little to do. Jack picked up a copy of station orders to discover that in his absence the Air Ministry had promoted him to Flight Sergeant; good news because it meant a bit more in his pay packet.

All three spent most of each day sitting at the far end of the airfield watching Royal Air Force transport planes landing on the runway that jutted well out into the sea.

It looked pretty hairy. We ate bananas, tossed the skins into the water and threw stones at the skins. There was no sign of enemy aircraft; the Germans were more interested in the threat from the Allied build-up in Malta so, early on, Gibraltar was mostly left alone. In any case, the Rock was well fortified with ack-ack guns and searchlights should the Jerries choose to make a surprise attack.

As I say, sightseeing wasn't really on the agenda for us three, though they did relent one afternoon and let us go unescorted into the town area. Larry and the Pole wanted to pay their respects to the Almighty so we all went into a small chapel we came across. We had been given a bit of back pay which, in my case, came to about five pounds, so I went on a spending spree buying little things to take home as presents. I bought Mary some silk stockings in the NAAFI, and a large shoulder of bacon that I knew would go down well back home with my mum and dad. I recall it only cost me a couple of pounds. I also splashed out on a bottle of Johnny Walker whisky for seven shillings and sixpence.

After a couple of days our isolation became a bit testing. Well, it was boring feeling so excited about going home, and having nothing to do to pass the time. The hours and days just dragged. Nobody seemed to know how I was going to be sent back from Gibraltar. From what I could gather the options were possibly a banana boat, a tramp steamer, frigate, or aboard an aircraft that was passing through. I was told I'd have to hang on until something turned up. Obviously, I was hoping it would be an aircraft.

Then I heard that a Sunderland flying boat was due in, but that it had been shot up on its way from South Africa. Was I prepared to volunteer to be its tail gunner to get back to the UK? Well, yes, I was, and then I was told that I'd have to be patient because the aircraft was scheduled to do an operational square search over the Bay of Biscay en route. I still said 'Yes'. But why was no tail gunner already on board? It turned out that in the attack on the Sunderland, the tail gunner had been shot up and killed, leaving his turret in a bit of a bloody mess.

I watched the Sunderland land, and taxi up to the dock. What a beautiful sight, and this was the plane that was to take me back home. I couldn't wait.

My departure from Gib on 13 January 1942 was just about as low key as my stay there. Brought in covertly across the Spanish border, the three of us didn't really fit in. As I have said, there was no slot for us. So there was not much anyone could do for us, other than give us a roof over our heads, something to eat, and let us pass the day as best we could. When the time came for us to go, I don't think anyone was too upset! Anyway, that was how it seemed to me, and it was understandable.

With Larry and Jurek it was different. We had been through a great deal together and leaving them was a bit of a wrench. There was a lot of back slapping, and sentiments that we would all meet up when the war was over – but it never happened. Maybe they didn't make it through the war. Many friends I made at that time did not; I was one of the lucky ones.

The morning it was time to go was like any other one on the Rock of Gibraltar, a clear blue sky, hot and sticky. I was picked up by a smart, very correct military police escort who took me by car to the dock where a single naval rating aboard a small rubber boat was waiting to take me out to the Sunderland flying boat. I could see her sitting majestically on the water, bobbing slightly in the gently rippling waves. I must have been in a big rush. As I hurried down steep stone steps to the boat, I lost my footing. I stumbled down the last half dozen steps, ending up virtually over the side and headfirst into the boat itself. But for the timely outstretched arm of another sailor on the quay, I'd have swallow-dived somewhat ungraciously into the Mediterranean! After a few minutes sitting back, as the boat skimmed across the water, I was climbing aboard the Sunderland with rather more care than I had exercised leaving the quayside. Then, surprise, surprise. My nostrils filled with the strong smell of a fry-up. Surely, I must be mistaken? No, it was definitely a fry-up and quite the best fry-up I think I had ever smelled from any kitchen, or galley, up to that time. It just struck me as so English. I really was nearly home, and it wasn't too long before I was not only smelling this English of English breakfasts, but enjoying what was a 'speciality of the house'. The Sunderland crew always had it on the slow burner, ready for hungry stomachs! A huge plateful was soon finding its way into mine. I was warmly welcomed aboard as the crew's new rear gunner for the last leg of the flight back to Pembroke Docks. The skipper asked if I knew why he had no tail-end Charlie. I told him I did, but he told me again anyway, saying how the turret had been in quite a mess. It had been badly shot up, and bits of the gunner spattered around. How the Gibraltar ground crew had the terrible job of cleaning it up, hosing it down and patching it up to make it fit for me to occupy on the last leg of the flight home. I guess he wanted to see if I'd turn green, and throw up, in which case I wasn't going to have much stomach for the job ahead, should there be any more trouble. But I didn't. This was no time for me to be sensitive. This was my ticket back to Britain and I was grateful for it. Besides, I already knew that on the way home we'd be doing an operational sweep over the Bay of Biscay, looking for German subs, so I'd be earning my ticket home.

I was kept apart from the rest of the crew and others on the dock, presumably for security reasons. But to me it was treatment fit for royalty! Who was I to argue? And once I was aboard, everyone made me feel at home. I was back in my job as aircrew, only this time in what was then the queen of the skies, a Sunderland, rather than aboard my own familiar Bomber Command workhorse, the Wimpy. I said a quiet 'thank you' to Him up there. He was quite definitely looking after me.

Within thirty minutes the huge solitary Sunderland taxied out for take-off, looking like some forlorn swan that had lost its mate. Jack couldn't help thinking that like swans, perhaps these huge and graceful flying boats should be paired off. Mated for life to another Sunderland! Nobody else on board seemed to be so concerned as the skipper called through headsets for a crew check. Then the thunderous roar of the four engines blotted out even clear thinking. The wind whipped up by the propellers churned the water into frothy turbulent whirlpools. From the rear gun turret positioned as he was high above the waves, there was no doubt about it . . . Jack was in the royal box. This was the place to be riding in a Sunderland flying boat. He could hear his heart pounding with the sheer exhilaration of the moment as the huge bird began its take-off run across the bay, before it lifted gracefully into the sky and out of the clutches of the clear blue Mediterranean sea. The moment was etched into Jack's mind for eternity. Next stop – England.

As the Sunderland turned to set course for the Bay of Biscay, Jack looked down at the huge Rock of Gibraltar rising from the mouth of the Mediterranean with all the grandeur of a British bastion holding its own against an enemy that lurked menacingly above and below the waves that all but surrounded it. The Union Flag fluttered defiantly from its highest point. It was a moment to be proud to be British.

Once the big bird was clear of land, over open sea, the skipper told Jack to 'squirt' his guns to check they were back in good working order after the nastiness that had befallen the previous occupant. It had been more than five months since that fateful flight from Binbrook to Aachen, but put Jack in a rear, or front, gun and what he had to do was second nature. The only thing that Jack noted about his new office was the slightly improved comfort factor over that of the Wimpy, and the slightly smoother flight of the Sunderland. Perhaps a bit like being in a five-star hotel, rather than a B&B!

For the next ten to twelve hours there was not going to be a great deal to do, other than keep his eyes peeled for enemy shipping and lurking submarines, although Jack had already been told by another member of the crew that it was unlikely they would see either. This was very much a routine exercise, on a par with those Wellington leaflet raids over Paris that kept Jack and his bomber crew busy before they delivered something heavier and nastier on Aachen.

As the droning engines took the Sunderland higher into the clear blue sky over the Bay of Biscay, and the plane began its coordinated sweeps, Jack's mind drifted back over the events of the past five months and his extraordinary run of good luck that had taken him more than 1,200 miles from Belgium, through France, over the Pyrénées and down to Gibraltar. How had he managed it? How had he been so fortunate to fall into the hands of so many brave and selfless Resistance men and women, who had put their own lives at risk in order to get him on that Sunderland, and back to Great Britain? And then there was Dédée, whose feminine fragility had proved the perfect camouflage in her dedicated work to help escapees like him. Without Dédée, and her gentle persuasion, Jack knew his chances of reaching St Jean de Luz would have been slim, and that crossing of the Pyrénées unthinkable. Dédée had been his guardian angel, and he owed everything to this young Belgian girl.

As the Sunderland banked first to port, then to starboard, there was time for Jack to reflect on the fate of Langlois and Tich Copley. Of McLarnon, Burrell and Porteous. Would he ever see any of them again? Would they make it back to Blighty? Were they even still alive? So many questions, and so few answers as he considered all the possibilities.

CHAPTER 14

Back Home!

Hour after tedious hour the Sunderland crew carried out a sweep pattern of the Bay of Biscay, hunting for prowling German submarines but not one showed itself. If the Jerry submariners were out there, then they were keeping under the waves, well out of sight. After some sixteen hours of monotonous flying, following a traditional square search pattern, the skipper finally decided to call it a day. 'We're going home,' he told his crew over the intercom, as he banked the huge flying boat to starboard and set course for Pembroke Dock. Jack says:

What a relief it was, too. It felt as though my head was in a kind of noose. And it would only take one hiccup to hang myself! I just didn't want us to get caught up in any nasty business and maybe come unstuck because an ME109 German fighter pilot got lucky. I was so nearly home and more than anything else in my life at this time, I wanted to get back on British soil. Huddled in a rubber dinghy in the middle of the Bay of Biscay was not what I had in mind after some five months on the run through France. Safety, and a nice hot bath held much more appeal!

Being back in my usual position, the rear gun turret, made it seem like old times in the Wimpy, but comparing the Wimpy and the Sunderland was a bit like comparing chalk and cheese! They hadn't very much in common – apart from wings. I had been given a flying helmet, but there were no flying boots available so I had to make do with two pairs of socks and my ordinary black shoes. I had managed to scrounge a pair of leather flying gloves and a scarf, which I double wrapped round my neck, so I must have looked a bit like Biggles. Who cared – it was very cold up there in the clouds. But I was hardly the best-dressed evader returning to the fold.

The Sunderland lobbed down on the water of Pembroke Dock on 14 January 1942, a very cold day as I recall. I had made it, but for some hours I just could not take in the fact that I was finally home. Back on British soil. I was in a kind of dream state. And it didn't help that even though my heart was pumping with excitement, for the rest of the

155

Royal Air Force it was without any particular significance that Flight Sergeant Jack Newton was back where he belonged. Not one person said even as much as 'Well done.' I was home and that was it. In fact, the feeling conveyed to me was more . . . 'You were bloody lucky to get back!' as though I had been on a back-packing holiday through Belgium, France and over the Pyrénées, and through my own fault had had a particularly hard time. Or, perhaps, they thought I'd been on some kind of orienteering initiative test!

I was quickly isolated from the rest of the crew, and taken to a room for debriefing; at least the debriefing officer had the kindness to shake my hand warmly and say, 'Welcome home'.

In my own funny way, I admit I did feel a bit special because I had been led to believe that I had done something no other non-commissioned British airman had done at that time, which was make it out of enemy-occupied Europe. But it seemed nobody else realised it, at least not until much later. Word even got back to me that officially I had achieved nothing in particular! Five months on the run, under the noses of the Nazis, being moved from one safe house to another, being mistaken for a German infiltrator and nearly being shot by the Resistance, doing what was virtually the impossible by crossing the Pyrénées in winter . . . all this and more, was nothing? Well, apparently, this was the way the Air Ministry saw it. I thought I might get some kind of recognition, and so did a certain Naval Lieutenant Grisar, who knew what I'd been through, but even his efforts to have my achievements officially recognised came to nothing. In fact, the Air Ministry rebuffed them rather curtly.

Of course, there was always the chance I might not be the real Jack Newton. I might have been killed and had a German infiltrator take over my identity. This, of course, was one of the purposes of the debriefing, along with the need to get all the information they could from me; vital information I had picked up on the run in German-occupied Belgium and France. I had to give my name, rank and number. Go right through my story yet again, from the moment of taking off at Binbrook, the names of the crew I flew with, the attack on Aachen, and the landing on Deurne airfield . . . right the way through to the eventual landing in Pembroke Dock. I had to give as many names as I could remember, details about the Resistance people who helped me, the safe houses where I stayed. Describe in detail how I got across the Pyrénées, and the route taken into Spain. It was all checked out to make sure I wasn't telling porky pies, and that I was who I said I was! After many hours of debriefing I even began to wonder myself!

Then I was given one pound, and told to go to the NAAFI canteen to buy myself a mug of tea, and a packet of cheese sandwiches. After that I was to report to the transport officer, a cocky young corporal, who would issue me with transportation papers from Pembroke Dock to Paddington, and the transit centre, in London, which was the Great Central Hotel, in Marylebone. There I would be further interrogated by the Army, prior to being returned to my unit.

On the twelve-hour train journey, which was severely interrupted by a German bombing raid, I consoled myself with the thought that I would soon be back in the arms of my sweet Mary. How wrong I was. When I arrived at the Marylebone hotel I thought I would be allowed at least a few hours to go and see my wife; after all, she was only fifteen minutes away in St John's Wood, I presumed, with my mum and dad. But nobody wanted to be responsible for letting me go. I was kept in my hotel room and had to endure five hours more interrogation. I wasn't allowed to even get in touch with my wife until they had finished with me. It did seem a bit heartless, but I suppose they couldn't take the risk. After the captain had finished debriefing me, I decided to take up my frustration with his senior officer, a Lieutenant Colonel. 'Please, sir,' I begged. 'I have been away missing for nearly six months. I only live some fifteen minutes away. Will you let me go to my parents' house?' The senior officer didn't even seem to know I had been missing in Europe. However, when I told him my circumstances, he was sympathetic and said he would do his best to get me an overnight sleeping pass. About an hour later, a corporal returned with a chit giving me permission to go to my parents' home in Townshend Road, St John's Wood, where I had to remain until recalled.

But Mary wasn't there, so Jack had to wait another day for her to come straight from work and her home in Twickenham where she was living with Jack's sister, Babs. It was a tearful and joyful reunion. They were back together again and with so much to talk about. Mary took two days off work to be with the husband she had to get to know all over again.

Then Newton was told to report to the Air Ministry and was given three weeks' immediate leave.

I spent the first week in bed, with hugely swollen knees, then I hobbled around for the remaining two weeks. Everything about those three weeks was great, apart from the swollen kneecaps. It was great to be back in a decent bed, and to get some semblance of a good night's sleep, although, by this time, London was being hit hard by Nazi bombing raids. At times, day and night.

Even so, for Newton it was still over-riding joy was that he was back in London itself; that he was back with his beloved Mary. And great that he was no longer hiding from the Germans. In fact, it was great just to be alive!

It remained to be seen if it was going to be great what the Air Ministry had in mind for Newton, now that he was back home, rested, and ready to get back to work as a non-commissioned officer.

When the Air Ministry asked him where he would like to be posted, Newton began to think that the rest of his war might not be so bad after all. Especially when he was told quite firmly that there was no way he could return to operational flights over Europe. With the enemy knowing that the other five members of Newton's original Wellington crew were now prisoners-of-war, and that he had escaped, he would be at risk if he was brought down again. His captors would know that he could not have evaded arrest in uniform, meaning he must have worn civilian clothes. They could have accused Newton of being a spy, and shot him. Newton was pleased the Air Ministry took this reassuring point of view; he had no wish to be shot as a spy!

Would he like to be posted to the Far East?

No, Jack said that as he was newly married, and had spent barely twelve weeks with his wife as a married man, he thought that would have been very unfair on Mary for him to fly off and leave her yet again. As he had only just returned home, he said he would appreciate a little time to settle down to married life. The Air Ministry was uncharacteristically sympathetic, and instead posted him to Bassingbourn, in Cambridgeshire, which was being prepared for the arrival of the American Air Force. Huge flying fortresses were landing there daily, and the resident operational training unit were flying out their Wellingtons.

Trying hard to conceal a smile, Jack said:

Then someone thought it might be a good idea if I went on a lecture tour of the squadrons to tell other aircrew how to escape if they were ever unlucky enough to be shot down, or forced down in enemy territory! I did a few such lectures and they seemed to go down very well, but the Air Ministry quickly decided it wasn't such a good idea after all, because I was giving too much away. I wasn't particularly bothered because I'd only escaped the once, and I didn't really consider myself an authority on escaping anyway.

Jack wasn't really surprised.

That one was quickly knocked on the head, and I seemed to be a square peg in a round hole. Nobody seemed to quite know what to do with me. Story of my life, really!

I was sent on various training courses, aircraft recognition schools and the like. I went back on a gunnery refresher course, and a navigation course. Then, one particular day, my brother-in-law, who was a travel agent, gave me some theatre tickets for Mary and me to go along to the London Palladium to see Tommy Trinder.

It was a fantastic show. Mary and I sat in the dress circle and all the way through the first half we couldn't stop laughing at Trinder's antics. When the curtain came down, Tommy Trinder walked on stage and called out: 'Is there a Flight Sergeant J L Newton in the house? If there is, will he report to the box office immediately.'

I could not believe my ears. 'It's you,' said Mary, nudging me in the ribs. 'Yes, I know it's me, dear,' I told her. 'Well, get up and go to the box office to see what they want,' she urged me, half heaving me out of my seat. At the box office my father was on the telephone to tell me he'd had a call from someone at Beaconsfield saying that I must ring a certain telephone number at the earliest opportunity. Mary and I never did see the second half of the Trinder show because I had to get back to Townshend Road to make that call. Within an hour there was a car at my parents' front door, and I was on my way to an address in Beaconsfield. I hadn't a clue what unit it was, nor had I a clue what it was for, or why I was wanted so urgently. They would not tell me.

When I got there I found out it was the home of MI9. The intelligence boys needed me for my experiences on the run in Belgium and France. They hoped I might be able to identify a certain person who claimed I had met him when I was in the hands of the Belgian Resistance.

I was introduced to Donald Darling and Captain Langley, two officers I had come across previously. Captain Langley was a one-armed officer who was running escape activities for MI9 at the time. He told me he had been interviewing a Belgian civilian who claimed to know me from my time in the care of the Brussels Resistance. That this man had helped me. But I didn't recognise the name Frédéric. I told Captain Langley that it was unusual for Resistance people to give their names. It wasn't done. But this Captain Frédéric Hulot insisted I knew him. Though, as I say, the name just didn't ring any bells with me. 'Perhaps I will recognise Captain Hulot if I see him?' I suggested. Langley grunted his agreement, and we moved off.

I was taken to a small room at the Beaconsfield MI9 address and through a one-way mirror, I was shown the man who claimed to be Captain Hulot. Yes, I recognised him immediately. Hulot was telling the truth; he had helped me.

I told Captain Langley to say to Hulot that if he had met Jack, the airman with long black sideburns, black moustache, black beret, and long coat; an RAF gunner, then he would remember giving him something before he left Brussels. 'Ask Hulot what he gave me,' I suggested to Captain Langley. Only the right man would know the answer – he gave me a pair of brown brogue shoes. In fact, I was wearing those same shoes at the time. The best pair of shoes I'd ever had!

I took off one of the shoes, and handed it to the interrogation officer who then returned to Hulot in the room on the other side of the one-way mirror. I watched with interest as Hulot was handed the shoe and asked its significance. 'Why, that is one of the very shoes I gave to the RAF man Jack,' he said excitedly.

There were no more doubts. Captain Frédéric Hulot was the man he claimed to be. And that shoe of mine had proved it!

We weren't allowed to meet, but I was pleased to help a man who had been such a help to me when my life was under such threat in Brussels.

Life in London was beginning to hot up as German raids began to increase in frequency and intensity. The dreaded V1, nicknamed 'The Flying Bomb', was also pounding the very heart of London, its throbbing engines the only reassurance that it was not quite ready to deliver its deadly payload. But when the engines cut, and the flying bomb dipped into a steep dive, then those on the ground below it dived for cover, held their breath and hoped for the best. If you were indoors and curled up under a steel Anderson shelter that, in most homes, doubled for a wartime dining room table, it was probably the best place to be. Jack had not seen anything quite like it. In the months he had been away, the whole tenor of the war had changed considerably. Germany was bringing its war to Britain, and London was suffering badly.

Trying to find Newton a job seemed to be taxing the Air Ministry more than it probably cared to admit. So when he was told he was to be posted to the Central School of Aircraft Recognition in Southport, Newton could not help thinking some desperate decision making was taking place in London. At least, in Southport, he would be doing something he enjoyed, and something – apart from gunnery – which he was good at. Jack was given officer status, too, with promotion and title to Flying Officer instructor. Second-in-charge to boot! Mary remained in London, at the Crystal Palace flat she and Jack rented.

It was while I was in Southport that my father-in-law forwarded a letter sent to his St John's Wood home, for the attention of JL Newton. My father-in-law sent it on, thinking it might be important because he could see it had come from the Cavalry Club, in Piccadilly. But I had no idea who the sender was, a Navy officer by the name of Lieutenant Commander Grisar. The only way to find out was to ring him, which I did.

Lieutenant Commander Grisar wanted to come to Southport to talk to me, saying he considered it important. He said we had never met, nor had he helped me when I was dodging the Jerries in Belgium. But Grisar had been there, too, about the same time and worked closely with Emile Witmeur. I learned that Grisar had directly helped two other members of our crew, Burrell and Porteous. So Emile had probably told the Navy guy my story, and it had obviously impressed him.

Grisar said he intended writing to the Air Ministry to tell them of my 'remarkable story' and to recommend that I receive some kind of official recognition for evading arrest, and for being the first British airman to get back to Britain. As it happened, the only one from my Wellington crew of six. Grisar kindly portrayed me as a hero, and said this deserved recognition. Coming from a senior Naval officer, this was high praise indeed. I wasn't going to complain, nor try to stop him!

The Lieutenant Commander promised to write to me when he had heard from the Air Ministry.

To my great disappointment, though, nothing ever came of the Commander's recommendation. The Air Ministry didn't think I had done anything particularly worthy of such recognition, but it would have been nice if they had. Did I think I deserved a medal, or a written commendation? Well, it could be argued that if I hadn't spotted the concrete runway when I did, we might have crashed into Antwerp itself, or into the estuary. Either way, none of us would have stood much chance of surviving the crash. And I was the only one of the six crew who bluffed his way through Belgium and France, across the Pyrénées, and into Spain. Come to think of it, maybe I deserved an Oscar for that particular performance, for an acting role it surely was. Even the Belgians and French said I looked more like one of them than an Englishman. Praise, indeed. But I had to put the disappointment behind me, and accept that what I had achieved was, in the eyes of my superiors, just a part of wartime's grief – and gravy!

I continued to miss Mary, so whenever it was convenient for her I would invite her to join me in Southport. One particular weekend, she left our Crystal Palace flat with Jacqueline, our first baby who was only a few months old, to take the train north. Obviously I wasn't in married quarters so I found a nice bed and breakfast for the three of us at 32 Alma Road, in Birkdale, a mile from Southport. Mary brought Jacqueline's pram, too, so being a proud dad, it was my pleasure to take my little daughter out on the Sunday afternoon pushing her in the pram along the Southport seafront. I was in my civvies enjoying the nice day and the fresh air that filled my lungs with an almost intoxicating effect when the orderly officer from the Central School rode up on his bike and handed me a telegram. 'I think you should read this,' he said, thrusting the piece of paper into my hand. When my eyes had scanned it I could see why. The telegram was from Mary's dad and read: 'Your flat has been hit by a V1. It is uninhabitable'.

The news was shattering. But what was uppermost in my mind was the fact that, but for a last-minute decision to bring Mary and Jacqueline up to Southport for the weekend, they would have been in our flat when it was hit by the flying bomb. And most probably would have been killed.

I was given time off to return to London with my family so that Mary and I could see what damage had been done. Would we still be able to live there? And if not, then I would have to arrange for Mary and Jacqueline to live with my parents, or with my sister in Twickenham.

Back in his Air Force uniform, Jack made his way to the flat. As the complex came into view he could hardly believe his eyes. It hadn't been a direct hit, but the damage was still considerable, with several apartments blown open as though someone had swung a huge sledgehammer at the building. The bomb had struck another building a few hundred yards away, but the blast had punched a whole into one side, spilling shattered brickwork and the contents of many flats onto the lawns below. Jack said:

My flat was ripped apart. Every window was blown out, and most of our furniture littered the ground. An old cuckoo clock, I had had repaired only a few days before, was on its side among the mess, and the dust. My uniforms were shredded, hanging in tatters from the exposed apartment. I could see our bed had collapsed and was full of jagged shards of glass. Mary and I could have been in that bed. And Jacqueline's little wicker cot, by our bed, was also full of shattered glass. What could I do? It was heartbreaking, but I was thankful my family were not there when death struck. Some were not so fortunate, and a number died as they slept.

I rescued one or two personal items, then returned to Southport with Mary and Jackie. And that is where they remained for the next six months, until the flat was finally repaired.

When I went back to check it out, someone was already living in my apartment. I couldn't understand what was going on, and as I knocked on the door of my own flat and waited to see who was squatting there, I was quite prepared for a bust-up. This was a private flat and I had been paying twenty-three shillings a week rent to live there. A man came to the door, and said, 'Who are you?' I told him my name was Jack Newton, and that he was in my flat.

The man's face relaxed visibly. 'Ah, I didn't know you were coming back,' he said apologetically. He pushed his right hand towards me, as he said, 'I am the housing manager. Let me take you down to my office and we will sort this out.' But I wasn't yet ready to shake anyone's hand, at least not until I got my flat back!

The housing manager said he would get me a requisition note, adding that I could come back to the apartments and I could pick any one I fancied. Even a bigger one, and for the same rent of twenty-three shillings a week. And that is what I did. Mary and I moved into a much better flat than the one we had before, and stayed there happily until we eventually bought our own house in Blackheath. By that time, the war was coming to an end. There were still many deprivations, a great deal of unrepaired bomb damage, shortage of many foodstuffs, but the raids had stopped and the Germans were on the run in Europe. The sun was beginning to shine on London again, its glow reflected in the faces of the capital's inhabitants. It was a truly remarkable time to be alive, in the thick of the jubilation that followed when World War II was finally over.

And the sun continued to shine on both Jack and Mary. They went on to have two more children, Christopher and Phillip. Jackie is now 59, with two children of her own, James and Jenny. Chris is 57 and has three children, Holly, Alice and Robert. Phillip is 55 and lives in Australia with his wife and their six children, Danielle, Hannah, Sam, Jack, Charlie and Joe.

Conclusion

When Jack Newton arrived home on 14 January 1942, there were still many tough days ahead, but as VE Day, in 1945, drew ever nearer, so Jack's own lifestyle dropped down a gear or two. It had been too risky to use him on further operational flights, and efforts to integrate him into the Royal Air Force home front were not exactly purposeful! He felt – and was possibly considered to be – something of a square peg in a round hole. The Air Ministry was not quite sure what to do with him. It was as though his contribution to the war effort had been largely packed into his five extraordinary months 'on the run' in German-occupied Belgium and France . . . and now he was out of work!

This is how Jack Newton puts it:

> I had said my fond goodbye to Dédée at the British Consulate in San Sebastian, and seriously doubted that I would ever see her again. Happily, that turned out not to be the case. Once I was back in Britain, I had a need to see as much as possible of my wife, Mary, and our first-born daughter, Jacqueline, when she came along. My priorities had changed. Besides, my head continued to be filled with all the trauma, sometimes even the excitement, of playing hide 'n' seek with the Germans. I had experienced its intensity and lived through it to tell the tale. By comparison, life in Britain, even in wartime, was so much lower key. I had difficulty making people understand why it had such a deflating effect on me.

By the time the church bells were ringing in peace, Jack had been sucked into a number of intelligence jobs, which then led him to Bryanston Square, just off Marble Arch, where he was directly involved with Air Ministry intelligence work. From there, he was suddenly transferred to the Foreign Office on security and intelligence duties. 'It was the beginning of what I call the "nasty business",' says Jack a little sheepishly, stressing it was a time in his life he prefers to set to one side. Even to forget. 'In any case, I am covered by the Official Secrets Act, so I cannot talk about the kind of intelligence work in which I was involved. Besides, I wasn't particularly proud of what I did there.' Jack remained at the Air Ministry until he retired in 1977.

Like missing pieces of a jigsaw, from 1945 onwards, many of these pieces suddenly reappeared and took their place once more in the overall picture. Dédée survived the horror of a German prison camp, though dangerously ill. Then on 16 October 1945 it was officially announced that she had been honoured with the George Medal, one of Britain's highest civilian awards, which she received from King George VI at a private ceremony in London in February 1946. A proud moment for Dédée and for so many of the brave British airmen she helped get home. Jack's five captured crew members re-emerged from German captivity relatively unscathed, and were again reunited through the Royal Air Force Escaping Society. Reunions in Britain and in Belgium were soon organised, as were visits to many of those safe houses – and their courageous owners, those who survived – in Belgium and in France. One such memorable visit for Jack Newton was his return to the de Voegts' for the ceremonial unearthing of the flying gear and the crew's possessions that had been hidden in a deep hole near the farmhouse.

As you will have read, at the time, and this was August 1941, the three of us – me, Langlois, and Copley – wrapped up all our gear and many of our possessions, then buried it all in a deep hole behind the farmhouse. A shed was put over the top to conceal the hole. Our stuff remained there, undiscovered, until 1946 when I was invited to Belgium on a goodwill visit to thank many of those brave Belgians who helped me, and other aircrew members. One ceremony was at the de Voegts' farm to unearth my buried belongings.

I recall that the shed had been blown down by the weather, so the farmer had replaced it with a patch of potatoes. But we managed to dig out three sets of buried kit. Some of it was a bit damaged, but most of it was OK.

Then M. Dumoulin, who lived in Antwerp and operated a cargo ship between Antwerp and Tilbury Docks, shipped the rescued gear back to Tilbury where I picked it up, and arranged to give back their kit to the skipper, Langlois, and the wireless operator, 'Tich' Copley. I donated part of my kit to the Bomber Command Museum, in Hendon, where it can be seen to this day in a section devoted to escape and evasion. It was removed on just one occasion, a few years ago when my son, Chris borrowed my old flying helmet, scarf and boots to use them in a sponsored parachute jump through the Royal Air Force Escaping Society. Afterwards, he told me: 'Well, I've done something you've never done, Dad – jumped out of an aircraft!'

In fact, that old scarf still has some of my blood on it, where I gashed myself during the Deurne airfield landing. And M.

Dumoulin, who shipped our belongings to Tilbury, was the same Richard Dumoulin I'd met in the Belgian Resistance.

After her recovery from the trauma of imprisonment in Germany, Dédée devoted her life to humanitarian needs in Africa, mostly as a nursing sister in a leper hospital in the Belgian Congo. But she never really recovered from the inhumane captivity which she had to endure under the Nazis. Finally, she had to return to Belgium to live a quieter, less stressful life with her companion, Thérèse de Wael, with whom she worked in the leper colonies. Belgium's King Baudouin honoured Dédée with the title of Comtesse, in recognition of her services to her country. Both Dédée and Thérèse still live in Brussels and Jack speaks to them regularly. Since his reunion with Dédée, when she came to London in 1946, they have never again lost contact.

Sadly, though, many of those Belgian and French patriots who hid him in their safe houses have since died. In 2001 the last of the Belgian Resistance and Royal Air Force Escaping Society reunions was held in Antwerp. 'We are all getting a bit past it now, so this was the end of the line,' says Jack a little wistfully. But Newton continues to do his bit to keep those wartime memories alive. He gives talks to interested groups such as the Rotary Clubs of Great Britain; he opens hospital wards when he is invited and makes sure a particular favourite picture of his beloved Wimpy bomber hangs on a wall or two. And Jack Newton has been interviewed a number of times on the regional television news when there is a particular anniversary to celebrate.

Now there is this book, which he hopes will jog the many memories of surviving escapers and their families, as well as the many thousands wherever they may be now, who made it possible for those like himself to live through one of the world's most savage wars.

'If I was a car I'd say I was now in second gear. I've still another lower gear left. I can still go slower. But no need for that just yet,' he chunters with his infectious, characteristic laugh. He has spent a couple of days each week in recent years, giving his time to hospital charity work, but on his doctor's advice, he has stopped that and, instead, puts the time into a bit more gardening.

His East Sussex home and his garden are his pride and joy. Here is his little piece of England that each day reminds him how very lucky he is to still be around to enjoy it. But for Dédée, and those like her, as well as his Mary, who never gave up hope that he would return to her, Jack Newton's time might have run out a long, long time ago . . . a long, long way from home.

*Why it is **Lucky 13** for me . . .*

Jack Newton says *Lucky 13* has entered so many parts of his life that to this day it has become accepted by his family as his lucky omen. His lucky number. It all began with this heart-shaped emblem made for him by a young WRAF at RAF Binbrook in 1941, but because he was not wearing it on that first flight to Aachen, a member of his crew jokingly blamed him for their bad luck and forced landing in Belgium. Here are the '13' coincidences which Jack believes have given him a charmed life . . .

- Born at 13 Lancaster Mews, Hampstead on 13 May 1919.
- Father and Mother moved to 13 Daleham Mews, Hampstead.
- Service number was 742570 (742 adds up to 13, and 570 adds up to 12. 'I was in 12 Squadron').
- Joined 13 Flying Training School, White Waltham.
- Crossed from Belgium into France on 13 November 1941.
- Left Gibraltar on 13 January 1942.
- First new house he bought had the postal address No. 13.

Jack Newton's family now always write '13' on all their letters and notes to Jack and Mary. 'That is, before the kisses,' adds Jack.

Index

171